'*Sea Changed* is honest, unapologetic, full of fun and insight, an absorbing account of a thoughtful and well-lived life.'
  – *Jane Atkinson, formerly media advisor to Diana, Princess of Wales and Chief of Staff of Global Poverty Project*

'*Sea Changed* is a riveting read. A beautifully-written personal odyssey of our times. It is full of rich images of Kate Nicholas's "eclectic life". An honest and moving account which takes her from an eccentric upbringing in rural England to the corporate offices of London before she leaves it all for a global search to fill the void she feels. What she finally finds is a heart-felt faith which opens her up to the world's marginalized as well as courage to face her own battle with cancer.'
  – *Tim Costello, World Vision Australia's Chief Advocate, Baptist minister, leading media commentator and author*

'I loved reading Kate's life story and witnessing God and his amazing love meeting her and caring for her throughout her journey. I marvelled at the complexity of Kate's searching, her striving, her determination to find Truth – and her growing realization that the truth she needed to find was God within her. Kate, you are a woman gifted with the ability to communicate clearly and beautifully. My prayer is that others find who they are seeking through your story. Abba connected you and I across the ocean, unveiling another facet of his infinite gift to you . . . his healing grace. May his truth continue to be revealed beyond your greatest vision!

'Reader, enjoy this book, and open your heart to becoming Sea Changed!'
  – *Cindy Cox, leader of US-based ministry Jesus Christ Heals Today, and author*

'To read *Sea Changed* is to take part in an adventure that spans decades and crosses the globe. It is a story of God speaking, gently and persistently, into a human life. It is the story of a woman searching after God, without knowing exactly what she was searching for, and finding him in places that surprised her. It is an inspiring story of coming home, of healing and of being at peace with God.'

– Revd Peter Crumpler, St Leonard's, Sandridge, Hertfordshire

'Like the best travel books, this one takes you on an internal as well as an external journey. In *Sea Changed,* Kate documents a life spent exploring the world, and at the same time recounts a profound and fascinating journey of the spirit. Reading it is like backpacking through life with a stranger who becomes a friend. Public Relations professionals are sometimes regarded as disreputable "spin doctors", and Kate has reached the heights of that glamorous world. But she tells her own story with honesty and authenticity, wit and wisdom. Nothing is being spun here except the threads of a fascinating life in progress.'

– Andrew Graystone, writer and broadcaster

'If, like me, you tend only to read the biographies of the historically famous, you'd be missing a treat with Kate Nicholas's beautifully written, haunting memoir. It is so much more than an autobiography – a travelogue, a social history of the late twentieth century with its uncomfortable disparity between plenty and poverty, a journal of pain, loss and joy, a spiritual adventure, a celebration of parental love, of courage, hope and survival against the odds, and ultimately, of life itself, written as only someone threatened with the loss of it can do. I sat down in the garden to read it for thirty minutes – and no gardening was done that day. Nor anything else. *Sea Changed* changed me, as it will you. And it has stayed with me ever since.'

– Michele Guinness, writer, journalist and former Head of Communications for the NHS in Cumbria and Lancashire

'I have always had faith in Kate Nicholas, though do not share her religious faith. She writes beautifully about her career and journey to find God in this remarkable book. As she writes of her challenges with cancer I realize that this book is the story of a Life Force.'

— *Professor Julia Hobsbawm OBE, social health expert and author*

'Reading about Kate's wonderful life has made this old sceptic too often say to himself "Oh, ye of little faith".'

— *Sir Bernard Ingham, current affairs commentator,*
columnist and former chief press secretary
to Prime Minister Margaret Thatcher

'*Sea Changed* is balletic in the way it delicately coaches us to listen for that still small voice. Every page contains the gentle message that the calm and the storms in our lives are God's perfect plan of preparation. Our disappointments and the unknowns become the rudder that steers our paths. *Sea Changed* helps us to understand that every encounter and experience we face is the currency that provides access to our destiny; allowing us to ultimately be leaders in life who are full of grace and humility, because of what he was done for us. Thank you Kate for expressing God's love so beautifully.'

— *Esther Kuku, Presenter of Family Hour, Premier Gospel Radio*

'Read this book! You'll be drawn in to an incredible story of adventure, spiritual discovery, and hope. Kate Nicholas's amazing journey is one of a kind, but in it we see the joys and pains that we all face – as well as the faith that carries us through.'

— *Rob Moll, editor-at-large,* Christianity Today; *and author*

'Kate's journey – from bohemian childhood through the joys and sorrows of family life, from first-world glamour to witnessing the world's most wretched poverty and from the top of her professional game to life-threatening cancer – illuminates a faith revealed by life's everyday experiences. Kate's inspiring story calls us to find an extraordinary God in the gritty challenges of our ordinary human existence. This is an essential read for anyone looking to spot the divine at work in their world.'

– George Pitcher, journalist, author, cultural commentator and Anglican priest

'Kate's story is a remarkable testimony to the grace of God. The reader is left with a powerful sense of the wonder of God, and a longing to discover a new level of the presence and touch of Jesus.'

– John Ryeland, Director, Christian Healing Mission and author

'In *Sea Changed* Kate Nicholas leads us on an eventful journey through life and healing, taking in people and places all over the world through which God has found her, called her by name, and made her his own. The story has its dramatic moments, but God has always been there underlying everything, like the double bass in orchestral music. She records her ups and downs in love and work with clarity and honesty, including a serious run-in with cancer. God is often veiled but always good. Kate's life has been touched by love and grace, vibrant with hope through all its changes and chances.'

– The Rt Revd Alan Wilson, Bishop of Buckingham

Sea Changed

**Coming home, healing
and
being at peace with God**

Kate Nicholas

Authentic

22 21 20 19 18 17 16   7 6 5 4 3 2 1

First published 2016 by Authentic Media Limited,
PO Box 6326, Bletchley, Milton Keynes, MK1 9GG.
authenticmedia.co.uk

British Library Cataloguing in Publication Data

A catalogue record for this book is available from the British Library.

ISBN: 978-1-78078-162-4
978-1-78078-163-1 (e-book)

All Scripture quotations are taken from the
HOLY BIBLE, NEW INTERNATIONAL VERSION ANGLICISED.
Copyright © 1979, 1984 by International Bible Society.
Used by permission of Hodder & Stoughton, a division of Hodder Headline Ltd.
All rights reserved. 'NIV' is a registered trademark of International Bible Society.
UK trademark number 1448790.

Quotation from LAST RIGHTS © 2006 by Stephen P. Kiernan. Reprinted by
permission of St. Martin's Press, LLC. All Rights Reserved.

Cover design by Mercedes Piñera
Printed and bound by CPI Group (UK) Ltd., Croydon, CRO 4YY

Contents

For my beloved husband John and my precious girls
Aly and Emily

You are the only truth
One needs to know
But never can
Because it is the one that does
Crest the storm of Being.
Ego is but the figurehead,
Your carved and gilded totem
Of hope against fear
Forced to nose all the seas,
Dip into desperate troughs
Mount each heady swell,
Crunch through splintering breakers
Mountains high, you're sure
You'll not survive.

But you do somehow, creaking, soaking
Surprised? Just long enough to glimpse
The next: you wished you hadn't
To reach a calm you had forgotten
Could ever be, or later
Ever was.

The prow cracked, intact – the figurehead
Contrite, and you're still there . . .
But where . . . must remain
A sense of You
That's true
Beyond our knowing.

Daniel Nicholas,
'Sea Change' from *Disposition of C90*, 1998

Prologue

How perverse that the closer we humans stray towards death, the more we become conscious of the sheer joy of being alive. One of the great ironies of the human state is that, in our attempts to keep at bay our mortality, we too often fill our lives with so much activity that we fail to fully appreciate the moments when we are living life to its fullest.

Only a few months before writing this book, I swam in the bracing waters of the Ardèche in Southern France, tumbling and laughing with my husband and children as we battled against the fearsome current that had already overturned our kayaks. My skin thrilled at the bite of the clear water. As I struck out towards shore, the dull ache in my left shoulder was numbed by the waters and I swam on.

In hindsight, for too long I had ignored the inner voice that whispered that all was not right. There had been too many distractions. It was only when I finally took time to simply be, to listen to my heartbeat under a clear Provençal sky, to finally acknowledge the pain and the hardness lurking in my flesh, that I recognized my passenger.

I already knew in my heart, even before the consultant confirmed my suspicions, that the cancer had quietly insinuated itself into my system leaving shadows, as yet unsubstantiated but with ghastly implications.

It was then I began to write this story. The tale it tells has taken a lifetime to weave. The process of sea change is a gradual one. As Shakespeare articulated, it is not one without suffering but over time the waters recreate us into something rich and strange.

The Holy Spirit is a patient teacher, never going in for the hard-sell; never forcing the issue or raising his voice. So gentle is the whisper of the divine that we all too often fail to hear or recognize our God when he speaks to us, but as Aristotle said, 'Memory is the scribe of the soul.'

The Greeks have two words for time: *chronos* which means chronological time – a sequential string of events hung out on a man-made time line – and *kairos,* an ancient Greek word meaning the sublime or opportune moment, pregnant with opportunity.

When we look back over our lives, when we seek to read the map of our existence, we enter a space between the two. We are guided by *chronos*, the sequence of our lives, but the memories, images, sounds and places that drift into our consciousness are those that are pregnant with meaning. And as the mundane of *chronos* fades away, we can see those moments when an unseen hand reached out to touch us, to shift our perspective, alter our trajectory or to lift us up. It is in the cracks between the *chronos* and *kairos* of our lives that we glimpse God.

Part One

The Launch

1

Provenance

A boat is a vivid metaphor for a human being. The reality is that we have two options in life: to live our lives in the safety of the harbour, sheltered from the wind and waves, or to take to the high seas, venturing out in search of lands as yet unknown; knowing that at times we may be tempest-tossed but that in setting sail we are fulfilling our purpose.

How we weather the inevitable storms will be dependent on the depth of our keel, that balancing guide that reaches down into the stillness beneath the breaking waves and centres us; a keel that grows throughout our life but which is shaped by our early childhood.

My vessel launched on 7 March 1963 to the resounding clang of London's Bow Bells. My mother was fond of telling me that as I was born in Charing Cross Hospital I was officially a Cockney. As a small child, I used to carry round a pocket dictionary of Cockney rhyming slang, peppering my early pronouncements with colourful references to the apples and pears (stairs) and dog and bone (phone).

While my mother strained to produce me, my father paced through the early hours of Covent Garden night market, taking rain-drenched black-and-white photographs of real Cockney stallholders. When the sun rose, he was summoned to the bedside to survey his first daughter. He took in my thick shock of spiky black hair and pursed mouth and declared, 'She looks like Marshal Malinovsky.'

My Cockney credentials were somewhat undermined by the fact that my parents actually lived in leafy and affluent St John's Wood, in a spacious top-floor apartment on Cavendish Avenue, close to the back entrance of Lord's Cricket Ground. Our front windows afforded a bird's-eye view over the high wooden green gates of The Beatles front man Paul McCartney's London home. Some of my earliest memories were the satisfying crack of a cricket bat, and the out-of-tune rendition of The Beatles' hit 'I'm Down' by the resident groupies whose mattresses decorated the pavement outside.

My mother became an avid Beatles fan, buying singles and watching out for the blacked-out mini as it returned from the nearby Abbey Road Studios, prising its way past the groupies to disgorge the Fab Four beyond the safety of the gates. Occasionally McCartney's slight figure could be seen walking his endearingly shaggy Old English Sheepdog in nearby Regent's Park, or quietly taking a pint in the pub at the end of the road, where the locals had the grace to simply let him be.

My parents played the part of an archetypal upwardly mobile north London couple with gusto. My father, Daniel Nicholas, wrote copy for advertising agency Saward, Baker and Co., conjuring up Old Spice surfers and Felix the Cat, and appeared in his own adverts for Nescafé. He could be seen – Savile Row suited and bespectacled – on billboards around the city taking in the heady aroma of granulated coffee. A cardboard cut-out of his bright red hair and glasses spun from the light fitting in the local greengrocers.

My mother, Maggie Pycroft, was already a journalist of some renown. In her later twenties and early thirties she reigned in Fleet Street as chief feature writer home and abroad on *The Daily Herald*, covering everything from the Munich Air Disaster to the Middle East crisis, travelling through Jordan and the Holy Land. Over the years she interviewed figures ranging from the Israeli Prime Minister Golda Meir to playwright Noel Coward, the founder of the Royal

Ballet Ninette de Valois to composer Vaughan Williams and conductor of the Hallé Orchestra Sir John Barbirolli, with whom she became friends.

A fledgling power couple, my parents had been set up on a blind date by a mutual friend, Mickie, whose husband Arthur 'Ches' Chesworth was the dashing foreign correspondent for the *Daily Express* newspaper. 'Maggie, he's in advertising,' she gushed over the phone conjuring up images of suave sophistication.

When the time came, Maggie opened the door to find a chunky young man with wild carrot-coloured eyebrows and a ruddy complexion. As she watched him hobble down the stairs on crippled feet, she determined that he was not her type. But there was something about this rather intense young man which touched her and, as she drove through the streets of London, she had a premonition that he held the key to her future. (She recalled something her friend Dorothy Salmon had said to her in Manchester, 'You'll go to London, Maggie, I'm sure of that. I don't know what it means but I can see a man driving up in a car and holding a car door open for you and driving away.' Dorothy, it was said, had 'second sight'.) But then came silence. Maggie was furious and strangely disappointed.

Then two weeks later, the newsroom was in uproar; the Palace had announced that press photographer Tony Armstrong-Jones was to marry Princess Margaret. Every phone was ringing off the hook when across the deafening clatter of the newsroom came a yell, 'Maggie, there's some chap called Dan Nicholas on the phone for you. Keep it quick. We need the phones.' Her heart leapt.

While they courted, Dan made her coq au vin in gleaming copper pans at his impeccable bachelor pad in Holland Park (a culinary skill he promptly lost following his wedding), took her to the theatre and introduced her into the world of the Nicholases.

His father, Nick, was the son of a tinplate worker in the industrial South Wales town of Llanelli who had fled his humble Welsh roots and his future as a student teacher to seek fame and fortune in London. Having nearly starved on the streets, Nick had stumbled into advertising, despite having no knowledge or experience. But he was a natural and eventually set up his own firm, Rumble, Crowther and Nicholas, and crafted clever copy for Ford – the affordable car for the up and coming – Pear's Soap and the National Savings Account, an important money raiser for the war effort.

His professional life, however, was a mere backdrop for his real passion as a painter, actor and moderately successful playwright. The theatre had been a forbidden pleasure in his childhood, decried by his Non-Conformist father as one of the devil's last strongholds on earth. So it was perhaps not surprising that when forbidden fruit arrived in town in the form of Gladys Conner, a young Irish opera singer on tour, he fell in love, upped sticks and pursued her first to Manchester and then to London where he eventually won her hand.

Gladys was a woman of indomitable spirit, individuality and strong judgements who humoured and militantly supported her idiosyncratic husband until she died of breast cancer in her early fifties. Sadly, Maggie never met Gladys but they were cut from similar cloth.

Dan's sister Theresa was a rather feisty young woman who, after her mother's death, had fled the constraints of English middle-class female existence to live 'in sin' on the Greek island of Corfu with a fellow renegade, a ruggedly handsome Greek painter and shambolic resistance hero called Christo Vlachopoulos (who was described by his friend the writer Gerald Durrell as 'a rather well-preserved bandit').

Most evenings, Maggie and Dan would join Nick at L'Escargot restaurant in Soho, where he would await them at his regular table in top hat and tails (the Nicholas offspring grew up eating in L'Escargot as an extension of their home and, with Gladys no longer available to keep the home fires burning, Nick treated the place like his own personal cafeteria). This behaviour seemed tantalisingly bohemian to my mother who had spent her young life in Poor Law institutes (or work houses as they had been known since Dickensian times), in the Yorkshire town of Pontefract and Mansfield in Nottinghamshire, where her father had handled admissions and her mother Elsie held a nursing post.

While Elsie scrimped and saved to send her clever daughter to grammar school on the family income of £15 a week, Dan had been sent off to board at Charterhouse public school where he excelled at fencing, developed a cut-glass accent and allowed inanities such as 'top hole' and 'wizard' to seep into his vocabulary.

During the war, Maggie cowered beneath the stairs of their council house listening to the thrum of German bombers overhead, while my father took to the skies as an officer and a gentleman, earning his wings in the British Fleet Air Arm, Royal Air Force and the American Air Force.

After the war, Dan went on to study at Worcester College, Oxford, under J.R.R. Tolkien (the linguist perhaps best known today as author of *The Hobbit* and *Lord of the Rings*) while my mother, despite being brilliant at English, could not afford such luxuries as university. Instead, she left school to join the local newspaper *The Mansfield Chronicle*; quite an achievement for a woman in the 1950s. Her inaugural reports were not illustrious and consisted mainly of parish rounds and 'dog stories', but she had fire in her belly and rose rapidly to *The Sheffield Star*, then the *Manchester Evening News* and ultimately to the heights of Fleet Street.

Maggie and Dan were married in September 1960 at the journalists' church of St Bride's in Fleet Street; their classic wedding photographs taken by the famous news photographer Terry Fincher. My mother promptly gave up her globe-trotting existence to become deputy features editor on *Woman* magazine. Two years later, when I was born, her editor Roland Vice sent a telegram saying CONGRATULATIONS. STOP. WHEN CAN WE HAVE HER FIRST PERSON TRUE LIFE STORY? – ROLAND.

Maggie threw herself into motherhood with the same ebullient optimism and dedication that had enabled her to rise through the ranks of the world of newspapers. Her offspring deserved the best that success could buy and my nursery and clothes came off the shelf from Harrods. She glowed with pride when the classical actor Sir Ralph Richardson stopped one day in the street to pat my head muttering, 'Charming, charming.' And when she returned to work, I was cared for by a succession of qualified nannies – one of whom tried to abscond with me which my mother took as a sign of my desirability.

As I became more mobile, I attended an exclusive and primarily Jewish nursery school in St John's Wood, where I became best friends with one of the offspring of the Baring banking family. I went to her elegant house for tea and played in her cavernous bedroom, rode her antique rocking horse and watched her portable television, while my mother lived in fear of having to return the favour. After one birthday party, I appeared with a hand-illustrated copy of Hans Christian Anderson's *The Nightingale* which I had won playing pass-the-parcel.

Then everything changed.

2

Larkland

A rather cool young vicar once told me that there were two types of people in the world: those who wake each day with the expectation that they know what that day will bring, and those who consider the world to be in a state of constant flux. He saw himself as part of the latter group and found it hard to understand how those who anticipated the status quo actually made it through the day, concluding that they must be in a state of permanent shock.

Change is perhaps the only true constant in any of our lives. From our first breath to our last, we are in a continual state of transformation. But between these two moments, we expend an inordinate amount of psychological energy on seeking reassurance of permanence; building artificial edifices to convince ourselves that the planet we inhabit is not in a constant state of movement, that the earth is not shifting imperceptibly beneath us. Most of us resist change to such an extent we would rather sit in the pain of our darkness and insecurity than venture out into the light of the new.

Change came suddenly upon my parents in the shape of an American parent company with a relentless 1960s focus on youth. At just forty-one, my father was deemed out of touch with the youth of the day and therefore expendable.

My father had for some time complained bitterly about the vacuous nature of his profession. Sitting smoking in cafés in Soho, he spent hours writing homilies on the evils of consumerism, while simultaneously devising jingoistic one-liners to sell the very products he despised (we never knew if the Americans detected that he was a man at war with himself, ferociously biting the hand that feeds, as he failed to secure a publisher for his diatribes). So while the prospect of redundancy might have been, for some, a mortal blow to the professional ego, being fired actually set my father free.

It was just after their wedding that Margaret (as she then became known) and Dan first began to look for a retreat from the city. They would buy copies of *The Lady,* combing the classified advertisements for country retreats and then set out on forays into the green zone around London, armed with picnic baskets and bucolic fantasies about country living.

They initially found a beautiful cottage for sale in Surrey which went by the name of Larkland, but their hopes were dashed when the surveyor found an unexploded Second World War incendiary in the field behind the house. It was deemed too explosive an option.

The search continued but to no avail, until one day Dan spotted an advertisement for a row of cottages on sale for £800 in the northernmost tip of Buckinghamshire, about fifty miles north of London; a no-man's-land of uncharted territory well beyond the respectable commuter belts of Surrey, Kent or Hertfordshire.

Seduced by the remoteness and the price (which even in the early 1960s was suspiciously low), my father took the day off work and, without consulting my mother, drove up the A5. Having reached an inauspicious market town called Newport Pagnell, he struck out along the country lanes until he came upon an improbable and grandiose neo-classical archway standing alone in the midst of rolling meadows and deep green hedges.

Driving below the arch he found an eighteenth-century formal bridge surmounting the slow rolling River Ouse, lined with plump bulrushes. Cattle grazed on the far side of the river under the glassy gaze of the windows of a neo-classical mansion and an ancient Norman-towered church. Dan had discovered Tyringham-cum-Filgrave; a pair of hamlets too small to be considered worthy of a map reference in their own right, but once the domain of a Sir William Praed who had built this grandiose hall to the designs of architect Sir John Soames.

My father was enraptured; it was as if he had stumbled into a painting by English romantic painter John Constable. Climbing back into his Ford Anglia, Dan tooted his horn and drove at the bridge, taking off at the summit and, with jarred bones, wound his way up through the sparse delights of Tyringham and on to the next cluster of housing.

Filgrave, which didn't even warrant a church, was also without either shop or pub which my father, who was less practical than my mother, saw as a definite plus in his flight from consumerism. At the centre of the village he found a low, squat farmhouse, the home of the local farmer who had placed the advertisement in *The Lady.* After knocking on the door he waited, listening in urban rapture to the lowing of the cows awaiting milking. Eventually the door was answered by a wild-haired character whose trousers appeared to be supported by a length of string; a stalk of ripened wheat firmly wedged between his lower teeth.

'What'll you be wantin'?' gnarled the stereotype. Slightly taken aback by this image from *Cold Comfort Farm,* my father produced the now dog-eared cutting. 'Agh the cottages,' the farmer continued, still in caricature.

Dan followed the farmer out through a dog-strewn yard, round a deeply dipped corner in the road and up a shaded lane; the canopy of elms touching each other gracefully overhead to frame the pale yellow of Cotswold stone cottages. It was love at first sight.

On closer inspection, the row of cottages turned out to be a terrace of two workers dwellings complete with lean-to pigsties. Built in the late eighteenth century for his shepherds by Sir William Praed (after an early workers' insurrection about conditions), the cottages had been empty for some time and had definitely seen better days.

Curiously, the cottages also appeared to have no doors – or at least none facing the road where the two men now stood surveying a set of crumbling steps amidst a tangle of nettles, cowslips and laburnum. But, having come this far, my father was not to be deterred. On unsteady feet, he waded through the nettles and up one side of the house, past a pigsty which appeared to be rapidly descending into the earth until, rounding the corner, he stepped into a long garden full of apple trees in full bloom. The hawthorn hedge hardly separated the garden from the fields beyond where sheep grazed and ducks circled on a small pond.

In fact, the cottages were facing the wrong way round or, rather, over the course of history the village pathway had shifted from the old Roman road, which lay behind the house, to the dried out river bed where the tarmac now ran. With a parallel set of windows on either side, you could look straight through to the fields rising beyond. My father later described the house as like a train; you could travel through the landscape and look out on either side.

Pushing open a low-slung door, he walked into a large square kitchen with red flagstones and an ancient timber ceiling. The two cottages consisted of a main living area below; a simple open kitchen space, where a family of anything up to twenty had eaten, washed, argued and laughed. Upstairs were three miniscule rooms too small to even accommodate a bed of sufficient size to fit a 1960s male, all linked by a shoulder-squeezing corridor. In one of the cottages, access between the floors was limited to a rickety step ladder and narrow 'coffin trap' (a hole in the floor just big enough to pass down an inhabitant's remains one last time).

As Dan shut the door on his dream retreat and walked back out into the field-fringed Buckinghamshire garden, he heard a lark cry high above. Leaning on the moss-covered gate he made out a cheque for £1,000 (just to be sure). The cottages would be called 'Larkland'; the only task that remained was to tell my mother.

Maggie had grasped at an early stage that her new husband was impetuous and a little eccentric. During the war, he had seen little real action but perfected his combat flying skills, initially, with the British Fleet Air Arm and Royal Air Force (RAF) and later with the United States Air Force in Texas where he was trained by Hollywood stunt pilots. After the war he had automatically become a member of the RAF Voluntary Reserve and when he went up to Oxford was able to join the university flying club.

Young, headstrong and unproven, he got up the nose of his more mature instructor by showing off aerobatic techniques. One day, full of testosterone, he and his instructor decided to stage a mock dog-fight for a gallon of beer in order to prove once and for all who the better man was. Both failed to recognize they were flying too low; two male egos locked in combat, neither willing to give way or pull out. When Dan's Tiger Moth stalled on a sharp turn, he was only one hundred feet above the ground. The church wall sealed his fate.

Brought to earth, the fallen Icarus lay in a restless coma with two badly smashed feet, a missing knee cap and a broken finger. The doctors performed miracles on his feet and, in a ground-breaking operation, knit his bones back together to form a solid mass which resembled, but never again functioned as, a foot. The spectre of amputation loomed for some time but in the end the operation was written up as a triumph in the medical magazine *The Lancet*. His co-pilot mercifully escaped uninjured.

But while his body healed his mind did not. There was, apparently, no physical reason for his coma. Psychiatrists were consulted and concluded that it was the fear that his co-pilot might have been killed that was keeping him from regaining consciousness. Gladys sat by his bedside carrying her secret hidden fear, revealed one day when

Theresa disturbed her and her mother rounded on her screaming, 'Don't you realize when he comes out of his coma he may be mad.'

When Dan finally came home on crutches, Theresa drove him to Portsmouth Aerodrome where, armed with his log book, he convinced the commander to let him take up a Tiger Moth in his socks. 'That fool,' Nick said when he found out, secretly proud of his son.

A few years later, his psyche took another blow, however, when he lost control of a car while driving his advertising colleagues to a meeting. This time he was not so lucky. Dan and his front-seat passenger were flung out of the car but a young man in the back seat lost his life. My father never got over the guilt, and the incident left an invisible wound.

Larkland was, however, to prove a sanctuary, an oasis of calm. One of my earliest memories is lying stretched out on the back seat of my parents' Morris Minor Traveller as they made their weekend pilgrimage to Larkland; still so small that, even if I stretched out my arms and legs, I could only just touch the leather-lined doors with the tips of my fingers and toes. I would watch the street lights pass like flaming beacons in the night, my face glowing golden, blue and pink from the neon shop signs of Cricklewood.

As we reached the outer reaches of the capital and the newly opened section of the M1 motorway, my father would speed up and the darkness between the street lamps would narrow, turning into a single stream of light winding its way north. Until, eventually, the light gave way to the darkness of country roads.

My body would rock gently from side to side without the encumbrance of a seat belt (this was the 1960s), and the hypnotic thrum of rubber on tarmac seemed to contain snatches of song, a distant voice singing me to sleep. Years later, as I sleepily steamed my way through the night into the deserts of Rajasthan, rocked on public buses along precarious Himalayan roads or bounced in four-wheel drives along rutted tracks in Zimbabwe, I again attained a childlike stillness that seemed to elude me when I was stationary. In the sensation of moving forwards I left behind the detritus of life, and in the rhythm of passage I would once again reach that place of peace.

On a Friday night my parents would pack the car with essentials – bread, wine, steak, hammers, wallpaper paste and matches – and head north. In a couple of hours we were in another world. On the first night in the cottage, my mother nearly had a heart attack when a cow bellowed in maternal agony near her window, only to be woken at the crack of dawn by the rooster who lived down the lane. Like many metropolitan types, she had presumed the country to be quiet.

My mother and father were determined to do the restoration work themselves and gleefully broke down walls, as I squirmed happily among the dustsheets. One night the farmer appeared with a bottle of whisky to survey the work. He sat with my parents in the downstairs room of the second cottage surveying the crumbling plaster walls and a hideous cherub-adorned plaster fireplace. 'Goin' to leave that there, are you?' he drawled.

'Well, we've still got a lot of work to do on the upstairs,' offered my mother, who had some doubts about my father's building credentials.

'Seems a shame. Got the old bread oven behind there.'

The farmer now had my father's attention, 'Shouldn't be too much fuss. My nephew did that, so it's bound to be no good.'

Half a bottle of whisky and a crowbar later, the fireplace lay smashed on the floor revealing the deep timber frame of the house and a fireplace with an old bread oven, where families once lay dough deep in the embers to bake. The farmer, it turned out, was after all a man of taste; a complex man who took comfort in confounding expectations. My father had found an unlikely companion, and in later years would use string to hold up his own trousers.

For five years my mother and father alternated between their urban and rural identities, until my father's redundancy offered him an opportunity to escape from a life he found increasingly meaningless.

So the three of us left the affluence of Cavendish Avenue to live in a half-renovated cottage with a bath in a pigsty, no telephone or discernible means of income.

The kitchen rapidly became the main base of operations and its old Aga the sole means of heating and cooking. My father would make nightly forays to the furthest reaches of the garden where the coal bunker lay beside an aromatic cesspit in order to stoke the fire (a ritual which continued after the installation of a rather idiosyncratic coal-fired central heating system). I loved the Aga but it was banished after I catapulted myself off a rocking chair and deposited myself on the sizzling surface like a Welsh cake. I survived the incident but the Aga was replaced by a succession of cookers, which my mother succeeded in setting fire to at one time or another. A fire extinguisher was installed but normally anyone in the vicinity would simply grab the flaming pan, run out the door with it and dump it sizzling on the grass outside.

With money in short supply, my father became an amateur electrician and insisted on wiring the house himself. The deep ceramic sink that had served as my bath was cracked, so he installed a stainless steel sink unit which he inadvertently wired up to the mains. For years anyone doing the washing up experienced a strange tingling sensation in their extremities.

At a local fair, they also bought the bottom half of a Welsh dresser so large that it spanned the width of the kitchen. It was invariably covered with various second-hand items of kitchen electrical equipment which my father obtained at local auctions and then tinkered with. One late afternoon, as the sun went down, a gin bottle which he had left beside a particularly suspect toaster expanded to the point where it exploded, setting fire to the curtains and nearly gutting the kitchen. When asked by the insurance assessor whether he could have done anything to control the blaze, his response was, 'Well, I suppose I could have drunk the gin.'

By this time, the honeycomb of bedrooms upstairs had been cleared out to create a landing and two open rooms with timber beams which creaked across the ceilings like the bow of a great ship. My parents' room always seemed filled with sunlight and the scent of gardenia. From the windows, I would spend hours looking out over the fields that rose up on either side. On one occasion, I spotted my father stalking a particularly nonchalant pheasant up the field with a rifle. Having failed to dispatch the bird from the bedroom window, he had set out in pursuit in his dressing gown but still returned empty handed.

My father also eventually insisted on building an upstairs bathroom with his own fair hand, installing a fashionable 1970s orange bathroom suite. Typically, it never quite functioned; the shower insisted on either scalding or freezing you and the sliding door had an alarming habit of falling off its hinges and hitting you on your head while you were enthroned.

Later, my parents expanded the house, demolishing the second pigsty and building another square carriage onto the Larkland train. The 'extension', as it was always known, enabled us to create a sitting room with French windows that opened out on to a terrace and glorious flowering cherry tree. The enormous stone fireplace became my father's favourite spot and he would lean, a glass of wine in hand, conducting an invisible orchestra as his spirits soared to the strains of Elgar, Gilbert and Sullivan, and dubious recordings of German fairground organ music.

Larkland brought with it a glorious freedom. We rarely considered locking the house and would frequently come back and find the doors wide open with a neighbour or two ensconced at our kitchen table. On the few occasions that my mother did manage to lock herself out, I would have to squirm like an eel through a miniscule pantry window, tumbling to the floor in a ball of carrots, onions and mouse droppings.

We lived largely outside. Meals, always accompanied by wine, were taken under the apple trees and, aside from in the depths of winter, I would be turned out of doors like a puppy first thing in the morning, with an expectation that I would reappear before dark.

I would spend the days wandering the fields above our house, sometimes with children from the village, but more often alone. I would sit surrounded by the ripening golden corn, filling sketch books full of field flowers; brilliant red poppies, deep blue cornflowers and purple knapweeds. Two fields beyond our house lay a small wood which in spring would be carpeted with pale primroses and delicate pendulous bluebells, and in autumn by a rich golden rug of leaves. At the centre of the wood lay a well and it was rumoured that the ghost of an old man who had fallen down the shaft still haunted the copse. I was fascinated and built myself a den out of fallen logs.

But what I loved most about the wide open fields was the exhilarating sense of space. I would climb up the hills behind our house until, reaching the summit, I could look out over the rolling valley beyond. The horizon expanded around in all directions and I felt giddy with excitement and sensed a deep yearning for something indefinable but almost tangible. The air, the hedgerows and the profusion of life around me felt pregnant with a supra-natural meaning that I could not decode. With little religious education, I had no formal framework with which to make sense of what I was experiencing. Instead, I would wander the hills, woods and fields clutching a notepad and crayons, recording the world around me like a frustrated miniature Victorian botanist, but always failing to capture that sense of the 'other'; the numinous, that touched me so deeply.

On school days, I would set my alarm clock for an unearthly hour of the morning and would sit at my window watching the dawn to the accompaniment of Beethoven's Seventh Symphony or Mike Oldfield's *Tubular Bells*. As the first light stole over the horizon and the strings soared on my portable record-player, I would feel again that sense of divine order; my soul crying out in wonder to the originator of the day.

I probably impressed people as a rather strange and intense child; the village kids certainly thought so. At the age of five I had transitioned from the London nursery, where I learnt rudimentary French and a smattering of Hebrew alongside wealthy Jewish children, to the village school in Filgrave which catered for a grand total of eleven children whose parents mainly worked on the local farm.

The school was run by an elderly spinster, an old-school educator. Every morning we would stand in formation to sing Bunyan's 'To Be A Pilgrim' and recite our times tables. The only concession to modernity was an ancient radiogram pinned high on the wall, on which we would listen to Enid Blyton's weekly nature talks.

The headmistress didn't know quite what to make of me, and vice versa. I instinctively felt that I needed to rebel, but wasn't sure what I should take a stand over. We reached a crisis point when I refused to eat my school lunch. Most schools in the area received their lunch from a central kitchen and the metal trays of over-boiled carrots and tapioca were driven around the countryside during the morning. Filgrave was at the end of the line and, by the time the food reached us, it was inedible.

I already had a black mark against my name for having refused to drink the small bottles of curdled milk which the government supplied, and which the headmistress left in the sun before serving to us (I was caught pouring the milk down the drain at the back of the playground). Then on the day of my rebellion, I was faced with a particularly distressing culinary offering of half-warm mince floating in oil and badly reconstituted instant potato.

The headmistress was convinced I would capitulate if I was deprived of my lunchtime play, but she had no idea what she was up against. I sat obdurately through lunch break but the offending plate was transferred to my desk for the next lesson and I sat glaring at her over the mince through maths and the Enid Blyton nature hour. Home time came and went and still I refused to give in. At five o'clock in the afternoon, long after my classmates had gone home, she admitted defeat and let me cycle home.

The issue of school lunches, however, remained unresolved, so I came to an arrangement with a pale and skinny vegan boy: my school lunches for his packed lunch of nut sausages and bean pasties. We were both happier and healthier as a result but I was now marked out as trouble.

3

Far Horizons

Despite being located in the middle of nowhere, Larkland soon became a hive of activity. My parents' bohemian lifestyle attracted other refugees from city life and they formed an ever-increasing circle of friends including ex-newspaper editors, musicians, writers, artists, scientists and some more open-minded locals. Their home was open to a wide range of characters although my father did not suffer fools gladly and, if bored by dinner conversation, would sometimes fall asleep under the table and snore loudly to the consternation of my mother.

Old friends would also motor up from London for the weekend filling the house with cigarette smoke, whisky fumes and outrageous stories about Fleet Street. Others came from further afield such as my godfather, *The Express* foreign correspondent 'Ches', and his wife Mickie and, later, Mickie on her own with her children who came to stay with us after being airlifted out of Cyprus following the Turkish invasion of 1974. And then there was Penha.

Penha arrived on our doorstep unexpectedly one Saturday morning with a bad-tempered parrot called Sessy who bit and had a penchant for Smarties. My mother had first been introduced to Penha in London by a friend who suggested that she would be a wonderful subject for my mother's first docu-journalist book. Penha was a roving Anglo-American geologist who had been hired by the US

Government to buy up all the industrial diamonds in Brazil during World War II to prevent them falling into enemy hands but had, like many others after the war, resorted to smuggling diamonds from Brazil to the US to pay off business debts (although by the time my mother met her she was dealing legitimately in emeralds and topaz). My mother had duly worked on the book but the market wasn't ready for an independent woman like Penha. But when I met her as a young girl it was love at first sight.

Penha had mahogany-tanned skin, short spiky grey hair and a voice like gravel. She wore dusty cowboy boots, smoked constantly and must have been about sixty years old. She would follow my mother around the house regaling us with hair-raising tales about her forays into the Brazilian interior, the Amazon rainforest and Nicaragua, and would even follow my exasperated mother to the toilet, continuing to talk outside the door as she went about her ablutions.

'Maggie, did I ever tell you about the time that I smuggled a load of diamonds out of Brazil in a case of boa constrictors and how they escaped in my hotel room in Belem . . . or how I was arrested as a spy in Caracas Bay . . . or how the Vargas regime tried to bribe me to defraud the US Government?'

I was quite convinced she was mad, but it was the first time I had met an 'explorer'. My mother was, however, wary. At an earlier stage, Penha had taken up semi-permanent residence with us in the flat in London while my mother researched the book. And as she was frequently of no fixed abode, my mother was alarmed to see her settling in once again. Every evening for weeks, she would wax philosophical with my father under the apple trees, looking very much at home.

When she and Sessy were finally dislodged, I felt that she took away with her some of the colour from our English rural haven. We would never see Penha again, although years later we received a postcard from her saying that she was living in a caravan on a building site in Agadir with a Dutch millionaire. When she passed away, Penha left my mother a valuable topaz and diamond ring which she then lost – money never hung around our family for long.

The other visitor who significantly expanded my young horizons was my aunt Theresa. I had heard so many tales about the renegade sister who had escaped England for a life in the Greek sun. Her country of origin had really let Theresa down; unlike her brother, she had had a miserable time at public school. 'I gave you a happy girl and you gave me back a donkey,' Gladys told the headmistress on her daughter's final day. After school she had drifted between jobs, trying out as a trainee copywriter at her father's advertising firm, briefly attending art school and working with a literary agency, but she felt trapped.

It was the spring after Gladys had succumbed to cancer that her father Nick decided they needed to get away on a painting trip. As Nick distrusted planes, they travelled by train to Brindisi in Italy and then by boat to what was then an obscure Greek island called Corfu. The day after their arrival, father and daughter were sitting in the main town of Kerkyra nursing a beer under the cool arches of the Liston when they were approached by a powerful-looking man with wire grey hair and deep laughing brown eyes, wearing a striped vest like a Breton fisherman.

The vision sallied up to them, 'Are you Englesse?'

'Yes.'

'Goot,' said the Greek who, satisfied, sat down at their table and introduced himself as Christo.

Christo continued to appear every time they had a beer in the café and Theresa decided he was 'a very nice pirate'. A law unto himself, this freewheeling combination of artist, electrician and dancer adopted Nick and Theresa. Wherever they ate, Christo had already been and arranged to cover the bill, which he paid for with his 'munitions' – skilful pen and ink drawings of old black-clad, bent widows and laden donkeys climbing winding Corfuit lanes.

At night, he took them both to a small smoke-filled taverna where he danced like a powerful prowling panther, shoulders raised, brooding to the sound of the balalaika. Wherever they went, Christo was recognized and feted.

After two weeks Nick left to continue his grand tour with a cruise on the Adriatic, leaving Theresa behind to fly back to her office job. But her flight to Athens was delayed by twenty-four hours and, that night, freed from their chaperone, Christo and Theresa kissed beneath the olive trees.

Back at the office in London, Theresa descended into a torpid state. She wrote to Christo to thank him for looking after her so well and sent him a book on Impressionist painters (which he sold immediately to the local bookshop, well satisfied with his return). Her note ended with a cry for help, 'How much I want to come back!' Fifteen days later, a card arrived with a drawing of a figure in a striped vest with his head on his arms beside two glasses of wine and the words 'Yes. Come back darling. I look after you. Christo.'

Theresa bought a plane ticket for the night of her birthday; a symbol of her rebirth. She told no-one of her plan but posted a note to her father at the airport which began 'PREPARE FOR SHOCK,' reminding him that 'it's what you did when you ran away from school-teaching in South Wales to London with only £6 in your pocket and two pairs of braces. I now know how you felt.'

Her arrival in Corfu immediately sparked a scandal, not least because it turned out that Christo already had a wife, who publicly threw his clothes into the street when she heard of Theresa's return. As an English woman, she occupied an ethical no-man's-land. Christo would park her in the cool darkness of wine shops for hours at a time while he disappeared with pen and ink to prepare his 'munitions'. By night he would fuel their hand-to-mouth existence by selling off his drawings and dancing – now with Theresa at his side – for the tourists.

Our only images of Christo were some black-and-white photographs and a raw hand-pressed clay bust that Theresa had sculpted of the 'nice pirate' that sat incongruously among our English pewter. Then one day, there he was: larger than life, his powerful presence filling up our cottage, roaring with laughter, wreathed with smoke, downing bottles of wine. Pushing back the armchairs in our sitting room he announced, 'Now we dance.' And to the accompaniment of a scratched record of Mikis Theodorakis, the two of them wove the magic of 'Zorba's Dance'. Arms on each other's shoulders, they advanced and retreated, spun and knelt, their movements becoming faster as fingers on balalaika flew. Theresa had found her dance, and my eyes were opened.

Despite our precarious financial situation, we always managed to scrape together enough funds to travel; not to the distant shores that I would explore later in life but to France, as my father spoke French fluently. We drove down the Bay of Biscay and up the Loire staying in small, cheap taverns where truck drivers propped up the bar downing their morning *vin rouge* and culinary wonders unfolded.

We were the masters of the road trip, staying a maximum of one night in any one place. This gypsy instinct, which stayed with me for life, was partially inspired by my father's sleeping habits. To say that my father snored was the understatement of the year. So resonant were his breathing habits that we would always take two rooms: one for my mother and me and a separate one for my father.

On one occasion, my father decided to push the boat out and pay for rooms in a hotel near Cherbourg. We retired for the night and within minutes the wall separating our two rooms began vibrating. My mother put her head under the pillow and appeared to be praying.

After a while, we heard indignant footsteps coming down the hall and a knock on our neighbouring door, '*Monsieur, vous ronflez,*' said an irritated male voice.

'Zzzz-grgh-zzzz.'

Rap, rap, '*Monsieur, vous ronflez Monsieur,*' the voice raised a little louder this time.

'Um, hang on. *Oui, oui. Pardonez moi,*' came my father's befuddled response.

The accuser sounded mollified, '*Merci, Monsieur.*' The footsteps moved away down the hall.

But the silence was soon broken again, 'Zzzz-grgh-zzzz.'

This time, two sets of footsteps made their way down the hall. Rap, rap, rap, '*Monsieur, vous ronflez.*'

Then a third and a fourth set of neighbours joined the posse who were out for the blood of my snoring father.

'*Monsieur, vous ronflez,*' they all cried in unison. Then, finally, sweet silence descended.

In the morning, my mother was so embarrassed that she refused to go down to the restaurant for breakfast. When we finally descended with our suitcases and made our way through the marble reception, every eye bored into the backs of our necks. In the car, my father informed us that, after his near lynching, he kept himself awake for the remainder of the night by taking artistic photographs of the bidet. The whole incident had confirmed his view that one shouldn't waste money on 'fancy' hotels.

When I was eleven years old, my father threw caution to the wind and took us to see Theresa in her natural habitat. We landed in Corfu late at night in July and the heat wrapped itself around us as we crossed the tarmac to the tiny airport building. The dark air resonated with the sound of cicadas and a complex aroma of sewage, fish and charcoal. (I would always savour those first sensory impressions of a new land, the warm air on my skin and the distinctive, pungent odours that were like the signature of a country. To this day, whenever I hear the cry of the cicada, I feel the thrilling anticipation of the unknown rise in my soul.)

Christo immediately took charge and steered us to a small, family-run hotel which stood among the olive trees on the curved aquamarine bay of Dassia Beach. We hired ourselves a small car and, like Nick before us, found it impossible to pay for this or anything else on the island. 'Christo he already paid,' we were told wherever we went. Unfortunately, this brought out my father's parsimony and if we were not immediately identified as Christo's 'family' he would name-drop shamelessly until the bill somehow disappeared. Although it was the furthest we ever travelled as a family, it was also one of our cheaper holidays, much to my father's satisfaction.

During the day, we explored the island meandering through tiny sun-bleached mountain villages, ascending the mountain of Pantokrator to see the monastery of the transfiguration of Christ, descending to the azure waters and exquisite bougainvillea-covered monastery of Paleokastritsa and out across the sea to the monastic island of Pontikonisi where Mikis Theodorakis had been held prisoner during the Second World War.

I was enthralled by the intense, claustrophobic atmosphere of the Greek Orthodox chapels; darkened caverns where gilded icons glinted through a mist of incense, where women knelt to kiss the embalmed bones of saints and chanting priests swung silver thuribles dispensing Old Testament aromas. It was so very different from the Baptist church to which my mother sometimes took me on a Sunday morning with its plain white walls, simple wooden cross and functional seating. Fascinated, I would stare intently at the white-bearded priests as they glided around the old town of Kerkyra wearing black robes and tall stove-pipe *kalimavkion* hats.

By this point, Theresa had joined Christo's 'atelier' and was turning out pen-and-ink drawings at a prodigious rate. I would sit with her in the shade as her pen captured the crow-like clergy and bow-backed widows in the sunlit squares around St Spyridon.

At night, Christo and Theresa would walk us down the beach to Diktia, an open-air dance floor surrounded by tables in the sand. There Christo would dance to the music of Theodorakis, circling the floor in even, feline paces – all power and passion. And then, to the outrage of the locals, the 'Englesee' would join him and, arm in arm, they would dip and turn, performing the centuries-old dances of the Greek mountains.

As Dan watched his sister dance to this unfamiliar rhythm, he admitted, 'She is more Greek than English now.' I shuddered with delight, revelling in the foreignness of it all.

4

Growing Pains

My sister Charlotte entered the world on 6 September 1969 and I was not wildly impressed. I had come to think of myself as an only child and I had become used to controlling my interactions with other children, engaging on my own terms. My sister's presence changed the rules of the game.

My first impression of my baby sister was that she looked like a banana. 'Why is she yellow?' I asked, when introduced by my cooing mother. In fact she had jaundice and as a result I was sent to stay with the next-door neighbours while my mother nursed her to health. So, not surprisingly, my second impression of her was that she was a cuckoo who had taken over my nest.

I am ashamed to say that the deep and enduring love I now have for my sister took some time to emerge. Eventually we would become closer than I had ever imagined possible, but as she grew into an enchanting toddler I preyed on her naturally sweet nature and gullibility, teasing her mercilessly. My mother once even caught me putting drawing pins, sharp end up, on her dining-room chair.

It is fair to say that I was not an easy child. I undoubtedly had a natural propensity for solitude but was also painfully aware that I didn't quite fit in with the other children in our local school. This contradiction manifested itself as a strange combination of shyness and flamboyance.

On my first day at middle school, I hid under the coats so that I wouldn't have to talk to anybody but, by the time I reached secondary school, I had embraced life on the fringe. I would 'ham it up' by wearing maxi skirts and large-brimmed hippy hats, fostering a cut-glass English accent and hanging out in the art rooms. My reputation, however, was sealed by my father when he realized I was faking illness to get off school one day and marched me up to the headmaster's office while still wearing his pyjamas.

On the physical front, I was an early bloomer and soon attracted a ragged coterie of unsuitable suitors: a wannabe rockabilly who wooed me with dead rabbits which he skinned in our back garden, a St Bernard look-alike who could hardly see through his motorcycle helmet for hair, and a trainee bank cashier whose mother liked to make floral lampshades. My parents couldn't decide which match they were most horrified by, but the bank cashier seemed most out of place in our family.

The male attention, hippy dress and posh accent hardly endeared me to the rough gang from the estate near the school; I might as well have walked round with a target on my back. As a result, I became so preoccupied with avoiding being beaten up (not always successfully) that my grades began to slip. My reports included comments such as 'has such potential', 'must try harder to concentrate' and 'can be a disruptive influence'.

At one parents' evening, my father was horrified to hear from my form tutor that I was looking to leave school at sixteen in order to train as a prison warder – until the hapless woman worked out that she had the file for the wrong pupil. But with the correct file, she went on to explain that I was failing in most subjects, had been caught smoking on school grounds and was generally seen as an odd-ball who failed to fit in. Enraged, my father stormed, this time fully clothed, to the headmaster's office demanding to know what the school had done to the bright, intelligent child he had given them.

'Katie is bright but she doesn't make things easy,' explained the exasperated headmaster. 'What you need to understand is that it would be easier on her – it is easier – to be average.'

My father rose unsteadily to his feet, fixed the headmaster with a look of withering disdain and spat out, 'To be average is the goal of the mediocre.' Then turning on his heel, he metaphorically shook the dust from his feet and left the headmaster speechless. Unfortunately I wasn't afforded the same luxury and had to return the following day.

By my fifteenth year I was not without friends but had, by necessity, learnt how to throw a painful right hook and spent many lunchtimes outside the headmaster's office. However, after a last-minute panic burst of academia, I managed to scrape the necessary secondary-level qualifications to squeeze my way into the sixth form. It was a close shave and my dismal results brought me to my senses. The departure of my tormentors, most of whom had gone to work in local butchers or hairdressers, also gave me the opportunity of a fresh start.

Until this point, I had been a reactionary without a focus (apart from my mission to keep myself safe through high school) but once the immediate threat had lifted, I discovered that rebellion was still deeply rooted in my soul. I had become a rebel in need of a cause.

My career as a low-level activist was initially sparked by a visit to a veal production unit. After vomiting copiously, I returned home and announced that I had become a vegetarian. For the next decade I ate in parallel to my parents, spending hours soaking beans and grinding nuts. Every Christmas, I would turn my nose up at the festive turkey in favour of a dry and tasteless cashew nut roast.

One year, my father decided to economize and buy two poussins instead of one turkey. 'How on earth are we going to get these into the oven,' exclaimed my exasperated mother.

'And what about my nut roast?' I pitched in, adding fuel to the fire. 'Never mind your nuts, what about our turkey?' she flamed.

Eventually my mother managed to wedge the two birds into the oven with just enough room to spare for my nut roast, but their removal proved more of a challenge. The trays were wedged in so tight that my father had to step in and try to prise them out again. After tugging away for about five minutes, the two birds finally shot out of the oven like a cork out of a bottle and landed on the flagstone floor. The cat jumped in like a flash and one of the birds quickly disappeared out of the open kitchen door. 'Oh no, we'll have to eat her nut roast,' groaned my mother.

Once I began to wear make-up, my interest in animal welfare took on a new fervour. I was shopping for eye shadow in the local town of Northampton when an earnest young man handed me a leaflet showing a laboratory rabbit, its blood-shot and poisoned eyes cruelly held open with clamps. I had a rabbit at home called Flopsy and the thought that this gentle creature could be tortured so that I could flaunt Mary Quant eyes was so ghastly that I nearly, but not quite, gave up using make-up.

Instead I joined the British Union for the Abolition of Vivisection (BUAV) and its brigade of leaflet distributors and petition gatherers. I wouldn't go as far as setting free animals and certainly never condoned targeting individuals (although later on at university I did get into trouble for breaking into the Student Union audio visual room and broadcasting a particularly graphic video of vivisection on the screens in the canteen at lunchtime).

I also began to absorb the newspapers that liberally adorned our house and was left with a growing sense of distress, even anger, at the injustices I began to see all around me. One day I came across a series of photographs in *The Sunday Times* supplement of the Dalits of Bombay, the historically 'untouchable' caste of India who have been discriminated against throughout history. The article focused on the most unfortunate of all, those who had fallen prey to the beggar masters of Bombay. One particular photograph bore its way into my consciousness and still haunts me more than three decades later; the image was of a man in about his thirties sitting cross legged, cradling a crying baby in his arms with such tender care. His face was raised as if to heaven, and where his eyes had once been were terrible whitened scars.

The image was like some terrifying Pieta. When I closed my eyes, all I could see was the beggar and his child. When I ate, all I could do was to think of their hunger. Years later I would view the terrible handiwork of the beggar masters at first hand, children with eyes gouged from their sockets and limbs lopped off – all to make them more effective beggars.

In my teenage angst, I was consumed by a sense of injustice and wept hot angry tears at the thought that a human being could be so little valued by their own that they could be tortured and mutilated in such a way. Surely the creator God must also weep in despair at the inhumanity of his creation. I felt so helpless; there were no marches to join, no leaflets to distribute and no petitions to sign. So I did what so many in my family had done before me and sought a way to express the emotions that tore at my soul: I began to paint.

5

The Prow Cracked

From the day we are born most of us seek to leave our mark upon the world. We may not be conscious that we are seeking immortality but even the graffiti artist who scrawls 'I was here' has his eye on eternity. This was the impulse that drove my grandmother to sing, my grandfather, aunt and myself to draw and paint, and my parents to write.

My mother had an insatiable curiosity about the world, a genuine love of people and a desire to record the world around her – attributes that made her a great journalist. She once told me, 'I am not a writer. I am a journalist. Ideas don't just unfold in my head; I need a news editor behind me, to guide me.' When she left *Woman* magazine, she was effectively cut adrift and in need of a guide. My father found him in the pub in the next village of Emberton.

Vic Mayhew was a new arrival in the village, a flamboyant larger-than-life character fresh out of Fleet Street who had set up a publishing company. My father waxed lyrical over a beer about my mother's newspaper days and Vic was hooked. When my mother met Vic for lunch the rapport was immediate and, over several bottles of wine, the seeds were sown for a lifelong friendship between the two families and the next phase of my mother's career.

Vic offered her two options: a book on gardening or another on eccentrics with the title *The World's Greatest Cranks and Crackpots*. It was an easy decision, 'I know something about eccentrics, I live with one,' she told him. She was given four months to research and write the book.

My mother set up the essentials in her bedroom: an upright typewriter, an ashtray and a kettle for making coffee. She said that the only way she could get the book done in time was to focus completely. 'So long as the pots are washed, beds are made and everyone has got clean knickers, we'll be okay,' she assured us. It was at this time that we discovered that, while my father once cooked sumptuous meals to woo my mother, he was now capable of burning a boiled egg.

Every morning she disappeared upstairs and sat wreathed in smoke, banging away at the typewriter keys until late at night. As it came closer to the deadline she would often sit until five o'clock in the morning puffing and typing away. Occasionally she emerged for a trip into the labyrinth of the London Library and would re-emerge like a scholarly mole clutching batty aristocrats.

My mother was fully immersed in the amphibious Lord Rokeby (who in the eighteenth century contrived to spend his entire life in water) when she received a call; Vic had been lured back to Fleet Street by newspaper tycoon Robert Maxwell who had made him production manager of the Mirror Group of newspapers, and Margaret and her crackpots were now the property of Octopus Books who wanted delivery *tout de suite*.

For the next few weeks, we barely saw my mother except when she emerged dishevelled to construct cheese sandwiches and replenish her cigarette supplies. My father, unable to sleep with her typing away, became nocturnal, dozing during the day on the sofa. Charlotte and I became almost feral and lived off muesli. I would sit munching my way through bowls of Alpen salivating as I read the enclosed recipe cards, while my father ate at the pub. Then finally, after months of smoky isolation, she appeared, transcript in hand. 'It is finished,' she announced with a biblical flourish and set forth to London to Octopus's Grosvenor Square offices.

Octopus were hard task masters but still had the personal touch of an independent publisher. 'You have your own editor and they take you out for lunch,' my mother enthused (lunch being a particularly important part of this transaction). In fact, the publisher contributed to keeping our family afloat for several years by commissioning titles such as *The World's Wickedest Women*, *The World's Greatest Lovers*, *The World's Greatest Psychics and Mystics* and finally *The World's Greatest Royal Lovers* (a blatant effort to cash in on the worldwide obsession with Charles and Diana which my mother hated and buried at the back of our book shelves).

It was at about this time that my father also began to write poetry in earnest. He admired my mother's prodigious ability to churn out prose but regarded poetry as 'the logos, the thing it-self at its best'. He had begun writing poetry while still working in advertising but now devoted a majority of his time to the po-etic form and, in 1988, self-published his collected works entitled *Disposition of C90*.

My father's poetry vividly reflected his lifelong struggle with his spirituality, sense of identity and need for meaning. As far back as the early 1960s he had written:

> *What must I do to inherit eternal life?*
> *Seems to be the parody of my plea?*[1]

Some of his later work was beautiful and evocative, such as the ode he wrote to his precious sanctuary Larkland:

> *The sweetest moment of the night*
> *Is nearing to the day,*
> *Never knowing, never telling*
> *When light begins again.*
> *Exquisite wonder drinks the warm still silence*

Of the night around the moon serene
Before the stealing tinge of day.[2]

But as time went on, his work also reflected his growing disenchantment with the world. His poetry became painful, and he howled in iambic pentameter:

The confusion of tongues is growing
Growing, groaning, growling, howling
At its own bloodletting;
The rational has become rabid with fear.[3]

He became increasingly nocturnal, craving the silence of the night for his creativity and he would fuss around impatiently until we had all gone off to bed enabling him to settle down to write. When inspired, he would often write through the night. I would creep downstairs in the dark and find him bathed in moonlight, silent, breathing, waiting. Sometimes he would take me into the kitchen, pour himself a large glass of whisky and, at three o'clock in the morning, read his poetry to me.

As time went on, he would sometimes stay up for days at a time often wearing only his underwear or pyjamas, writing all night and dozing fitfully during the daylight. At these times he would become almost feverish with excitement, his wit rapier-like, until finally exhausted he would crash and burn, his excitement turning to anger and despair. At these times, he would lash out at inanimate objects and his skin would betray his inner turmoil by breaking out in terrible, disfiguring eczema. My father became like a black vortex and all we could do was to hold on to the sides hoping not to be dragged down into his darkness.

My mother blamed it all on Jung. My father had always been interested in symbolism and mythology and one Christmas she had bought him a copy of the analytical psychologist's great work *Memories, Dreams and Reflections* – a move she came to bitterly regret.

There was something about Jung that resonated with my father at a very deep level but which became distorted in his mind. He became obsessed by the idea that we are connected by a collective subconscious, a psychic repository of symbols that have appeared in mythology and dreams throughout history. On most mornings my sister and I would face a third-degree interrogation while we hurriedly inhaled cornflakes in our mad rush to catch the school bus.

'So Charlotte, what did you dream last night?' he would enquire, cigarette in hand.

'Dad,' Charlotte would squirm with embarrassment.

'No, tell me.'

'I can't remember, Dad.'

At which point my father would embark on a monologue: 'It is in dreams that we tap into the mind of God, the unconscious. They are not rational. They are confusion, logically confounded. Freud had it all wrong – this focus on the sexual, the oedipal, I find his assumption irritating and absurd.'

'Dad, the bus is coming.'

I occasionally humoured him by sharing some of my wilder nocturnal reflections and thus became his favourite subject. He was particularly fascinated by a recurring dream in which I beheaded a series of identical doll-like figures on a conveyor belt. Apparently this was a positive sign of my burgeoning non-conformity and indicated a deep fear of mediocrity, something he heartily approved of. 'What you are revealing is your disdain of bourgeois life. I feel it too; it pains me,' he told me.

My father also began to categorize people according to Jung's psychological types of introversion and extroversion. He regarded his own introversion as a sign of intellect and spiritual depth, but extroversion as a sign of superficiality and a failure to grasp the meaning of life. Whenever my mother pestered him to change out of his pyjamas, he would pour scorn on her concern for social niceties telling her, 'Oh Margaret, you are such an extrovert!' He also decided that I was neurotic and would say to me, 'You are so like me. It is like watching a mirror image. It's awful. It is like watching my anima acting out.'

Such analysis wasn't just reserved for the family. To my mother's horror, he would pin guests in corners at social gatherings and psychoanalyse them. In a bank in Vitry, he once cornered an unsuspecting victim and talked to him about Jung for half an hour in fluent French.

My father was continually concerned about our intellectual diet. He had always been widely read, a polymath, and was impatient with lesser pursuits. Whenever my mother tried to watch a television programme, he would stand behind her chair interrogating her:

'What's that you are watching?'

'*Neighbours.*'

'What is this all about?'

'Neighbours in Australia.'

'Is it a soap?'

'Yes, Dan, it's a soap.'

'Soap operas. It's another example of Tao,' he mused. 'It is named perfectly. You know the big detergent people sponsored it – so soap operas. It still speaks true . . . Soap opera . . . Soap emotion . . . Soft soap. It is sound without meaning.'

'Oh, Dan!'

And having finally harried her away from the television set, he would put on a worn VHS of his favourite film, Marcel Carné's poetic realist *Les Enfant du Paridis*, which he felt was more suitably pregnant with meaning.

Despite, or perhaps because of, his obtuseness I adored my father and took a strange satisfaction in the fact that he saw me as some kind of psychological experiment. I was also more willing to listen to his Jungian rantings than my mother and sister. I would often sit with him until dawn listening to his monologues interspersed with readings from Jung as he drank whisky and chain smoked. 'We are seeing the split in the psyche that took place when Adam and Eve were ejected from Eden, which is of course unconsciousness itself. We have been ejected out of unconsciousness to consciousness,' he would explain to a baffled teenager. I would sneak a sip of his whisky and became lost in his rhetoric.

His reasoning was not always easy to follow as his mind made rapid connections between the rational and the irrational, the concrete and the mythological, the fictional and the spiritual. But I was dazzled by the breadth of his knowledge and his easy recollection of classical and biblical references. I also recognized that my mother was right; as his obsession with Jung grew, he was becoming progressively more introspective and despair had begun to creep in.

Who knows where my father's depression first began. Perhaps Gladys was right and the plane crash unleashed a madness, nurtured by deep-seated guilt over the death of his passenger in the later car crash and finally fanned into full flame by the words of a long-dead Swiss psychoanalyst.

Like Jung, he believed that the decisive question for man was whether he was related to something infinite or not, but, like Jung, he found God to be an absent and heartless landlord. In society, he saw only the collective neurosis of the age, loss of soul and a profound superficiality and conformity to consumerism. He had little time for the superficiality of the 'persona' that people wear to make themselves acceptable to society and became obsessed with the shadow, the dark area of our personalities which most of us struggle to keep under control for fear of rejection and isolation.

Nowadays my father would have been labelled as bi-polar but the older term of manic depression better describes the extraordinary roller coaster that he travelled from enormous heights of creative imagination, extroverted wit and even joy, to the dark depths of introspection, frustration, inwardly focused anger and despair at the world. When on good form, my father was eccentrically urbane, charming, erudite and entertaining. When the 'black dog' caught up with him, he would rage at the world, or sit silently, sadly, moving me to tears.

One of the main triggers of his depressive episodes was, ironically, a very worldly one – money. He would declare his disdain, 'It is all materialism, what is money?' but then make himself sick obsessing about the lack of filthy lucre.

Money always seemed to be in short supply in the Nicholas household. After an initial three years of redundancy, my father had become a taxi driver, much to my mother's embarrassment and to his delight; he thoroughly enjoyed having a captive audience in the back seat. But, in reality, my father was an appalling driver. He was officially categorized as 100 per cent disabled and therefore was meant to drive Motability cars, but preferred second-hand 'bangers' bought at auction houses which he regularly put in the ditch up the lane from Larkland.

His cars were always in the process of being reconstituted. When his passenger door had to be removed to be beaten back into shape, he continued to drive the car, the wind whistling through the interior. The local publican told my mother that he had watched him drive up and park outside the pub and meticulously lock the driver's door, leaving half the car open to the elements as he walked in for his habitual half of lager.

Eventually he gave up the taxi driving to become an insurance broker. The irony was that, although my father seemed incapable of managing our domestic budget, he had a good grasp of finance on a larger scale. When he wanted, my father could be both professional and highly engaging and he came close to landing some very large corporate accounts. However, he insisted on operating his business out of a small cupboard under the stairs in which the cat would pee on a regular basis, ignoring my mother's plea that he rent an office in the local town. When the smell got too much he would commute to the dining room table.

The fact that we kept our heads above water was mainly down to the Open University which provided a rich source of potential clients. When we first moved to the area, Milton Keynes had been little more than a picturesque thatched village but in 1967 the Government decided that this small corner of Buckinghamshire was sufficiently unimportant to be the site of a new city. The development never impinged on our rural idyll but the Open University did attract a large number of professors with alternative lifestyles who recognized a kindred spirit in my father and were willing to trust him with their financial arrangements.

Money, however, continued to be my father's bête noire. He became obsessed about our use of electricity, plunging us into darkness as we read in order to save a light bulb and turning off 'excessive' electric heaters in the midst of winter. He also developed a theory about saving petrol and would turn off the car engine whenever he was on a downward incline to let gravity do the work and save a few pennies.

One Christmas Eve, his fears about our financial situation came to a head. 'We can't afford Christmas,' he sank down into his chair in despair. 'I don't know where the money is going to come from. I can't cope anymore.'

I had grown accustomed to my father's melodramas but something in his voice seriously worried me. So, to protect my father's sanity, I spent Christmas Eve interrogating the family finances; and in doing so discovered that we were being kept adequately afloat by a generous veterans allowance from the RAF. I was able to restore equilibrium by working out a weekly allowance for each of my parents.

My mother, despite her perennially sunny disposition, undoubtedly found his behaviour hard to handle. She had incredible powers of denial and when my father was at his worst would walk around the house singing loudly 'la, la, la, la' as he plunged philosophical. It didn't help that she was also caring for her elderly and highly hypochondriac mother, going to her nearby flat to cook her three meals a day and negotiating with the local doctor's surgery where she had been blacklisted. (As my sister once observed, 'Nana has had everything except for Dutch Elm disease.')

My mother always had an emotional relationship with food that I could not understand. As a war child she had undoubtedly suffered real hunger and had developed an attachment to some extremely unhealthy but comforting food stuffs and, when stressed, she resorted to eating. My sister and I would regularly discover emergency bars of chocolate hidden down the side of her favourite chair, and slabs of Battenberg cake secreted away behind curtains. We felt we were doing her a favour by polishing off whatever we found, secure in the knowledge that she would never confront us.

Christmas always seemed to be a flash point in our house. One year, when my father had been particularly difficult in the run up to Christmas Eve, my mother barricaded herself in the kitchen and seemed intent on eating the entire contents of the larder; she had already made her way through the Christmas cheese, polished off the 'spare' Christmas puddings and was eyeing up the turkey trimmings. My father, Charlotte and I huddled in the dining room and drew straws on who would be brave enough to save my mother from herself.

Having lost, I gingerly opened up the kitchen door and crept up behind her. 'Mum, are you okay?'

'I'm fine, except for your father. He's determined to ruin Christmas.'

'It's going to be fine, Mum. Just don't eat all the food.'

The next minute I was sitting outside in the snow, having been forcibly ejected with a broom handle, while my sister and father fell about laughing.

Ironically, it was my father who drove my mother back into the arms of Christ. Having grown up a Baptist, she drifted away from the church when she left home. But when I was a child she began to attend the local Baptist church in the nearby town of Olney, occasionally dragging me and my sister along. Then, as my father's depressive episodes became more frequent, my mother's attendance and need for spiritual succour increased in direct proportion to his intensity.

My sister was by far the most enthusiastic and willingly underwent a full-body immersion baptism in the pool of water ingeniously hidden under a large and imposing pulpit. I had been christened with due pomp and ceremony in the Anglican church near Nick's house in Itchenor at three months old but was never confirmed or baptized in my mother's adopted church. It wasn't the concept of the second immersion I objected to; it was the ethos of the church.

Perhaps my father's analytical fervour had rubbed off on me but I found it very hard to accept the congregation's rather literal interpretation of the Bible; nothing could convince me that the earth was only 6,000 years old. While philosophically I accepted the 'concept' of God and had even felt his presence as I had wandered as a child bathing in the beauty of his creation, I could never sense his presence in the church. I found the whole Baptist experience too unremittingly upbeat and I baulked at the tambourine waving, Pollyanna-like positivity, knowing that my father sat at home periodically sinking into darkness.

I wanted to know how God could love my father yet allow him to suffer such despair, but no-one could give me a satisfactory answer. I struggled as I watched my father weighed down by a world he did not seem to understand, and my mother eating her way towards an early grave in jolly denial. God seemed very distant and lacking in empathy – more like the unfeeling God that Jung struggled with.

So, in anger, I turned my back and walked away.

Part Two

The High Seas

6

Celtic Shores

I still dream of Aberystwyth and the magical journey through the mountains to the town by the sea. A transformation begins at the Welsh borders where the English roads begin to give way to narrow, high-hedged lanes, and orderly, productive, striped fields turn into rambling, sheep-strewn meadows cut through with meandering and cackling streams. As you drive deeper into Wales, the well-watered greenery gives way to deep purple heathers and brash mustard gorse-covered granite mounds which rise up out of the earth like ancient funeral sites to meet the glowering sky.

When my parents drove me up to 'Aber', we would occasionally turn off at the grey-stone market town of Rhayader and climb the narrow pass between the cowering Cambrian Mountains until we broke through onto the high pale-green and golden moors and the vastness of the skies. There, only ghosts roamed among the black ruins and copper-stained ground of the Cwmystwyth mines, while red kites wheeled overhead.

But my favourite route to Aberystwyth took us through the inconspicuous market town of Machynlleth where, back in the fifteenth century, Owain Glyndŵr was crowned the last Prince of Wales. The town also held a special place in the hearts of students as the county of Dyfed was dry on a Sunday and it was the only place to get drink for miles around.

From Machynlleth, the road wound upwards, eventually breaking through the thick dark-green woodland just above the university buildings on Penglais Hill, to reveal tumbling rooftops ranged around a glittering, white-flecked bay and a protective horseshoe of green hills. It was like a Welsh Shangri-La and something deep inside told me I was coming home.

Although my birthplace was irretrievably English, my mother and father had long recognized the Celt within their daughter. In fact at times of exasperation, my mother would fling at me, 'Oh you are such a Celt,' which I took as a backhanded compliment as I treasured my Celtic roots.

My grandfather Nick came from a long line of Welshmen and had been brought up to speak only '*iaith fy man*' ('my mother's language') outside of school. His siblings had melodious names such as Anulum and Handel. I can still remember my ancient, creaking great-aunts who laid out lace tablecloths, gargantuan hams, browned rice puddings and Welsh cakes for 'high tea' in their dark, grey-stone terraced cottages.

My grandmother Gladys Conner was of Irish Celtic descent. In the 1850s, her grandfather Charles O'Conner, a flaming redhead, had escaped Galway and the deadly grip of the potato famine and crossed the forbidding Irish Sea. His daughter Lizzie Burridge, another redhead, went on to marry a 'feckless' Irishman by the name of James Fynne, who died at the age of twenty-six with photographs of five women in his wallet, but not before giving Lizzie three children including the opera-singing Gladys.

My mother, on the other hand, always thought of herself as a Yorkshire woman and had little truck with Celtic sensibility but her mother, the unfortunately named Elsie Beard, was actually born in the South Welsh mining town of Maesteg, a mere 10 miles from Neath where her future in-law Nick trained as a teacher. So as I looked down on the rolling Irish Sea, I reasoned that I was returning to the land of my fathers.

After being brought up in a house full of my grandfather's Post-Impressionist paintings, my aunt's bucolic images of Greece and countless books on the impossibly romantic lives of artists, I had enrolled to study Fine Art at the University College of Wales. In this day and age of tuition fees and vocational degrees, I would probably have steered another course but at the time my choice of degree seemed entirely logical.

There was something profoundly unreal about the Aberystwyth experience; this was where children came to play-act at being adults and the beauty was incandescent. I can still see the town in my mind's eye: the walk down Terrace Road towards the glittering blue horizon, the pale pastel houses overlooking the Irish Sea, the monstrous bubblegum-pink Kings Hall where I head-banged enigmatically to a variety of heavy metal bands, and the Marine Bar where I spent one memorable day glued to the televised rock charity extravaganza 'Live Aid', swigging beer as rock stars sang their hearts out to raise funds for victims of the Ethiopian famine.

By day, the glittering arch of the bay drew students who would sit between lectures on the pebbled beach or lounge in the pretty pastel Victorian shelters. By night, the seafront Parade would come alive like a South American *paseo*, boys and girls promenading in their best charity-shop rags in order to see and be seen before dancing the night away on the ancient sagging pier.

The actual student population of Aberystwyth was around seven thousand but you would be forgiven for thinking that it was a lot higher given the number of students who have 'gone local'. Aber has a strangely narcotic effect on those who go there. It was a bit like a Welsh *Hotel California* which you could check into but never leave.

A large number of students arrived each year with good intentions only to succumb to the slower pace of existence, giving up their dreams of academic achievement in order to take to the hills to live the good life. As a result, the land around Aber was littered with ex-students growing organic vegetables.

The town has always had a strong alternative vibe; a majority of my friends were also vegetarian, vegan or macrobiotic. On my first day in the university hall of residence, I was handed a slab of cheese and a plate of chips and coleslaw but from there on in subsisted primarily on industrial quantities of muesli. The received wisdom was that the more roughage the better, so I soon began supplementing my diet with lashings of bran meal until, one night, I ended up in Bronglais Hospital with a blockage and was told by an incredulous doctor, 'You are not a horse, go and eat some fish fingers.'

The place also offered a range of what could loosely be termed New Age doctrines. Everything was available in Aber – statues of Buddha or Ganesh, 'purifying' crystals, books on the Mother Goddess or Wicca, and courses on everything from transcendental meditation to the origins of the Green Man – all mixed up with a healthy dose of Arthurianism. (Dyfed features as the site of many early Arthurian legends in the medieval Welsh literary masterpiece *The Mabinogion*.)

The area had also once been a hotbed of Celtic Christianity. The ancient Celts who had wandered Dyfed were animists who believed that every mountain, river, stream and spring was 'inspirited'; certain trees were revered and the spirits of water were honoured as givers of life and a link between this world and others. So when Christianity came to Wales in the fifth century, its adherents naturally focused on sensing the creator in his creation, and ancient Celtic prayers spoke of God and nature in one breath. Apart from a couple of crosses cut from standing stones in the churchyard of Llanbadarn Fawr, not much remained of Celtic Christianity by the 1980s but it was still hard to escape the long arm of the church.

Churches were as ubiquitous in Aber as pubs (of which there were fifty-two) and the two establishments existed symbiotically despite the local legislation about being dry on the Sabbath. During a period spent living above a pub, I would wake every Sunday to the sound of strong Welsh male voices belting out the hymn 'Bread of Heaven', only for the same dulcet tones to resonate around our back door as the church doors closed, 'Hey, Dai Bach. Give us a pint.'

Perhaps it was the inherent musicality that spoke to me. My grandfather Nick, who was brought up as a Welsh Non-Conformist, always said it was the rhythms, open vowel sounds and grand rhetoric of the Welsh language – rather than any innate spirituality – that appealed to him. He said pronouncing the Welsh word for Lord – *Arglwydd* – was like climbing a mountain range, 'Oh we had good prayer-makers in Wales in those days,' he recalled. 'Men who could buttonhole the Lord for twenty minutes at a time and hold him enthralled with those Welsh biblical rhythms.'

So one Sunday morning, I snuck into the back pews of an imposing looking Baptist church. The preacher was spectacular, terrifying and had about him a whiff of brimstone. 'There's sin in our midst,' he roared and, convinced his flaming eyes were boring into me, I bolted back out onto the street and decided to explore some of the alternatives on offer.

Encouraged by a rather attractive hippy, I attended a weekend of transcendental meditation high in the mountains above Capel Bangor conducted by a 'guru' with a strong Liverpudlian accent. I was attracted to TM primarily because it was sold as a mental technique, unrelated to a specific religious doctrine, which focused on everyday benefits such as inner peace, stress reduction, well-being and reduced anxiety.

I didn't have high expectations and at first, flushed full of camomile tea, I could only think about how much I needed the loo. But within a matter of hours, I was astonished by the change in my mental state. At first my mind became quieter but then I began to lose a sense of connection with my body. I felt as if I was looking out over a vast horizon.

At first, this endless landscape seemed empty but then I began to feel a presence, something awesome, formless, and powerful but caring and I had an overwhelming sensation of being loved. Unnerved, I brought myself out of this transcendent state like a panicking diver rushing for the surface (and ended up with a terrible migraine – the mental equivalent of the bends). I had been looking for off-the-shelf stress relief but once again had connected with something more and was shaken.

In my first year at university, I had to study an additional subject and, just to ensure that my degree would have absolutely no practical value in Thatcherite society, I chose to study philosophy which I found something of a mixed bag. I didn't really take to logic primarily because of the timing of the seminars. At five o'clock on a Friday while every other student headed for the student union bar, I'd be engaged in painful debates on such critical issues as why an elephant was not a table. I was far more attracted to the religion and philosophy lectures which took place on a Tuesday morning, where I immersed myself in the complexity of the ontological, casual, cosmological and teleological arguments for the existence of God until my head felt like it would explode.

My confusion probably wasn't helped by the fact that, for a short time, I had a British Muslim boyfriend. I never quite understood how this hirsute and rather intense young man was able to justify our relationship to himself, but I was fascinated. He gave me the Quran to read, had a beautiful silk prayer mat which he dutifully knelt on five times a day facing Mecca, and tried to illuminate Islam for me. However, we soon went our separate ways, not because of issues of faith, but because I helpfully offered to wash his karate suit and turned it pink. My next boyfriend was a dead ringer for Robert Powell's Jesus of Nazareth complete with long hair, beard and sandals (a development my father found highly amusing).

My main love, however, was art. Laden with books and art materials I would walk miles up and down Penglais Hill to attend lectures on Russian revolutionary art and the lost wax process. I threw myself into my work with gusto, attending live drawing classes – at which my Jesus-look-alike boyfriend would sometimes rather unnervingly pose in the nude – and even learnt how to weld in order to major in sculpture.

I began to specialize in large abstract pieces which I hoped spoke of man's condition in this less than perfect world. I would drag great pieces of driftwood, metal and other flotsam off the beach and merge them with glass and other materials to create large-scale – completely unsaleable – sculptures and installations. My *tour de force* was a large-scale resin and metal sculpture of a screaming head cut through with intersecting prison grilles. It was meant to represent the concept of prisoners of conscience and was entitled *We see nothing, we hear nothing, we say nothing*; although it later became known as 'the head in a grid' and was used by my family as a hat stand.

The problem was that I was really a rather average artist. It wasn't that I didn't have any talent at all – I did a roaring trade in watercolours of local churches – it was just that I struggled to adequately express my angst at the human condition in my chosen metier. The light began to dawn when my tutor asked me, 'Why do you write so much in your sketchbooks?'

At the end of three years, I received a respectable but not spectacular II.i Hons degree but was granted the Sir Francis Williams Award for Art History, reinforcing my growing suspicion that I was a better writer than artist. The award paid for a place to study for a Masters in art history and also bought me some valuable time to rethink my career options. I was still fascinated by the idea of art which conveyed a social message so decided to focus my studies on Marxist art theory, Russian revolutionary and feminist art.

Second-wave feminism was in full swing in the UK in the early 1980s and there was a whole range of radical women artists, such as Judy Chicago, using modern art and installation techniques to bring female issues to the fore. (In an effort to radicalize my younger sister,

I once dragged her to see Judy Chicago's *Dinner Party* in London but she was mortified to discover that all the exquisitely painted dinner plates represented the vaginas of famous women.)

I was also highly influenced by writers such as Rozsika Parker, author of *The Subversive Stitch*, who gave a new prominence to crafts traditionally associated with women, such as embroidery and textiles, that had previously passed beneath the respectable art world radar. Enthused, I curated an exhibition of women's textile art in Wales and spoke fervently at various seminars and symposiums. As a result I was granted access to the mysterious world of feminist academia and sat through earnest conference sessions on everything from 'Women and Electricity' to 'Menstruation'.

I also decided that it was time I took a stab at following in my mother's footsteps and try to write for a living. On the basis of a few articles in the university newspaper, I managed to secure some work as a freelance arts reporter on the local paper *The Cambrian News*. My first by-lined article headlined 'Actors and Activists' was a rather worthy review of the Fall Out Theatre Company's performance of *Two Plays for a Nuclear Age* but it was deemed acceptable and from that point on I was able to attend the theatre for free.

Emboldened by my regional newspaper success, I reached out to *Spare Rib*, a radical feminist magazine founded and edited by Marsha Rowe and Rosie Boycott (who went on to become a legendary editor of *The Independent*). In the early days, mainstream retailers had refused to stock the magazine which aimed to challenge the traditional gender roles of women as virgin, wife or mother and showed how to make Christmas tree hangings out of tampons. To my surprise, I was taken on as a freelance arts correspondent and asked to write in-depth features on issues such as women's education.

By this time, I had been in Aberystwyth for nearly five years. At first I relished the sense of isolation from the world and fondly imagined myself growing old in a hillside cottage surrounded by sheep and organic vegetables, writing radical papers on Welsh art and women's issues. But while I dreamed, my Jesus-look-alike boyfriend had decided to make this life a reality. In the second year of university he dropped out of college, took jobs ranging from chicken plucker to barman, and preferred to frequent 'local' pubs away from the student crowd where he would spend many an evening swapping yarns with characters who appeared melded to their bar stools. He was a poetic soul and seemed at peace with the world but I could feel the mountains closing in around me.

I knew I had to get out but, in order to do so, I needed to convert my rather esoteric academic experience into some kind of money-generating venture. I aimed high and somehow obtained an interview with the head of news at HTV in Cardiff. My colossal lack of knowledge about Welsh current affairs and my plummy English accent didn't make me an obvious candidate but he was both patient and charming and gave me the advice I needed: 'The only way you are going to get in is pester power,' he explained. 'You've got to keep on turning up on the producer's or editor's doorstep. And be willing to do anything to get in . . . and you need to be in London.'

So, accompanied by 'the head in a grid' and several boxes of boxes, I left the sea and made my way back through the mountains.

7

All That Glistens

I arrived in the capital at the age of twenty-three with a rather grand idea of my own abilities. Sara, my flat mate from Aberystwyth, had moved to London a couple of years previously to study at the London School of Economics and had secured a bedsit for me in Camden. The room was situated directly above the basement flat of the elderly and miserly Italian landlady (who later made the news by leaving over a million pounds to her cat). Her mission in life was to catch any of her tenants 'sinning' – transgressions being punishable by eviction – and as I was located directly above her, I came in for special attention. If she ever heard more than one set of footsteps cross my floor, she would stand on a chair and bang on the ceiling with a broom handle, bellowing, 'I know what you're up to. I know what you are up to.'

The room was a hovel. The first thing I did was to wash the sticky curtains that covered the windows and the cooking area, and scrub the yellowing grease-covered walls with sugar soap and paint them white. When my landlady spotted the improvements, she insisted she had organized the decoration and tried to charge me for the paint and labour. But I loved the fact that the bedsit was so centrally located, literally on the doorstep of the wonderfully vibrant Camden Market.

I walked every inch of the capital from the Dickensian alleys of the Docklands to the sordid and rubbish-strewn streets of Soho where I peered into dark sin-filled doorways. I spent hours in the National, Portrait and Tate Galleries revelling in the reality of artworks I had previously only seen in books. My mother would often join me and treat us to cheap tickets for West End Shows – *Phantom of the Opera, Les Misérables, Miss Saigon* – and afterwards we would splash out on a taxi-cab, carving our way through the late-night crowds and neon lights of the West End. Even today I thrill at the sight of the Thames by night and love to be lulled by the passing neon lights as we make our way out into the darker outer suburbs of the city.

What I didn't have, however, was any money or realistic prospect of employment. So as an interim measure, I signed up with a temp agency that placed me as a receptionist and the only white employee at the North London Development Agency for Afro-Caribbean businesses, and then as a trading floor secretary in the City, where the hands-on approach of the brokers reignited my feminism.

In the meantime I sent my curriculum vitae and folio to over two hundred publications, television and radio stations including *Spare Rib*, where I went through an excruciating interview for a sub-editor's job.

'So how do you feel about working with women?' asked an intense woman in Doc Martins and dungarees.

'I would prefer it because I wouldn't have to worry about sexual harassment,' I replied, tossing my long blonde hair and adjusting my floral shirt. Not surprisingly I didn't get the job.

I needed work experience, so Sara and I went to volunteer at Amnesty International for the price of the bus fare. Volunteering involved everything from stuffing envelopes to occasional copywriting in the basement of Amnesty's offices in Bowling Green Lane. But after reading graphic accounts of torture in South America, all I could do was put my head in my hands and cry. I came to the conclusion that I needed to acquire a greater level of maturity and pragmatism before I could be any use in the not-for-profit sector.

I was reaching the end of my tether and financial resources when I spotted an advertisement in *The Guardian* asking 'Are you creative, are you full of ideas, can you write?' It was almost identical to the advertisement that my grandfather Nick had answered back in the 1920s, and, like him, I didn't have a clue what job the advert was actually referring to, but it involved writing and was based in Fleet Street so my curiosity was piqued.

I called and spoke to a rather enthusiastic woman who invited me in for an interview and, a couple of days later, I found myself down an alley off Fleet Street, in a tiny second-floor room with a sloping floor, packed to the ceiling with pink fluffy bears and assorted toys. Swept away by my interviewer's vehemence, I signed up for a career which I only later discovered was called public relations.

So I began work in PR, or at least a rather specific subset of consumer PR. In later years I would apply these skills to nobler causes, but in the early days I did everything from dressing up as a bear at a press launch, to running press notices on new toys to nearby newspaper offices. I would enter the pewter-coloured portico of the *Daily Express* building with the kind of awe usually reserved for cathedrals.

The nearest I experienced to the rumoured glamour of PR were press calls with former child star Bonnie Langford and TV conservationist David Bellamy, although in 1987 a joint venture with *Woman's Own* called 'The Most Caring Child in Britain' was shortlisted for a *PRWeek* Award. My boss and I duly turned up to the glittering ceremony in a grand hotel on Park Lane but left minus a gong.

My deliverance from the world of toys came in the form of a consultant who briefly worked with us and recommended me to the company she had moved on to, called Broadstone Communications: a fledgling company of just five, tacked like a barnacle onto the side of the advertising agency Holmes, Knight, Ritchie (which later merged with legendary agency TBWA). At this stage, advertising agencies had just woken up to the potential power of 'below-the-line' (that is, non-paid-for) media endorsement and a few like HKR were experimenting with their own agencies; but paid-for advertising still ruled the roost in terms of client spend and kudos.

When the agency moved to a swanky new waterside location in Battle Bridge Basin in Kings Cross, the PR offices ended up literally below the water line. We would watch the canal barges pass by while upstairs the 'real' creatives sat in airy, open offices equipped with juke boxes, basketball hoops and big sofas. The reception area was covered in wall-to-wall television screens which played loops of the agency's advertisements or the trendy music channel MTV while the fridges in the kitchen were packed with merchandise from our well-known whisky, champagne and beer producing clients.

As PRs we were regarded as the poor relations but were bringing in clients left, right and centre and, as we worked together with the guys upstairs on an increasing number of integrated campaigns, they became more convinced of the power of PR. As our credibility grew, I found myself on a fast track with increasing responsibility. Professionally, I seemed to have secured a foothold on a ladder. Like my father, I had some trouble drumming up enthusiasm for the promotion of car seats, vinyl flooring and home appliances but I seemed to be fairly good at my job and particularly enjoyed working with the media.

Personally, things weren't quite so clear cut. Although I had moved to London I had not quite severed all ties to Aberystwyth. Before my departure I had become involved with a third-year student with a passion for sailing. It was not an obvious match, but his passion for the sea appealed. He would take me out sailing around Cardigan Bay, stopping off at harbour-side pubs along the coast line. The problem was that the only way I could continue the relationship was by sailing – and I was not a natural.

One New Year's Day, I found myself plunged up to my neck in ice-cold water in Lake Bala while my boyfriend screamed at me, 'It's a trapeze. You're not meant to jump right out of the boat!' I also made the fatal mistake of agreeing to join him on the return leg of a cross-Channel race between Dieppe and Brighton. When I arrived in France, the crew hit the town for the evening before setting out for our return journey just after midnight. As we sailed into the darkness, the wind began to pick up and within a couple of hours we were facing a force nine gale. On deck, we tied ourselves to the boat to prevent being swept overboard by the twenty-foot waves. When we broached all I could do was scream blue murder, so I was sent below decks where I spent the rest of the journey throwing up into a bucket.

When we finally moored in Brighton, the rest of the crew bounced off the boat in high spirits and headed into the yacht club for a fried English breakfast while I crawled on the jetty thanking God for delivering me onto dry land. The relationship was doomed and, after I refused to live on a yacht in a London dock, our paths slowly went separate ways.

So, at the age of twenty-six, I joined the burgeoning ranks of singletons. According to the media, the single person living pattern was becoming the norm. Whereas once being single had been seen as a sign of social failure, it was increasingly regarded as an indication of strong-minded individualism. Self-reliance had become fashionable and vulnerability something to be hidden at all costs. A new breed of YEWs was emerging: young executive women who were married to their careers for richer or poorer, for better or worse.

In reality, however, life as a single white female in London was something of a mixed blessing. As I progressed through my twenties, an increasing number of my friends began to settle down and the downsides of single life became more obvious. Weekends, being a time for couples, were the worst. On a Saturday morning, I would wake to the deadening silence of an empty flat, dreading the vacuum of the weekend ahead. The transitory nature of life in London fuelled a sense of insecurity. Landlords would only allow you to rent for a maximum of a year to avoid being burdened with sitting tenants, which meant that you were continually in the process of looking for somewhere new to live.

Renting in London was also not a cheap option and as a result I often lived in less than desirable areas of the capital. During a short sojourn in a damp ground-floor flat on the run-down fringes of Wimbledon, I came home one evening to find a lump of concrete in the middle of the sitting-room floor and a complete absence of electrical items – from the TV to the toaster. A rather ponderous investigator examined the flat and then asked me, 'Madam, I have to enquire, are you missing any items of continental lingerie?' I thought the question seemed rather irrelevant but duly went and checked my underwear drawer and, sure enough, my one and only pair of French knickers were missing. Apparently the perpetrator was a pervert with a penchant for French underwear as well as re-saleable electrical items. Two days later, the heavy-breathing phone calls began and I decided to cut my losses and move on.

Later on, while living in Stockwell, a rather run-down area of south London, I was wrestled to the ground for my bag. Two weeks later I was attacked in the stairwell outside my flat by a tall man in a long, black trench coat and a baseball cap. I was pushed back roughly against the wall and a pair of dissecting scissors pressed into my stomach while he rifled through the bag slung across my body.

'What's this?' he demanded holding up my make-up bag, cheque book, and plastic A4 folder of draft press releases. But when he found my purse only contained £2 worth of change he became angry, 'Haven't you got any more than this?'

When I shook my head, he began to scream at me, 'You're lying,' and I felt the scissors pressing into my flesh. I felt sick but indignant and pointed out, 'What possible reason have I got to lie to you? You have a pair of scissors stuck in my stomach.'

Amazingly, my assailant seemed to accept my rationale and simply turned away and walked down the stairs. I only understood what a lucky escape I had when the police arrived. As they took my statement, a radio call came in to say that the scissor-wielding mugger had struck again in the other side of the block of flats and that a young girl had been stabbed.

To escape the loneliness of a London weekend, I would often board the train back up to Larkland. By that time my sister Charlotte had also headed to Aberystwyth to study English and Drama and, left to his own devices, my father's depression and associated eczema seemed to have intensified. When his skin condition became too bad, he would be admitted to hospital. Wrapped like a mummy, he would bash out poetry on my mother's old upright typewriter. The nursing staff even allowed him a steady supply of red wine but drew the line when he escaped to the local pub in his pyjamas.

I would regularly receive packages of poems, some obscure, others funny, many heartbreaking, as well as tape recordings of his reflections on Jung. Sometimes my father would call me at the office, and pour out his despair down the phone line. I felt so helpless.

I don't know what prompted me to go and see Billy Graham speak. Since my experience in Aberystwyth, I had not sought out a church in London. In fact my only exposure to Christianity tended to occur in Oxford Street where I was regularly accosted by a fervent and slightly deranged young man who would yell at me that Jesus loved me, and a more sombre and muted elderly gentleman sporting a sandwich board warning that the end was nigh. But when I heard that the larger-than-life American evangelist was coming to Britain, my curiosity was piqued. Unfortunately, I seemed to be alone in my interest; I tried to persuade various friends to come with me to see Graham in Earls Court, prompting responses ranging from hilarity to atheist anger.

In fact, my own scepticism was at an all-time high as I entered Earls Court. American Evangelicals had been given a bad press in Britain with scathing reports on the fundraising missions of mega churches in the US. But as the hall filled with the worship music of George Hamilton IV, I began to give myself up to the moment.

I didn't know what to expect but was surprised when, after a stirring introduction, a small and sober-looking man rose from his seat at the edge of the stage and walked to the microphone. Without any theatricality he spoke eloquently of the inadequacy of the church in filling the needs of many people, and told the story of an alcoholic gambler who was invited into a church by a congregation but was thrown out when he owned up to his dissolute lifestyle. 'When I tell a lie they vote me in but when I tell the truth they throw me out,' he had told the evangelist.

Graham also spoke movingly of the gap that we all have in our lives; the universal feeling of an emptiness, a God-shaped hole wired into our DNA. And as the thousands of voices rose in praise, tears ran down my face. I recognized all too well that yawning chasm within myself, an emptiness I tried to fill with a blur of activity, misplaced love, late nights and bottles of wine.

Many in the crowd began to push past me eager to reach the stage and give their lives to Christ. I felt caught up in the tide and my feet began to move. I craved that sense of belonging to this throng and found myself propelled forward towards the stage where Graham stood hands raised. Yes, I was ready to give my life, but to what? As people moved forward like a wave, I was hit by what felt like a rush of cold water. What was I doing? How was I allowing myself to be manipulated like this, to be caught up in mob mentality? And who was this Jesus? I had no idea. How could I give my life to him?

When I reached the stage, I just couldn't do it, I couldn't make the commitment. I mumbled apologetically and incoherently, was handed a copy of Luke's Gospel and, crying, made my way back out into the neon night of the city. The disease had been diagnosed but I had not taken the cure.

Instead I began to stock up on self-help books. I read Paulo Coelho's *The Alchemist*, Susan Jeffers's *Feel the Fear and Do It Anyway*, M. Scott Peck's *The Road Less Travelled* and even tried Jung. I went to evening classes in yoga and tried to tie myself in knots like a pretzel while connecting to my inner chi. I even began to revisit the transcendental meditation techniques that I had briefly learnt in Wales, using my lunch breaks for breathing and relaxation exercises.

One day, when I was feeling particularly tense, I lay down on the floor of my office to do some deep breathing. I was just beginning to drift off when I heard a voice through the open window, 'Heck, look there. Can you see? There's a body on the second floor.'

'Where?'

'There. Look, by the desk.'

'Do you think we should call the police? Perhaps she's been murdered.'

It slowly began to dawn on me that they were referring to my prone body and I had to stand up and wave to the secretaries in the office over the road in order to convince them that there had been no foul play.

Despite my inner turmoil, I was making real headway at work. I had been made an account manager responsible for my own clients with a generous salary and the prospect of a directorship dangled before me like a carrot. I was increasingly travelling out of London and even to Europe to pitch to clients. Then the managing director mooted a potential management buyout from the parent advertising agency. I tried to convince myself that this was the future that I wanted, and that given material wealth and status, personal happiness would surely follow. But deep down I had misgivings.

Around me the whole world seemed to be falling apart. After singing 'Give Peace a Chance' at a candle-lit vigil in Trafalgar Square, we watched in horror as the first air strikes on Iraq were televised. In Africa, twenty thousand Ethiopians once again faced being plunged into famine. Closer to home, the Provisional IRA were launching mortar attacks on Whitehall and Downing Street and bombing commuters at Paddington and Victoria railway stations. Unemployment was rising faster in the UK than any other European country and in Birmingham, Dudley, Tyneside and even genteel Oxford, the unemployed and the disaffected rioted and looted stores, carrying off the kind of consumer goods that I was being paid to promote. The stark gap between the consumer lifestyle peddled by advertising and PR agencies, and the reality of life in the grip of a relentless economic downturn, was becoming painfully obvious. I struggled to see the relevance of my work.

All I could see ahead of me was a life of mediocre achievement, a daily struggle to convince one's self of meaning, and I shuddered. Then one day, during an interminable meeting to plan the launch of a new range of kettle jugs, I had an epiphany. As the meeting droned on, I found my attention straying. As my colleagues' voices faded I reached perhaps for the first time that stillness that is the goal of meditation. And there in the calm, a single thought came to me with clarity and force, 'I don't know what God wants me to do with my life, but this isn't it.'

It was simple, definitive and impossible to ignore. And when I finally zoned back into the room again to find my colleagues still debating the merits of white goods, I comprehended with a cold, hard, unnerving certainty that I could not continue down this path.

So, at the age of twenty-nine, while everyone else around me fought to hold on to their jobs and to pay their mortgages, I handed in my notice, sold and gave away all my possessions (apart from a couple of boxes of books and 'the head in a grid') and bought myself a plane ticket.

8

The Roof of the World

I have always loved flying. One of my earliest memories is of soaring over Larkland with my father in a tiny Cessna light plane, my little body strapped into the bucket seat as my father performed loop-the-loops over the house; my mother hugging her body anxiously in the garden below. (My father never lost his love of flight, and continued to keep up his flying hours from the local airfield in Cranfield even when the family seemed to be teetering on the edge of bankruptcy.)

I loved everything about the process of flight – even when I graduated to flying on commercial airliners. I would revel in the cosmopolitan crowd at the airport and the sense of possibility conveyed by the exotic names on the flight bulletin boards: Abu Dhabi, Bogota, Caracas, Dhaka, Harare, Jakarta, Khartoum, Lusaka, Manila, Nassau, Phnom Penh, San Salvador, Taipei. All of them seemed attainable, as if once cut loose from the moorings of home you could wander the world at will.

I loved the cacophony of different languages in airport lounges, and the multi-lingual loudspeaker announcements inside the airport. On the tarmac, I was thrilled by the rush of the engines as the pilot prepared to career down the runway before taking to the skies. And most of all I loved the view of our planet from high above the clouds. Over the years I have looked down on the icy tundra of the Arctic Circle, the great empty expanses of the Sahara and the forbidding mountains of Afghanistan and wondered, in awe, how such beauty came to be.

As a child I mainly motored with my family in Europe and rarely flew but, as soon as I was old enough, I took to the skies. At the age of sixteen, I travelled to Crete with a school friend and as a student I spent a summer in Paris with a fellow art student at the Cité University, living off French bread, tomatoes and three-franc wine. Another summer I headed to Florence where I spent the days hanging out in the Piazza della Signoria, sketching and eating wafer-thin slices of pizza watched over by Michelangelo's *David* and the Medici Lions.

At one point I stayed in a Renaissance apartment close to the Santa Croce and in the early mornings tiptoed across the cool, worn, stone floors, out through the heavy wooden doors and into the street, and in the wide open Piazza, drank bitter noisettes of coffee and watched Florence come to life. (I never lost that love of solitary mornings in strange cities and, on business trips, would wake at dawn and creep out into the half-light in order to explore the great sights before meetings. I have a collection of photographs of myself outside the closed gates of great landmarks such as the Coliseum and the Louvre, taken by passing street-sweepers.)

Later, while working in London, I travelled to Amsterdam, Germany, Malta and Greece but never further than a few hours' flight away. However, a yearning for far-flung places ran in my family. My paternal great-grandmother, Lizzie Burridge, once temporarily relocated her family to New Zealand. When she had misgivings and decided to return to Britain, her eldest and adored son Sidney stepped off the gang plank at the last moment and waved goodbye as the boat departed. He was never heard from again but it is likely that I have unknown relatives down under. On my mother's side of the family, an offshoot of Baptists made their way permanently to Utah and established a large and flourishing Mormon community.

So, having given up the security of a job and flat, I decided that I must make use of my new-found freedom to explore further afield. Unsure of my desired destination, I bought a round-the-world ticket which afforded me a high level of flexibility – as long as I returned within a year. At first I planned a solo trip but, once I had announced my intentions, Juliet, with whom I had been sharing the latest flat, decided to join me. We left the country on 22 November 1991 in the middle of a major economic downturn.

As I hugged my mother, father and sister at Heathrow airport, I was struck by a momentary sense of foreboding. My parents both seemed so vulnerable and almost childlike. A wave of guilt washed over me but it was too late, my bridges were well and truly burnt. So, weeping quietly, I passed through immigration, casting one last look back at their dear smiling faces.

Juliet and I left the UK on an Aeroflot plane which resembled a giant aircraft hangar, its interior covered with green flock wallpaper. After a late-night stopover in the snow-bound Moscow airport, we flew on over the glittering blue of the Gulf, landing in Sharjah at dawn. Even at 3.30 a.m. I could smell the heat as we stepped out onto the tarmac. Then from Sharjah we headed to our first official destination in Nepal.

As we neared Kathmandu, a great white peak rose above the cloud line and we circled, open-mouthed, down around the summit of Everest. As we broke through the clouds, vivid green rice paddies climbed up the side of the mountains like contour lines.

Tribhuvan International Airport, like all others, felt like a no-man's-land, an air-conditioned neutral ground. Juliet and I retrieved our backpacks which contained all we believed we needed to sustain life for the next six months, and stepped boldly out through the automatic doors into the Indian subcontinent.

Within a few feet of the entrance, we were met by a wall of shouting rickshaw drivers, taxi touts, hotel 'ambassadors', tour guides and beggars. The cacophony of sound and the aroma of spice and sewage were overwhelming. In shock, the two of us backed up gingerly until we stood once again behind the automatic glass doors surveying the melee. 'Well, that was interesting,' Juliet ventured, as we stood immobile in the airport entrance with our backpacks. We needed a strategy. So from behind the glass, we picked out a taxi driver, took a big deep breath and sallied forth into the pungent warmth of Nepal.

The following day I was woken at dawn by the sounds of the hotel kitchen; unfamiliar voices competing with Indian film music from a tinny loudspeaker. From across the street, I could faintly hear devotional *bhajans* crackling out from a television set. A symphony of car horns and calls from street-sellers and rickshaw drivers rose up from the street below. A rich blend of aromas – coffee, street food and exhaust fumes with an underlying counterpoint of stagnant fetid water – drifted through the open window. As the hazy sun rose, I lay in bed luxuriating in the alienness of the sounds and smells of the morning, contemplating the fact that, by getting on a plane, I had somehow altered the trajectory of my life.

When Juliet awoke, we walked through the crowds and colours of Kathmandu, past the profusion of meat shops selling buffalo feet and live chickens, the women seated on the street amongst great baskets of brightly coloured fruit and vegetables and up to the towering, terraced temples at the centre of the city. We strode through a sea of pigeons that rose en masse into the air, relocating to the ornate, crenellated pagoda-style temple roofs which stretched across the three interconnected Durbar squares.

Inside the red three-storey Kumari Ghar, we stood in the courtyard, faces upraised to the intricately carved wooden balconies and windows waiting for a glimpse of the kohl-eyed, legendary 'living goddess' or 'Kumari': a pre-pubescent girl from the indigenous Shakya clan, idolized and worshipped by Hindus and Nepalese Buddhists as an incarnation of the demon-slaying goddess Taleju.

Chosen at the age of four or five from hundreds of others on the basis of thirty-two signs of perfection, she had been separated from her family and prevented from leaving the temple except on formal occasions. While considered immortal, her feet would not touch the ground, but the moment that she menstruated, or bled for any other reason, she would be cast out of the palace to pick up the threads of her life (not an easy task as many still believed that anyone who married a former goddess would cough up blood and die within six months). We stood for hours in the rising heat, waiting to see this pathetic paragon of virtue but she never appeared, which only reinforced the impression that this child was a prisoner in a gilded cage.

My first days in Kathmandu left me reeling, overwhelmed by the sheer density of population, the beauty of the city and the complexity of the vibrant spiritual life. To the west of the city, we visited one of the most sacred of the Buddhist pilgrimage sites, Swayambhunath, also known as the Monkey Temple. Crawling up 365 steps we emerged, gasping, at the top of a high hill from which the eyes of Buddha looked out in four directions over Kathmandu valley. Above our heads, washing lines of red, yellow and green prayer flags fluttered in the wind earning merit for the devout. Holy monkeys, said to have originated as the lice of a *bodhisattva*, scampered among the shops and gilded shrines while saffron-draped monks and resident weather-beaten Tibetan Sherpas energetically span prayer wheels, inscribed with sacred mantras.

To the north-east of Kathmandu, we found Nepal's most sacred Hindu shrine, the Shree Pashupatinath Temple, one of the greatest holy abodes of Shiva and the seat of the national deity, Lord Pashupatinath. Down by the Bagmati River, we watched a family group gather around a diminutive body wrapped in gold silk on a funeral pyre. The son removed the golden fabric, throwing it billowing into the air whereupon it fell into the water and drifted downstream. Each member of the family stepped forward to pour a little water into the open mouth of the corpse before the son lit the pyre. Then, having performed this final act of love, the son returned to the Bagmati to bathe as funeral attendants piled wood on top of the body. All around, life continued; monkeys scampered shrieking along the bridges over the river where worshippers watched the proceedings. Down below, small children played with the discarded silks and orange garlands in the water.

Before leaving Kathmandu, I had my own act of devotion to carry out – not for the dead but for the living. From her first sight of a photograph of a snow-covered peak, my mother had developed a profound fascination with mountains. As a young woman, she had been taken climbing in the Alps and Dolomites by her first serious boyfriend, a German-Jewish amateur mountaineer called Gert. But her real obsession was with the Himalayas and the legendary Nepalese Sherpa Tenzing Norgay, who, together with New Zealander Edmund Hillary, conquered Everest in 1953.

During the early years of her marriage, she continued to climb and followed the careers of mountaineers such as Chris Bonnington (dragging me along to hear him talk about his leadership of the British Mount Everest South West Face expedition in the 1970s). My mother was always convinced that she would one day reach the Himalayas but by the time I was a teenager she was plagued by increasing ill health. A serious thrombosis in her right leg, followed by a life-threatening embolism in her stomach and early signs of heart disease, rendered long-haul flights and scaling mountain peaks an impossibility. Her dream of seeing Everest may have faded but I could see an opportunity.

We left Kathmandu at three in the morning and headed east to Nagarkot, winding our way up through the foothills until we reached a hill station located at seven thousand feet, from which it was possible to see all the way from the Annapurnas to the Mahalangur Himal including the great peak of Everest.

We stood silently, patiently in the darkness as children appeared from nowhere and tugged at our trousers. Nearby a group of Japanese tourists tested their camera equipment, their flashlights providing brief glimpses of the hills around us. Stealthily, the first glimmer of dawn revealed the glories before us and, as the first shafts of sunlight moved steadily over the ranges, they revealed the glittering snow-covered peaks. In silent wonder, I gazed across the vast panorama, scanning the horizon in vain for the great peak of Everest. It was only when I threw my head back and looked up into the sky that I cast my eyes on the highest point on earth.

Saying a silent prayer for my mother, I took from my pocket a small locket containing a curl of her grey hair. I knelt and, using a rock, began to scrape away an indentation in the hard earth with the aim of burying the keepsake there in the sight of Everest. Within minutes I was surrounded by curious faces and small hands and realized that the locket would only remain in the ground for seconds. So, instead, I opened the casing and, accompanied by children's laughter, scattered my mother's hair on the wind coming off the Himalayas. At least part of my mother reached the land of her dreams and would now forever be part of it.

As the day unfolded fully, we drove back down through mist-covered villages to Kathmandu and on to the next leg of our journey. Before leaving London, we had suffered a last-minute crisis of confidence and arranged to join an overland group travelling from Kathmandu down through India to Bombay. The whole concept was geared towards travellers with the desire, but not the guts, to be fully independent. As soon as we reached Kathmandu and talked to some backpackers, we realized that we had made an unnecessary investment, but there turned out to be some definite upsides.

We set out from Kathmandu the next day at dawn in what appeared to be a small converted lorry with large open sides and a roof to protect us from the rising sun. We joined a group of fourteen travellers of differing ages from Britain, Canada, Australia and the US. I sat beside a middle-aged woman who read piously and audibly from the *Book of Mormon* as we ricocheted our way along the precarious Prithvi highway.

The road was about the width of our truck. On one side we were hemmed in by a sheer rock face and on the other we had an uninterrupted view of the tumbling Trisuli River below, traversed by precarious rope bridges. The road quickly gave way to a rock-strewn track which tilted the truck alarmingly. Down in the valley below, we spotted the carcasses of less fortunate vehicles – lorries and buses like the one that careered its way down the road ahead of us packed to the brim with people, live chickens and hay bales. The roadside was lined with the tarpaulin huts of migrant construction workers; men lolling on *charpoys*, smoking; women in dull-coloured saris cooking over open fires; and children splitting rocks to surface the growing road. As we progressed, tarpaulin gave way to small red, mud-roofed shacks, where we stopped for chai and dal bhat.

After twelve hours, we rolled into the outskirts of Pokhara, only to be informed by an elderly man on a bicycle that the main bridge had been destroyed by an earthquake. Determined to help us, he teetered precariously ahead of our truck along an extensive but successful detour to our designated lodging. It wasn't until morning that I grasped how close we were to the Annapurna massif; the mesmerizing fish-tail peak of Machhapuchhre appearing to rise up from the edge of the town. The air was warmer than in Kathmandu, almost sub-tropical, but clear and crisp in the early morning – full of potential. From the roof of the world, we would now head south, like migratory birds soaring through spectacular mountain gorges and down across the great open plains to India.

9

The Beguiling Soul

So began my lifelong love affair with India. Much has changed in the couple of decades since I first came face to face with Mother India. She has modernized, urbanized, globalized and sanitized but, despite the glossy shopping malls and fast food joints, the soul of India remains intact, unchanging through the ages. Foreign companies may have finally obtained a foothold in the country believing that they are bringing with them a brave new world but, like many before, they only find that India forces them to adapt to an immutable land, people and soul.

There is something so subtle about interactions in India; by comparison, Westerners seem crass as if, in our desire to pin down the very essence of the thing, we somehow let it slip through our hands. As soon as one begins to uncover one layer of what it means to be in India, one only realizes how many more depths there are left to reveal.

I still find India as bewildering and beguiling as I did when I first crossed over into the country at the no-man's-land of Sunauli. As we drove on down through Uttar Pradesh, I felt as if I was watching an unearthly film of iridescent beauty. In the early moist mornings, solitary, dark silhouettes carrying bundles of wood would merge with the mist. In the searing heat of the day, we would pass young girls in saris which shimmered pink, orange and yellow against the white dust of the roads. In stately progression, they would glide beneath large terracotta pots of water or baskets of brilliant yellow bananas. As we passed through villages as inconsequential as the air, small children would leap with inexplicable joy, poignantly shouting 'bye-bye' – the name given to the ephemeral who only pass through.

Feeling like an outsider is inevitable in India. She is like a lover who takes more than a lifetime to know, let alone understand; a jealous suitor who wants to engage but only on her terms. There was so much about India that challenged my assumptions, my expectations, and my prejudices. I yearned to be an enlightened global citizen, but she continually tested my worldliness.

This was a country that wore its deep and complex spirituality on its sleeve. Having come from such a secular nation which compartmentalized and hid any business it had with deities, the omnipresence of the divine in everyday Indian life felt uncomfortable and uncontrollable; the extroversion of worship, the profusion of colour, emotion and expressions directed towards a rainbow pantheon of deities, the glimpses of a god's blue skin framed by marigold coloured garlands through smoke-darkened kitchen windows. In the towns and cities, sacred cows scavenged on street corners with nothing to eat but muddy torn-up cardboard but, when a stray bovine blundered into the ticket queue of a train station, one was expected to step back in reverence.

Out in the countryside, coloured ribbons blew in the trees and food was left at the wayside together with rocks covered with paint, coloured powder or glinting silver foil in an attempt to avoid the displeasure of female ghosts or *bhuts* and local goddesses – some of whom had been deified after ending their lives as *sati* on their husbands' funeral pyres.

As I travelled through India, I tried so hard to interpret the world unfolding around me; to untangle Hinduism from Buddhism, Sikhism from Jainism, and Zoroastrianism from Christianity, and to penetrate the historic and shadowy divide between Hindus and Muslims. I tried to compartmentalize, to make sense of the sheer exuberance of the divine connection but, at every turn, the picture became more confused. Over 80 per cent of the population was Hindu but so much of spiritual life seemed to be a merger of creeds. It was unclear where one religion ended and another began.

Varanasi – the eternal city – and other key temple sites seemed to be littered with pale white women in saris, earnestly seeking to cast off their origins and to embrace Hinduism. What attracted them? The physical and mental strictures of yoga, westernized versions of meditation, vegetarianism, or perhaps something deeper? What were they trying to embrace? An ancient culture, an entire socio-economic caste system? Was it even possible?

I tried hard to understand the all-embracing idea called Hinduism that encompasses every aspect of so many lives, but I was hampered by my own upbringing in a nominally Christian country. The multitude of scriptures, the expansive variety of teachings and the lack of a central institution like the church all seemed so alien.

As we travelled, I was lulled by the mantra of motion and able to zone out the American, British and Australian accents of our fellow travellers. I began to read a copy of *The Bhagavad Gita* which had been given to me by a rather chilly saffron-robed Hari Krishna adherent on the corner of Leicester Square (which, inexplicably, I brought with me to India, as if no copies would be available, and promptly lost).

I loved Krishna's description of the soul in the *Gita*: 'It cannot be pierced, it cannot be burned, it cannot be wetted, it cannot be parched. It is invariable, everywhere, fixed, immovable, eternal',[1] and was fascinated by the idea of a single life force, the Brahman, who is not only the supreme being but lives within devotees and appears in the guise of multiple and colourful 'avatars'. What kept me awake at night was a suspicion that life, being seen as a repeatable event, was somehow regarded as more disposable.

In Western Rajasthan, I spotted the body of a young boy laid out on a dirty mat on the side of the road. It was unclear if he was dead or in the process of dying but he was already covered with a cloud of flies. Villagers passed by without a glance, going about their business while a life seeped away in their midst. I didn't know who the boy was, whether he had parents who mourned or the ultimate fate of his sorry corpse, but this image of a life discarded bore its way into my soul. I began to realize how deeply I clung to the idea of one God-given life and how, from my Western perspective, this concept of spiritual recycling led you down a dangerous path.

As a quasi-feminist I was also challenged by the role of women in Indian society at the time. Every day, the English-speaking newspapers seemed to carry gory accounts of dowry deaths: young women attacked with acid or set alight with kerosene when their families failed to produce an ongoing flow of funds for their daughters' new in-laws. The request or payment of a dowry was outlawed in the early 1960s but the practice continued.

In Jaipur, an erudite and encyclopaedic guide told us about the difficulties he'd had in getting his daughters married due to his rejection of the dowry system saying, 'I am a Christian and a father. It can be difficult. I have only now found a husband for my daughter who is twenty-eight years old.'

'Some families will demand ridiculous sums and for many years,' he explained. 'If a woman is ugly they will have to pay more. They will do this because it is a terrible stigma to be unmarried. If the family fails to provide the presents, the bridegroom will often pour kerosene over the bride and burn her to death. A law was passed which said that the family would be prosecuted if the woman died in suspicious circumstances in under seven years, but they just wait eight years.'

In some cases the deaths were self-inflicted when young brides could no longer bear the beatings, torture and isolation. These tragic footnotes in newspaper columns reminded me of the *sati* marks on the gates of the great Rajasthan palaces, tiny childlike handprints of wives who had joined their husbands' corpses on the pyre. The fact that in 1987 a young Rajput woman, Roop Kanwar, either climbed or was forced onto the funeral pyre of her husband of eighteen months made my blood run cold. Several thousand people attended the event and afterwards she was hailed a *sati mata* – a modern-day goddess to whom offerings would be left on the side of the road. This was the stuff of nightmares.

As we progressed down through Rajasthan, the landscape became even more ethereally beautiful but water became scarce and life even harder. Men rose up like medieval mirages out of the desert in simple white dhoti, long sand-coloured shirts and turbans. Women carrying water lined the roadsides, seemingly miles from the nearest habitation.

As we travelled, we stopped at roadside shacks to drink chai and eat puri and dal bhat. Sometimes we parked up outside a village and bought food to eat sitting on the ground. Wherever we stopped, no matter how remote, we would rapidly find ourselves surrounded by men, women and children who seemed to appear from nowhere. Eating in the presence of their hungry eyes felt grotesque.

On one occasion, we stopped outside a tiny village in which a small hut displayed strings of boiled sweets and *beedi*, the thin Indian rolls of tobacco wrapped in leaves. A couple of us walked into the village in search of some food to buy but when we came to the shop we found that the ancient *beedi* and sweets were the only stock. As we walked along the dirt street, eyes bored into us from gaunt faces. I began to take in the emaciated frames of men, women and children. There were no cries of 'bye-bye', just silent stares. As I looked around, I felt a creeping sense of shame at our intrusion and it finally dawned on me that the reason we could not buy any food was that there was none to sell. We gave what we could but were very aware that it would meet only the most immediate needs and, with heavy hearts, we did what all the other 'bye-byes' did and drove away with our sense of inadequacy.

By this point, time seemed to have lost its relevance. Occasionally it would strike me as odd that it was a Monday morning and that, if I had made a different decision, I might have been at that moment crushed like a sardine into a sweaty tube train, anxiously checking my watch to see if I would be late for work. As we drove on down through Madhya Pradesh and into Maharashtra, I reached a state of stillness that was almost meditative. So our entry into Bombay came as something of a shock to the system.

The slums began not far beyond the international airport. Nothing could have prepared me. As the sun began to go down, resigned faces, aged beyond their years, peered out of ramshackle structures cobbled together out of cardboard and, occasionally, corrugated iron. Here and there a dim lightbulb flickered, illuminating the fetid water running in the cracks between the houses. The road seemed to be lined with rags but slight movements revealed them to be old men and young children. Along the deep gutter, men defecated as children bathed their emaciated bodies. The smell that rose from the mass of bodies, even in the cool of the night, made me retch. As our vehicle slowed, the stump of an arm was thrust into my face and numerous hands grasped at my clothing.

Central Bombay was beautiful, spacious, vibrant and cosmopolitan, but even the wealth of the city could not insulate against the poverty; it only served to make the contrast more painful. One night we made our way through a phalanx of emaciated and truncated beggars – their nerves killed by leprosy and their limbs eaten away by infection – to the legendary Taj Mahal hotel. Once inside, we shrunk against the walls and watched the glitterati of Bollywood and Bombay society parade by; manicured, coiffured, self-satisfied and dripping with gold. All that divided this juxtaposition of obscenities was a sliding glass door.

On the streets of Colaba, I found myself face to face with a girl of about twelve years old, pretty and petite, with raw white round scars in the place where her eyes must once have been. It had been many years since I had first been shaken by the images of Dalits in *The Sunday Times* supplement but I immediately recognized the work of the beggar masters, those soulless traders in human misery who take children and mutilate them in order to increase their profitability. Above our heads hung government information boards telling you not to give to tragic phantoms like the one before me as it only encouraged the ghastly practice. It went against all human instinct not to give, but I was beginning to understand that poverty was complex and multi-layered and that its alleviation required something much deeper than the well-meaning, emotive, knee-jerk reactions of outsiders.

We left India on Christmas Day 1991 on an Air France flight to Bangkok. As we incongruously sipped champagne at thirty thousand feet I felt a disconcerting sense of loss and wondered if I would ever make my way back again.

10

The Silent Depths

We landed in Bangkok on Christmas night and took rooms in a cheap hotel in Sukhumvit Road. Outside on the street, I recognized a Frenchman from the plane draped over a fantastically beautiful Thai ladyboy. The next day we transferred to Khao San Road, the backpacker epicentre of Banglamphu, in which travellers from different points on the South East Asia trail greeted each other like Cotswold villagers.

We found a set of rooms in a quiet road just behind the Wat Chana Songkhram which afforded a view down into the tranquil teak housing area where saffron-clad monks wove their way between wandering cows and the scabrous dogs to the glittering white-and-gold temple. In the street below you could buy delicately fringed squid from street carts or squat on a pavement stool over a steaming bowl of noodle soup.

This quiet retreat became our base of operations as we explored the city, a bewitching juxtaposition of ancient and modern, and the sacred and profane, before setting out to travel the country. We initially headed north by train to Chiang Mai, and from there joined a leech-infested five-day trek across the mountains, sleeping in mountain-top mist-covered Lisu, Lahu and Akha tribal villages. One night I slept under a blanket on a dirt floor, another high on a bamboo platform which shook as the pigs below rubbed themselves on the struts holding up the house.

Early one chilly mountain morning, I sat with the owner of the house, who was dressed in a combination of silver, cotton and highly coloured lycra, exhaling smoke-like breath in the morning air. As we nodded to each other in lieu of speech, I couldn't help wondering what on earth she made of these *farang* interlopers or how long it would be before we destroyed the way of life we came to see.

A diminutive but handsome guide called Kamon took a shine to my beautiful travelling companion Juliet and, when we returned from the mountains, offered to take us to the Golden Triangle and to the country above Chiang Rai. We travelled by motorbike through the night, reaching Mae Sai as the day dawned pink, and looked out on the neighbouring countries of Laos and Burma. We then travelled up the Mae Kok River on a boat equipped with an ancient rusted rifle (in case of bandits), threading our way through tiny villages and elephant camps. We passed through Yao and Mien hill tribe villages and began to take in the complex ethnicity of the area; the village of Mae Salong, which was populated by Yunnanese KMT refugees from nearby Burma, seemed more Chinese than Thai. We spent weeks wandering the region by boat and bike with Kamon as our guide and I sensed that he hoped Juliet would stay on with him when I left. But it was an unrequited love and, when I headed south, Juliet was beside me.

Back in Bangkok, we decided to head down to the Thai islands to relax on their pristine palm-fringed beaches. We took a small boat from Ban Phe to Koh Samet. Few of the Thai islands were completely undeveloped, even in the early 1990s, but Samet, as part of a National Park, was afforded some protection from developers. On later darker days, I would relive that journey to Samet, picturing the tranquil aquamarine waters, so clear that you could watch the fish swimming beneath the painted bow of the boat. And I would recall the glorious moment when we were told that, as the jetty was too small for the boat to dock, our backpacks would be taken in by raft while we swam to the brilliant white shore in the distance. To this day, I can remember the sense of utter freedom as I leapt off the side of the boat into twenty-five feet of crystal-clear water and swam with great lazy strokes to land.

On the island, I lost track of time. I swam in the cool of the early morning then, as the sun rose, wrote in the shade of a palm tree, often losing hours looking out to sea. The island wasn't completely unspoilt; young male ladyboys paraded their wares on the beach and a few makeshift bars had sprung up in between the palm trees, but only a few open-topped *songthaews* traversed the one dirt road; in the interior, you could lose yourself in the lush, deep forest.

Dotted between the trees and the simple huts were countless white and gold shrines with ornate pagoda-style roofs. Early in the morning, women would come out to lay offerings of rice, grain and flowers before miniature gold Buddha and bow obsequiously, clutching bundles of fragrant smoking incense to their breasts.

Buddhism fascinated and confounded me. In India, I had encountered the Mahayana branch of Buddhism and, in Thailand, the Theravada. There were so many different sects, schools and interpretations of Buddha's original teachings that the concept seemed, to my untutored mind, rather like his own fabled elephant (differently interpreted by blind men) and mired in contradiction.

This was a religion which dispensed completely with the idea of God but which inspired grandiose gestures of devotion to its founder who seemed to have assumed a semi-divine status; every small town boasted a temple, or *wat*, of unsurpassed beauty, and across the country great golden Buddha reclined before observant followers. Every layman was expected to adhere to the five precepts – forbidding killing, stealing, sexual immorality, lying and taking intoxicants – yet children were trafficked into the sexual hellhole of Patpong, injected with heroin and expected to peddle their vulnerable bodies to passing *farang*.

While in India I had visited the birthplace of Buddhism and sat beneath the tree where Siddhartha Gautama first outlined his *dharma*, or teaching, that existence is comprised of suffering, caused by our own thirst of life, but that it is possible to end this suffering, to reach nirvana (literally 'quenching' or 'blowing out' those states of mind that trap us in suffering). That by following the Buddhist eight-fold path one can ultimately achieve a state of formlessness where human beings exist as pure mental energy, which in its purest state goes beyond even the thought of nothingness to a state of mind known as neither perception nor non-perception.

Key to this process was meditation. In Bangkok I had visited the Wat Mahathat near the Grand Palace whose meditation training centre was open to the public. I came away with various leaflets and books on Samatha meditation, which focuses on calmness and concentration, and the Vipassana practice which stresses mindfulness.

It was many years since my first flirtation with transcendental meditation but, on this serene island, I sat by the lapping waters and tried once again to clear my mind. I spent hours in the lotus position on the burning sand, focusing on my breath and the sound of the waves but my thoughts kept on intruding. The more I strived for peace the more a rebellious voice inside me kept crying out that it wanted to be exposed to the full, rich tapestry and messiness of life and that nirvana was in fact my idea of hell. Until finally, when I stopped trying, I lost awareness of my surroundings. The sound of the surf and birdsong in the forest and the sensation of sand beneath me all faded away and in the silence I sensed, once again, a presence, something indefinable, vast and comforting. The experience was unnerving, but I sensed only goodness. I was curious, but cautious. However, as I compared notes with others on the island seeking nirvana, I was forced to face the fact that, as a Buddhist, I had failed in my pursuit of nothingness. Puzzled and frustrated, I abandoned my introspective pursuits and headed off in search of life.

I found it in the form of another group of travellers who had been working their way through the islands escorted by a rather eccentric and extrovert American with surf-blonde hair who said that his mother was an English aristocrat. I found him rather intimidating; he was extremely intense and unpredictable which made him challenging but exciting company. But to my bewilderment, he seemed attracted to me and I ended up spending most of my time with him. During the day I would swim, while he sat and drank coffee on the beach surrounded by his 'followers'. In the evenings, we would all eat together in a beachside bar and dance in the dark shallows to the tinny strains of R.E.M. emanating from the barman's ancient cassette player.

Then one morning I swam too far. Lulled by the silence out at sea, I didn't notice the wind that had begun to whip across the surface. I soon found I could only catch glimpses of the beach through the peaks and troughs of water. I tried to swim back towards the shore but found that I had to fight to keep afloat and, as I breathed deeply, salt water stung my throat. I eventually began to tire and the waves broke over my head until, aching, I began to sink down through the pale green water. Above my head I could see the churning waves but below I drifted in silence.

My chest ached but my eyes were clear as I gazed around me. I sank further down and let the waters enfold me. All was still. A profound sense of peace stole over me. I turned over the thought of my potential demise in my mind, and felt an inexplicable sense of calm. And as I sank down, I had the impression of being comforted, of being held. In the depths of the water I sensed that I was, once again, not alone and that I was loved.

Then suddenly all I could feel was pain. Light and water choked me. I could feel my legs rubbed raw as they were dragged across sand.

My chest was on fire. It was as if heavy weights bore down on my ribs, crushing me. I lay on my side, choking, vomiting and heaving great pain-filled gasps of air. I could see blonde hair, blue eyes hovering over me and could hear a voice shouting.

As the sun began to fade, I woke in my room, bruised but calm. Apparently my American paramour had seen my arms flailing and had correctly interpreted that I was not waving but drowning and had flung himself into the water, swum the considerable distance out to sea and then dived deep down to draw me back into the air. I was awash with gratitude but I also felt a strange sense of loss. I couldn't shake the conviction that, down in the depths, I had fleetingly encountered the numinous of my childhood; that presence in the stillness. I found myself yearning for that sense of being held, of being wrapped in warmth, that had come to me as I sank beneath the waves.

I loved Koh Samet and after my ordeal entered a dreamy and introverted state but, by sheer force of personality, my American paramour persuaded a group of us to continue travelling in Thailand. At this point, Juliet and I amicably parted company. We both knew that we had different paths to follow and this journey was too important to each of us to compromise.

As she retraced her steps to Nepal, I was accompanied by this character with whom I was increasingly enamoured but also wary. He told me, rather impetuously, that he loved me and wanted me to wait for him in Indonesia. His plan was to return to Texas where his father ran an oil company; he would arrange to work on oil rigs off the coast of Kalimantan. He also told me he had worked in Africa and had dreams of eventually moving to Kenya to work in the safari business. I occasionally wondered if there was a touch of the Walter Mitty about my companion but I so wanted to believe him. I had set out on a journey to find out what I was meant to do with my life but to date enlightenment had eluded me. What I did know with increasing certainty was that I couldn't simply return to the way of life I had left behind, and I seemed to have met someone who was offering me an alternative to the life that awaited back at home.

I was far from sure about my feelings but, as we drifted on the exquisite turquoise-fringed islands of Southern Thailand, I allowed myself to be seduced by the dream. I spent hours sitting beneath the palm trees, writing, drawing and dreaming of a future in the sun. And on return to Bangkok, we made practical arrangements about how to contact each other – I was to fax him at his father's business and let him know my latest contact number – which made the prospect of reuniting seem more real.

Then on the day his Thai visa expired, I went to see my travel companion off at Suvarnabhumi airport. As he disappeared through security, I realized that I was finally alone, six thousand miles from home.

11

The Freedom of Solitude

As a child, I had always rather revelled in the freedom of my solitude. It was only in my twenties, when that solitude became involuntary, that I began to interpret the concept of alone-ness as loneliness. It was this creeping sense of unease that had originally led me to grasp at the offer of a travel companion.

As I strode back out into that Bangkok morning, my emotions were mixed. On the one hand I was terrified, like a child abandoned in an unfamiliar city; on the other, I felt giddy with freedom. Up until that point, my journey had had to adapt to some extent to the needs of my companions; we had travelled like a wandering back-packing committee, negotiating temple trips. I was now completely free to travel at my own pace.

I had originally planned and budgeted for a six-month trip and, following this logic, I should by that point have been roaming the Australian Outback. Instead, I still had most of the globe left to circumnavigate. My funds were running alarmingly low but that morning I mentally tore up my schedule and expectations of return. I knew only one thing, that I had to keep on travelling until I found the right direction.

My own Thai visa was soon to expire so I decided to head on down to Malaysia, taking the train to Hat Yai in the south of Thailand, before going on to Kuala Lumpur. My new-found sense of freedom was, however, somewhat dampened by the fact that I was hobbling around on a painful left ankle. I had been consistently falling down the gaping and fetid holes in the Bangkok pavements and presumed that I had twisted my ankle. I also felt very tired but put this down to a last night imbibing Mekhong whisky on Khao San Road. I was also down to my last few bhat so, hugging my backpack, I set off in one of the polluting motorized rickshaws known as tuk-tuks to change one of my last few travellers cheques.

The Bank of Thailand near Hua Lamphong train station was teeming with snake-like queues at every counter. I glanced anxiously at the imposing clock above my head and shivered despite the oppressive heat. The minutes of waiting gave way to hours and, when the pain in my foot became unbearable, I sat on the floor and sweated profusely. By the time I finally heaved my backpack up to the counter, my hair was plastered to my head and sweat ran down my face. I signed one of my last travellers cheques in a rather feeble hand and handed it to an expressionless bank teller who studied the paper for some time before barking, 'You have passport?'

I handed over my passport and shifted from one foot to another to alleviate the pain as he meticulously studied the documents. Eventually he said, 'You stay here.'

He disappeared for what seemed like hours before returning with an even more stern-looking man who turned out to be the manager. 'You are Catherine?' he asked sceptically.

The manager held up the passport to eye level, his eyes shifting left to right, comparing the sorry, sweaty creature before him with the glamorous blonde in the passport photograph. The teller pushed a piece of plain paper towards me and said, 'You sign here.' Together they then held up my signature and the travellers cheque and frowned, 'You come with us.' I felt an arm pull on my right elbow and turned to see a uniformed security guard.

I was taken to a small, tobacco-coloured room with a barred window and a simple table and chair, and then left alone. By this point I had begun to shiver quite uncontrollably. After half an hour the manager returned accompanied by a young uniformed police-man with a firearm hanging in a holster (I don't know what it is about Thai police but they can strike fear into even the most inno-cent heart).

The policeman sat down before me: 'I tell you problem. These people from bank. They look at your cheque.' He pointed to the top right-hand corner which contained my original beautiful script, written on a relaxed day in an air-conditioned office in London. 'See here is signature of Catherine.' Then he pointed to the sorry spi-der crawl that I had produced earlier that day on the bottom of the cheque, 'See here is you. They say maybe you are not Catherine. They say maybe you take the cheque.'

I felt a cold chill creep over me. On arrival in Bangkok, I had got talking to a well-dressed woman in her sixties who had a haunted look about her. With little prompting, she had revealed that she was visiting her son who had been arrested two-and-a-half years before on Koh Samui for cocaine offences and was serving a lengthy sen-tence in Klong Prem prison. Visits were sparse but over Christmas prisoners were given a special concession and she had come to spend three hours with her son with an intervening grill. In the interim she sent him *The Sunday Times* on a weekly basis. He was thirty-six years old and she had no idea how old he would be before he tasted freedom.

With Klong Prem in mind, all I could do was protest my inno-cence in mime. I pointed to my foot and my sweaty hair, hugged myself to show that I was shivering and emptied out my backpack in an attempt to find items to prove my identity, only to be surprised how few I was actually carrying. All I produced could have been stolen from some unsuspecting backpacker. I mimed writing and asked for more paper and began a desperate attempt to replicate my own signature, each effort proving worse than the last.

Looking up in desperation, I saw a smile steal across the face of the policeman and for the first time I noticed that he had kind eyes. I smiled feebly back. The two of them got up and left me on my own in the room. A few minutes later, the manager returned with my passport in one hand and a wad of bhat in the other. 'Catherine, here is money. You go now.' I never knew what convinced them that I was the hapless soul I claimed to be but the sense of relief as I walked out the front door of the bank was even more overwhelming than my need for a toilet.

I caught the train to Hat Yai after chasing it by tuk-tuk to its first stop in the suburbs of Bangkok. Settled on the train with a banana leaf of sticky rice, I propped my foot up on the chair opposite and drifted in and out of dreams featuring exquisite teak villages and lush rubber and palm-oil plantations.

I arrived as the sun was coming up but had little intention of staying around. Hat Yai was known as the sin city of Southern Thailand and a popular dirty weekend getaway for more decadent Malays. So I found a bus which was due to leave mid-morning and would get me into Kuala Lumpur at six o'clock in the evening. As I hobbled up the steps, the bus driver gave me a rather quizzical look and, as I settled into my seat and looked around at the full bus load, I realized I was the only woman on board. A rank odour of stale Mekhong whisky and cigarette smoke seeped down the aisle.

As the bus rolled out of Hat Yai, I was able to peer around at the various sleeping forms and it finally dawned on me that I had inadvertently booked myself onto a 'pleasure bus' taking night trippers back to Malaysia after their debauchery. After a few miles, the television monitor at the front of the bus crackled into life and began to beam out Asian porn. The seat in front of me cranked back for a better view and an exploratory hand appeared over the top of the seat and reached for my breast. This was baptism by fire into the joys of being a solo woman traveller. I was not completely naive and had dressed modestly in a *salwar kameez* that I had bought in India and covered my blonde hair with a scarf but the journey was to prove educational.

After about an hour, the bus stopped at a small tea shop and we were told to get off; one of the tyres was flat and our driver didn't have a spare. While he borrowed a motorbike to look for a garage and the passengers drank tea and sugar-cane juice, I headed to the back of the bus and, adopting a defensive posture, smoked furiously and prayed that we could get under way again. After a while, I was approached by one of the men. I was prepared to bat away another exploratory hand but, instead, he smiled at me and pointed to the sugar-cane stall, 'You like drink?' I nodded chastely and I was soon equipped with much needed hydration.

Two hours later, our driver reappeared with a tyre and we resumed our journey but it was only another couple of hours before the engine started to give trouble and the whole exercise was repeated. This time we came to a halt at a large truck stop and I was able to buy rice. Once again a polite posse offered to buy me tea which I accepted with my eyes lowered.

Back on the bus, the TV monitor once again cranked into sordid life but just a few miles down the road the bus again came to a halt. I groaned inwardly; it was now late afternoon and I had been relying on being able to find a room in Kuala Lumpur during daylight hours. But then I felt a hand on my arm and, looking up, saw the bus driver smiling down at me, 'I put on English video for you now,' he said kindly. And as the film *Terminator* roared into life on the screen, men throughout the bus turned and grinned at me, giving me the thumbs up.

After further mechanical difficulties, we finally drew into the bus station at around two o'clock in the morning and, as the passengers left the bus, many grinned rather sheepishly at me and said, '*Selamat malam.*' As the bus departed, I began to look around for a taxi but the station seemed deserted. I felt a rising sense of unease that spiked dramatically as a group of eight young men appeared around the corner and made their way towards me. I stepped backwards towards the wall but they came closer without saying a word. I thought about running but could hardly walk on my swollen foot. Instead I found myself inwardly praying, 'God, please help me. God, help me.'

Then I heard a voice, 'Lady, you should not be here alone.' I turned to find one of the passengers, a middle-aged Muslim who had been seated a couple of rows ahead of me and had bought me tea at one of the stops. As he led me away, he told me that he had got into a taxi and had been heading to his hotel when he began to wonder about the strange English girl. Something had made him turn the taxi around to check on me.

My rescuer bundled me into his taxi and took me to his hotel and, after giving up his room for me, slept on his coat behind the reception desk. When I woke in the morning he had already left and paid the bill, so I was unable to thank him. In retrospect, I could easily have been jumping out of the frying pan and into the fire but there was something about my guardian angel that made me trust him and believe that he had been sent to take care of me that night.

By the following morning, my foot was swollen to almost twice its size and was bright red, so, with the aid of the hotel manager, I found a doctor who told me that it was a 'naughty mosquito' and gave me antibiotics for a severe infection. I had planned to travel extensively in Malaysia and particularly wanted to visit the Cameron Highlands, Malacca and Penang but it was clear that I was going to be immobile for some time.

I waited out my time in a gloriously faded old colonial hotel on the Jalan Tuanku Abdul Rahman. After plugging various peepholes in my room with chewed-up paper, I set myself up in an atmospheric old planter's bar, complete with Hemingway-style ceiling fans and great ragged brown leather chairs. With my foot propped up, I spent my days writing and talking with the regulars, including a local satirist and cartoonist whose work covered the walls.

Alone, I had more time to reflect on my journey, to read my rambling journals and organize my thoughts. I saw an opportunity to have a go once again at journalism – this time focusing on travel. I befriended the daughter of the hotel manager who let me borrow her ramshackle typewriter and some carbon paper and I soon became lost in words.

In between days spent writing, I would hobble out to Chinatown to eat spiced chicken, cucumber, soup and rice and, in the evenings, I would head out to the night markets for satay. I wandered the exquisite red and white Masjid Jamek, enjoying the cool of the marble on my aching foot and reflecting on the amazing care and hospitality I had enjoyed from the Muslims I had met on my travels. As I began to feel better, I took a taxi out to the ancient Batu Caves where every year Hindu devotees celebrated the Thaipusam festival by carrying religious ornaments on steel pins embedded in their flesh. Following in their footsteps, I hobbled the 272 steps up to view the plethora of Hindu shrines within the great Cathedral Cave.

My hiatus in Kuala Lumpur was quite magical. I found that I truly enjoyed my own company and relished the time to reflect and write. But once I was fit and well again it was time to move on. My funds were dwindling and I was only a third of the way into my journey so I made the tough decision to continue on to Singapore, even though I had seen so little of Malaysia, but vowed to return one day.

12

'La Vie En Rose'

Friends who live in Singapore love the island but I always had the impression that the city suffered from a mass neurosis. It is a city of signs: at the railway station, letting you know that the import of fire crackers is punishable by caning; in public parks, banning dogs, bicycles and chewing gum; in restaurants, banning smoking after 9.00 p.m.; in public toilets, threatening an exorbitant fine if you didn't flush. (How can they tell? Is there somebody watching you?)

The pedestrian crossings were unnecessarily complex as they forced you to walk two sides of a triangle, instead of directly from A to B. The road rules brought out the worst in me and I found myself wanting to risk arrest for jay walking by crossing the road as the crow flies. My one skirmish with the law, however, came when a policeman ripped a cigarette from my lips as I stood waiting for the American Express office to open.

I found myself a cheap room in a flat with a phone on Bencoolen Street and was finally able to speak to my absent paramour. Over the previous weeks, I had found it harder to recall his features and it was disconcerting to finally hear his voice. He said he loved me, that he had some loose ends to tie up but would hopefully be arriving in Borneo in three weeks. I simply had to make my way to Indonesia and wait to hear from him. I had a feeling the loose end was female.

I took a late-afternoon flight from Changi to Denpasar in Bali, the next stop on my round-the-world ticket. My first impressions were not promising. When my backpack failed to appear at the airport, the Balinese staff seemed unconcerned. After an hour of miming my distress, I resorted to wandering around the runways in the dark and monsoon rain until I stumbled over a large object which turned out to be my backpack which had fallen off the cart coming from the plane.

The main backpacker strip of Kuta turned out to be a nightmare: a neon collage of 'Aussie cafés', nightclubs dedicated to 'The Lost Boys' and streets populated by drunken Australians, scabrous dogs and aggressive touts selling everything from hotels to narcotics. I managed to find a palm-thatched *losmen* at the quieter end of town and passed out in despair.

I woke the following morning in time to watch the sun rise over a litter-strewn beach. I vowed to spend as little time as possible in this hellhole but, before I left, I had to establish communication with the absent American. I squeezed myself into a *bemo* – one of the overcrowded local jeep buses – and headed into the main town of Denpasar but at the Post office was told that international telecoms was in its infancy in Bali and that I would be lucky to get through to the hotel down the road let alone the US. My best bet, apparently, was an international hotel.

Through a small archway on the Jalan Legian, I discovered a group of quiet hotel rooms surrounding an exquisite courtyard garden which was dominated by a large lily pond traversed by delicately crafted stone bridges. The Mastapa Garden Cottages was a serene oasis in the midst of the sordid madness of Kuta. It was also equipped with a fax machine and an international telephone service.

At this point, I also had a short-lived reunion with Juliet who had resumed her round-the-world trajectory but was once again contemplating a return to Nepal. Both of our journeys had taken unexpected turns in the name of love and both of us were in need of an international telephone service. We couldn't afford to stay at the Mastapa but persuaded the staff to let us use their fax machine and to wait for a responding phone call in their exquisite garden.

So, every afternoon, we sat patiently on the exquisitely carved veranda, mesmerized by the monsoon rains and the discordant tones of a small gamelan orchestra. Every day, I would send a missive into the ether only to be disappointed. But on the third day a fax emerged; I would receive a call at midnight. Juliet and I were undoubtedly out-staying our welcome, so I reluctantly raided my dwindling resources to pay for one night in an exquisite air-conditioned room overlooking the lily pond.

Determined to maximize the investment, we took long, hot showers and repaired to the balcony to watch the sun descend in a haze of crimson, followed by a spectacular display of lightning as the evening wore on. As the minutes ticked away and midnight loomed, I felt a frisson of almost fear. What new direction was my journey now to take? Was I prepared to alter the course of my destiny for this man? How much did I really know about him? Then, almost on the stroke of midnight, the room was illuminated by a great flash of lightning and the whole of Kuta was plunged into darkness. Deprived of electricity, the phone remained silent.

Juliet was more successful in contacting her paramour and set off once again to retrace her steps. I was devastated that I hadn't man-aged to make contact with the American and had no idea whether I would ever see him again but time was moving on and I decided I could wait no longer. I sent a final fax to say that I was heading out to explore Bali and that I would provide another contact number in due course.

As much as Kuta bitterly disappointed, the remainder of Bali exceeded all expectations. Driving inland from Sanur, I felt as if I was in a different country. The rains had replenished the land which seemed to burst forth with abundant life; rivers carved their way through verdant valleys and villagers bent industriously in palm-fringed paddy fields. The landscape seemed like an imagined Eden.

Eventually, I stumbled on my own temporary paradise in an un-spoilt village called Lalang Linggah: a modest group of huts hidden in a forest, looking out over a deep river gorge that led out to the rolling shoreline. In the mornings, I walked on the shore watching the surf break. As the sun came up, I swam in the river estuary. Lying on the sands, I delighted as the waters pulled me along in their rush towards the wide open horizon. I then washed the sand away standing in the rain in the open-air Indonesian *mandi* at the back of my hut. In the afternoons I sat under the mosquito net writing, listening to the rain on the roof and the familiar croak of a resident gecko. Time stood still and I relished the silence and the solitude.

Some mornings, I would walk down to the village and watch drivers bathing and blessing their *bemos* and motorbikes in the stream (this blessing and venerating of inanimate objects ranging from postcard stands to boulders was the fruit of an idiosyncratic blend of animist and Hindu beliefs, called Agama Hindu).

One afternoon, I came upon a rainbow snake of women dressed in red and purple skirts and jackets and men in brilliant white robes with richly embroidered gold cummerbunds and hats, processing in stately fashion down the beach. They were led by musicians ringing bells and beating large skin drums and some carried tall poles fringed with multi-coloured streamers, others towering ornate umbrellas or delicate statues of deities.

The group turned off the beach and down a banana-fringed lane leading to a temple. I turned to leave but a young woman held my arm and pointed to my sarong indicating that it was okay for me to follow. At the temple, the musicians seated themselves on a covered platform and continued to play while the women placed bamboo trays of offerings in front of the spirit huts and returned the statues of the deities to their shrines. I was offered strong coffee and small cakes made of rice and sugar and gave myself up to the moment.

That night, the ex-pat owner of the guest house, who looked like a pirate complete with grey beard and pet monkey, explained that the ceremony was a preparation for Nyepi, the Balinese day of silence to mark the New Year. He explained that what I had participated in was the Melasti ritual, which takes place three days before Nyepi, in which all the effigies of the gods from the village temples are taken to the river and bathed by the Balinese god Baruna, before being taken back to their shrines; the aim being to purify, and to take the Amerta (the source for eternal life) from the ocean.

Apparently, there was also an exorcism ceremony to come at the main village crossroads, the meeting place of demons. Then on the eve of Nyepi, great effigies would be made of Ogoh-ogoh monsters which symbolized the evil spirits that have to be cast out of the villagers' environment and lives. At the following sunset, the villagers would then progress to the sea to the sound of gamelan and cast the burning effigies onto the waves.

On the day of Nyepi itself, everyone would dedicate themselves to reflection and meditation in order to prove their control over themselves and the 'force' of the world. Every street would be quiet and no traffic, work, entertainment or lighting of fires would be allowed. Lighting had to be kept to an absolute minimum. We were warned that the silence was rigidly enforced by black-uniformed *pecalang*, or security men, and that *farangs* who flout the sanctity of Nyepi took their lives in their hands. I shuddered, recalling a story about an Italian journalist who was rumoured to have been killed by locals after infiltrating a secret ritual on Mount Agung.

As Nyepi dawned, the only sound was that of the sea. I sat on the steps of my hut, writing. The day passed quickly and when dusk fell together with the rain, I wandered up to the main eating area where other guests gathered in hushed tones among candles and gas lamps.

After dinner, our host turned down the lights and his partner, a voluptuous Australian cabaret singer, arranged herself and her Indonesian daughter on a chair in the centre of the restaurant. Two candles were placed at her feet, the flames casting shadows on the ceiling and single wall. Beyond, all was dark.

Everyone fell silent and, in slow measured tones, she began to tell us about the song she was about to sing, '*La Vie en Rose*', which she had performed at the opening of the new temple in Lalang Linggah dressed in head to toe sequins and stilettos. She told us, 'When I finished, the crowd stood in silence and one man came to me and said, "Tell me about your religion."' They were so moved, they thought it must be a form of worship.

The candle flames fluttered. We could just make out the outline of the cabaret singer and her child. Then out of the darkness rose a voice of utter purity and beauty. We sat rapt, hardly able to breath, until the last tremulous notes hung in the air. The silence was complete.

Then came a loud crash. A large stone landed close to my feet, closely followed by another and another. Stones and rocks started falling like rain on the tin roof and tables. The owner quickly extinguished the last two candles and we sat in the darkness, stones raining down around us.

Suddenly a lamp swung into view and a Balinese voice demanded, 'No more singing. No more people.' The angry *pecalang* strode imperiously between the tables shining his flashlight into our faces. The chanteuse sat stone still, staring straight ahead as the father of her child examined us all then walked away full of hatred and bitterness at the foreign interlopers.

From Bali, I took a boat to the nearby island of Lombok where I tried again unsuccessfully to make contact with Texas, and from there took an outrigger to the exquisite and unspoiled Gili Trawangan, the largest of an archipelago of three small islands north-west of Lombok. I found myself a hut in the small group of dwellings down by a beach which led directly out to a coral reef teeming with life.

During the day, I snorkelled an underwater wonderland and wandered the island where the only traffic was a single horse-drawn cart. After dark, I watched the southern sky until turning into bed with no light other than a candle. The old woman who owned the guest house seemed to grow fond of me and, when I finally left, gave me a simple brass ring. As she slipped it on the fourth finger on my right hand, her son translated, 'Your happiness waits for you.'

From Lombok, I made my way to Java, setting out from Ngadisari in the freezing dawn to climb the great volcano Mount Bromo. I spent three hours scrabbling through vertical undergrowth behind a cocaine-fuelled guide, finally breaking out onto the volcano rim at Cemoro Lawang, only to be greeted by a busload of Japanese who had taken the road that ascended the other side. On the way down, I discovered that my fellow climber had gone to school with my sailing-mad ex-boyfriend and knew his family. The world suddenly felt very small.

I made my way up through Java to Solo, on to Yogyakarta and embarked on a 'pilgrimage' to the fabled Mahayana temple of Borobudur, where I stood amongst the 504 images of Buddha gazing out on the mountains beyond.

I also sent yet another fax to Texas with my telephone number. I knew that my time, visa and money were all running out and that if I didn't hear from my paramour soon, I would have to take my scheduled flight to Australia. I felt angry, let down and puzzled by the silence. If anything, I had been cautious about the relationship but he had pushed me so hard to believe in him that I had allowed myself to be persuaded. But was I being unfair? Was there some other reason why he was unable to contact me?

I had one more day in Java and could not face waiting by the fax machine so hired a bicycle and set off on a seventeen-kilometre ride to the great Hindu temple of Prambanan. I set out in the cool of the morning but by the time I reached the temple it was unbearably hot. I sat in the shadow of Shiva waiting for the heat to die down and drank the last of my water. On the ride home, I was overcome with thirst and stopped at a roadside stand where I was given cola in a glass complete with ice, which I presumed came from the block on the side of the road which a young boy was using for a seat. Turning away so as not to offend, I fished the ice out of the glass, flung it away and downed the cola in one. I felt so much better. As the sun went down I managed to complete my cycle marathon and made it back to my *losmen*. No faxes were waiting for me.

So the following night, I caught a flight to Cairns in North Queensland. The plane was eerily empty and I was able to stretch out over four seats and slept blissfully until I was woken by a crimson sunrise. I passed over the great red centre, my face pressed against the window, the land unfolding below me like the surface of Mars.

By the time I landed in Cairns, my stomach was turning. I dearly wanted a room of my own in which to rest but soon realized that solitude was a luxury I could no longer afford and, instead, I ended up in a lower bunk in a room populated by teenagers. I slept little that night as they wove their way drunkenly to bed in the early hours.

The following morning I woke bathed in sweat and overcome with nausea. My insides seemed to have turned to water and I was unable to leave the hostel for the first few hours. I lay on my bunk overcome with emotion at the apparent failure of this latest relationship, torturing myself over imagined failings until finally I could bear it no longer. I had to know what had happened.

One of the greatest frustrations of the previous months had been the fact that all communications had been on his terms. However, I had an ace up my sleeve. I wasn't proud of myself but, one day, when the American had left his bag with me, I had found his passport and an emergency number. I didn't have any idea whose number it was but it was obviously important, so I quietly wrote down the number and buried it in the bottom of my bag, never dreaming I would look at it again.

I roused my sorry body and walked down the esplanade to a phone box overlooking the pelican-dotted mud flats of Cairns and dialled the number. The phone was answered by a woman, then a familiar voice come on the line, 'Kate, where are you?'

'I'm in Cairns. I couldn't wait any longer. I had to go on to Australia . . . Where is this? Where are you?'

'Look, I can't talk to you right now. Give me your number at the hostel, and I'll call you back in half an hour.' I gave him the number of the hostel and the line went dead.

I stepped back out into the sunshine and the horizon shifted before me; sweat ran down my back and my stomach felt on fire. I wandered unsteadily back to the hostel and, as I passed the reception desk, the manager called out, 'Hey, I've got a message for you.' He handed me a slip of paper which simply said, 'Kate. Please don't ring this number again.'

The ocean blue walls began to rush away from me. I somehow made it to the bathroom and watched myself as if from afar as I vomited blood over the clean white floors.

13

Homesick

According to a doctor in Cairns, I had a severe case of amoebic dysentery. In the sweltering heat of Java, a microscopic passenger had made its way from the suspect ice cubes into the cola that I had downed on the way back from Prambanan. I spent a week languishing on my bunk-bed with a raging fever and intestines which felt as if they had been burnt out with acid. Between this, the 'nasty mosquito' and near drowning, I was beginning to feel like a walking disaster zone.

I was so weak that I could barely walk to the telephone but in my vulnerable state I needed my mother and father. I had spoken to both of them whenever I had been able to access an international line and each time had extended my period of absence a little further, but this time I told them I was coming home. I was extremely ill, thousands of miles from home and miserable. Moreover, I didn't have enough money left to explore Australia, let alone complete my round-the-world journey. Steeped in self-pity, I decided to use my last funds to buy a ticket back to Britain.

I fully expected my parents to be delighted at the prospect of seeing me again but, to her eternal credit, my mother told me, 'If you come back now, you will regret it for the rest of your life.' I felt like a five-year-old being told that I wasn't too sick to go to school but, later, I would be profoundly grateful to my parents for not letting me give up on my journey at that point.

However, in the near term I was obviously not fit to travel, so I looked for somewhere to recuperate and found a haven in Kuranda, a hippy town nestled amidst the mist-covered rainforests above Cairns. Once again, a Good Samaritan took me under his wing; in this case, a t'ai chi teacher and his New Age healer girlfriend who practised her reiki on me. Wrapped in the temporary comfort of their friendship, I slowly came back to life. In the mornings, I would walk up through the rainforest until I broke through the tree line to look down on the glittering ocean. I breathed in the sheer enormity of the landscape and felt my soul expand.

As I regained my strength, I took a bus and ferry over the crocodile-infested Daintree River and stayed in a camp deep in the rainforest surrounded by prehistoric fan palms and sinuous vines. The canopy was so dense that the whole camp sat in shadow during the day but, at night, vibrated with life which occasionally made its way past the canvas into my sleeping bag.

I still found it hard to sleep and would wake at dawn and walk down to the inelegantly named, but perfectly formed, Cow Beach: a sheltered bay surrounded by mangroves. One morning, as I sat there watching the sun rise, I was entranced by a giant lace monitor, the size of a large dog, stepping stiff-legged across the pure white sand.

Despite the differences in flora and fauna, the atmosphere and ethos reminded me of Aberystwyth. It felt comfortingly familiar and, like others before me, I could imagine myself lingering here for years. But like many other havens, Daintree was economically challenged. There was no work and I needed to replenish my coffers so I reluctantly accepted a lift from the hostel owner. Sitting in the back of his pickup truck, I made my way out from under the protective covering of the rainforest, back into the sunlight and down the mountainside to the comparative metropolis of Cairns.

I had originally flown in to Cairns with the aim of learning to dive and explore the Great Barrier Reef but every outlet I approached took one look at me and shook their heads. Looking in the mirror, I could see why. I had lost considerable amounts of weight, my skin looked sallow despite the tan and my eyes were sunken deep in shadows (ironically I look like a model in photographs taken at this time). So I contented myself with snorkelling over the damaged and rather disappointing reef before making my way slowly down the Queensland and Sunshine Coasts.

I rolled into Sydney on a local bus from Byron Bay one crisp and sunny winter's day. The chill in the air was a not unwelcome surprise after so many months of tropical heat and I felt a real spring in my step as I strode out into the morning. I took a dorm bed in a hostel in the leafy lanes of Glebe, a pretty district lined with ornate wrought-iron Victorian balconies. The street which I was to call home for a while backed on to the waters of Sydney Harbour and sported a road sign which read: 'No Swimming. Sharks.'

After buying myself some more suitable clothing and footwear, I set off to find work. As a 'prisoner of mother England' (or POM) on a work permit, I had fairly humble expectations about what type of employment might be available. The only working backpackers I had encountered had been locked into what amounted to bonded labour in Bundaberg picking fruit and vegetables, earning only enough each day to pay for their accommodation, but I was so low on funds that I was willing to do anything within reason. In the end, my nascent typing skills came in useful and a temporary secretarial agency told me they could find me some work.

Having had such low expectations, I was delighted to be told that my first assignment would be as a stand-in assistant to the Executive Director of UNICEF Australia. I arrived at the UNICEF offices in the midst of a major campaign to raise funds for those affected by the ongoing war in Somalia. The staff at the tiny office were stretched to the limit as the information officer had been sent to Mogadishu to collect stories and photographs.

The first morning, the Director called me into her office to welcome me. 'I have your CV here. How did you come to be doing secretarial work?' I explained that I was travelling but had jumped at the opportunity to work for an international development agency, particularly given my recent eye-opening experiences in Asia. When she asked if I would also do some work to help fill in for the absent PR, I grasped at the chance to apply the skills I had acquired in the commercial sector to something more meaningful. She was able to offer me work for five months; this was the total amount of time I had allotted to travelling in Australia but it seemed too good an opportunity to miss.

My main focus was on Somalia. I would watch the fax for incoming news from the information officer in Mogadishu and repackage it for a highly insular Australian audience. It was an uphill struggle as even the major outlets, such as *The Sydney Morning Herald* or *The Australian*, mainly focused on domestic stories, peppered with a bizarre smattering of news about strikes or transport issues in Britain. I suspected that the majority of their readers had little idea of where Somalia was, let alone cared about the plight of the children caught in the crossfire between rebel warlords in a land without law. But as I learnt about the plight of the people in the crumbling country, the unwillingness of the media to engage with their story broke my heart. It was a painful education.

I threw myself passionately into the work at UNICEF but the pay was modest and I knew that I needed to earn more to fund the remainder of my journey. I eventually managed to secure some evening work at one of the achingly trendy restaurants along Glebe Point Road. The restaurant, which was frequented by the likes of Australian rock band INXS lead singer Michael Hutchence, was an early adopter of the open-plan kitchen, which enabled customers to witness every aspect of food preparation, and forbade its waitresses to use anything as pedestrian as a notepad.

My career as a waitress was short-lived. First the maître d' found my roughly drawn aide-memoire stuck behind a pillar with descriptors such as 'fat pink dress – steak'. Then one of the customers complained when I nearly gave myself a hernia trying to open a bottle of wine at their table. However, when I succumbed to a lifelong octopus phobia and dropped three plates of baby molluscs on the back room floor, it was the last straw. Having scraped the tentacles off the floor, the manager took me to one side and said, 'Look, love, I am sure you have many talents, but this isn't one of them.'

Having lost my waitress job, I pulled out the number of a small PR agency based in Redfern which my old boss had given me before I left my job in England. I was greeted by the agency owner with open arms as if my time in PR in London had turned me into some kind of guru. I was immediately given freelance work on a major international soft drink account, which netted me around three times what I was earning per hour at UNICEF, but my heart really wasn't in it. I found it difficult to wax lyrical about the merits of sugared water, so I was shocked when I was offered a full-time job as director on the account.

The offer threw me into a tailspin; for the first time I was being offered a real chance of making a life away from Britain. I loved Sydney with a passion. Every morning I would walk with a spring in my step, down through leafy Glebe and across the glittering Darling Harbour. In the evenings, I would wander down to Circular Quay and sit at a bar under the Opera House watching the evening ferries taking commuters back to Manly as the sun set over the Harbour Bridge. It was a glorious crisp, vibrant city but small enough to feel like a village in comparison to London. At the same time, my work at UNICEF had also opened my eyes to the potential to use communications to do more than just sell consumer products.

There was also another complication. One beautiful crisp Saturday morning, the British girl who slept in the bunk-bed above mine had asked if I wanted to come out for the day. 'There's this Australian guy who has spent the last year or so cycling around Australia. His bike broke and he's here in Sydney getting it fixed and it's his birthday today.'

The 'Australian' turned out to be a giant of a man standing six-feet-six-inches tall with an unruly mop of long dark hair, shot through with a single streak of grey. His skin was so dark that I thought he might be part Aboriginal. He had a large, generous mouth that always seemed to be laughing and his blue eyes were creased around the edges from smiling. Despite his obvious presence, he was quietly spoken and seemed rather shy, hiding under his battered Akubra hat.

A group of us wandered down to Circular Quay and I shivered as the breeze came in across the harbour; I still hadn't adapted to the idea that Australia could be cold and didn't possess a jacket. Without saying a word, my tall companion took off his grey fleece and put it over my head; the hem and the arms reached nearly down to my knees.

Falling into stride with each other, we wandered up to the Rocks, the old quarter of Sydney, to find something to eat. He told me that his name was John or Jonas Vilkaitis, that his family had come to Australia from Lithuania as refugees fleeing the Soviet Union following the Second World War and that he had been cycling alone down the east coast of Australia, sleeping in a swag tent under the stars.

As the sun went down, we walked back across Darling Harbour and up to a pub in Glebe, where more backpackers from the hostel joined us. But he only seemed to have eyes for me. He told me he wasn't a city person and had only been in Sydney a couple of days and, as his bike was now fixed, he planned to head on out again tomorrow. He also revealed that it was his twenty-third birthday. As I was nearing my thirties I felt a pang of sadness on both counts but, when the pub closed, he walked me back to the hostel and asked, 'If I stay around tomorrow, would you like to spend the day together?'

The following day, I found myself face to face with a large octopus at Glebe fish market. My giant friend was on fine form and wandered between the pungent trays of red mullet, squid, tuna and swordfish picking out the choicest cuts of the fresh fish. After he had finished shopping, we sat on the deck drinking white wine, eating mussels and swinging our legs over the shark-infested harbour waters. I felt so comfortable and when he leant over to kiss me, I allowed myself to forget about the age difference.

That night, John made hand-rolled, hand-fanned sushi in the cramped kitchen of the hostel and told me that he wouldn't be leaving the following day.

14

The Centre

I had always scoffed at the idea of love at first sight but now had to face the fact that I had fallen instantaneously, hopelessly and utterly head over heels in love with this marvellous, gentle and generous-hearted bear of a man. The chances of our paths crossing had been a million to one but somehow we had been brought together.

Every day that passed, I wondered when he would leave, but every evening we sat in the garden of the hostel talking until the early hours. During the week, he would come and meet me for lunch. We would walk to Chinatown and buy delicately sweetened pork buns which we ate in a park overlooking Darling Harbour. At the weekend, we explored Sydney, walking for miles. One day we took a ferry to Manly and he told me how, as an eighteen-year-old, he had broken his neck by diving into a pool cut into the rocks while celebrating New Year. Unaware of his injuries, he had wandered the town before his aunt, with whom he temporarily lived, forced him to go to hospital where he was quickly clapped into a neck brace; the doctors told him he must have a charmed life as he could easily have ended up as a paraplegic.

He told me about his childhood in Canberra: how he had left school at just fifteen years of age with undiagnosed dyslexia; how he had learnt to be a butcher; and finally how he had left home to travel in the hope of finding an alternative future. I sensed an old soul in a young man's body and, although our lives to date had been radically different, I instinctively knew that we shared a perspective on the world. When he wound his great arms around me, I felt as if I had come home. Every day I wondered how much longer he would stay, until one evening he announced that he had taken casual work in Central Station. I began to relax.

We talked a lot about travel; he had come into his own during his solitary cycle ride and was keen to see more of the Red Centre and the north and west of Australia. He suggested tentatively that we might undertake this journey of exploration together. But as our love deepened, I began to erect imagined barriers. I was happier than I had ever been before but I struggled with the age difference and the fact that our life trajectories seemed to be so divergent; although I was in temporary backpacker mode, I still envisaged a glittering career for myself, but John had no qualifications, prospects or seemingly any ambition other than getting the most out of every day. He was a happy hippy on a bike.

I knew that my time and my round-the-world ticket were running out and I convinced myself that when I eventually returned, as I must, to the 'real' world, that we would make a very strange pairing. So, with a heavy heart, I turned down the offer of a job with the PR agency and prepared to continue my journey alone.

Five months after meeting John, I boarded a bus out of Sydney; my heart breaking as I watched his tearful face slide past the window. He had suggested meeting up when he had enough funds to continue his journey but I suspected that I had severed the cord of trust that had bound us together and that I would never see his beautiful smile again.

Once again, I resumed my transitory existence, town-hopping my way down the coastal road from Sydney to Melbourne. I imagined that the pain would lessen when I was back on the road again – that being in motion would restore my peace and equilibrium – but instead I was wracked with emotion. And as my journey progressed it became clear to me that I had made the worst mistake of my life.

By the time I reached Melbourne a couple of weeks later, I was an emotional wreck and incapable of thinking about the next leg of the journey. As if seeking some familiar connection, I headed for a hostel in St Kilda which I vaguely remembered John talking about. I located the doorway hidden among the cake shops in Acland Street and lugged my backpack up a steep set of stairs. As I waited in the tatty reception I glanced up at the notice board and there, to my amazement, among the multitude of ephemeral residents was John's beautiful face. The photograph had obviously been taken in the hostel garden and he was surrounded by friends, laughing. I felt sick.

The receptionist appeared and, as I signed my name in the register, said, 'Oh Kate Nicholas, I've got a letter for you,' and handed me an envelope from a set of pigeon holes behind the desk. I was puzzled, no-one on earth – not even I – had known that I would make my way to this non-descript hostel. I leant against the wall, opened the envelope and gasped. A familiar hand had written, 'My Kate. I love you. Have faith. I am coming for you.' In tears, I called through to the hostel in Glebe.

Two weeks later, at six o'clock in the morning, I squatted outside Adelaide Central Bus Station wearing full make-up and the best clothes I could muster. At 6.30 a.m., the bus from Sydney rolled into the station and began to disgorge its motley group of passengers until the vehicle appeared empty. I felt regret rising like gorge in my throat; I was sure that he had changed his mind but then, belatedly, a battered Akubra bobbed up inside the bus, followed by a backpack and an enormous grin. As John tumbled down the steps, I fell into his arms.

Our commitment to each other grew incrementally. At first, we simply decided that we would travel around Australia in each other's company, which would in itself be a challenge as we would be together on the road for twenty-four hours a day. Many a long-term relationship had not survived such sustained exposure, let alone a fledgling romance. But I reasoned that the journey would be a valuable test of our relationship. If we were meant to be together, we would only grow closer.

As we both had very limited funds, we decided to hitch around the continent. My mother was appalled when I let her know of my plans; the Australian and British media were in the grip of an obsession about the murders of two British women in New South Wales. And I, too, began to question our wisdom when, alerted by the hostel, a reporter from the local newspaper turned up to interview us. The resulting article was full of foreboding and featured a noir photograph of the two of us looking suitably perturbed, although the journalist did point out that I was luckier than most as my travel companion was an Australian who looked as though he would be able to defend himself. In the end we compromised and organized a petrol-share through the hostel.

We left Adelaide in an ancient white Falcon station wagon driven by a British plumber who looked reassuringly sane and had plentiful supplies of water and gas in case we broke down during the 1,500 km trek to Alice Springs. 'You're famous,' he grinned as he loaded our backpacks into the boot. Since appearing in the local press courtesy of my mother as a child, I had become rather entranced by the idea of featuring in the media but I wasn't sure the exposure was helpful on that occasion.

With windows cranked down and Chisel's iconic rock anthem 'Khe Sanh' blaring out of the loudspeakers, we left behind the green fields around Port Augusta. The road stretched out in front of us as far as the eye could see and we entered a multi-coloured wonderland. As we drove north new colours emerged one by one as if painted by numbers: the purple of Paterson's curse followed by the yellow of the scrubland wattles, their roots reaching deep into red sandy soil.

Entering the desert proper, I asked if we could stop the car. I stepped out alone and turned on the spot, my arms held high, looking out to the horizon in every direction. I was the highest point in the landscape as far as the eye could see. I couldn't speak. It was as if in this desolate place, hundreds of miles from habitation, I could feel the pulse of life more clearly. I thought of John the Baptist eking out his strange existence in the desert and about Jesus who, after being baptized by his cousin, was driven by the Holy Spirit into such a wilderness for forty days. I tried to imagine the impossible hardship of living in this terrain for that length of time without food and water. There were plenty of stories of modern-day travellers who strayed from the main road, only to be found many years later, their flesh long since dried from their bones. (The local paper had recently run a story about a twenty-seven-year-old who had just been found dead in his car; he had committed suicide just thirty metres from the Stuart Highway and had only been found five months later.)

John was in his element. While in Sydney he had bought himself some good-quality professional photographic equipment and began to capture the colour, emptiness and eeriness of the Outback. At dawn, he would shoot the sun rising red over the land and, at the end of the day, the surreal quality of twilight in the desert. At Uluru (or Ayer's Rock), we respected the Aboriginal land-owners' request not to climb the ancient natural monument; an act they likened to scrambling over an altar. Instead we walked the twelve-kilometre circumference of the unearthly rock formation while John photographed textures and formations that appeared to have been created by an alien hand.

From Alice Springs, we picked up another lift to Darwin and made our way up through the tiny settlements of Barrow Creek, Tennant Creek and Daly Waters and on to the crocodile-infested wilderness of Kakadu. The roads were eerily empty apart from giant road trains that would suck us up into their wake, and a dogged and determined lone cyclist, who we continued to pass throughout our journey.

It was so hot that we didn't even bother putting up our flimsy tent but lay on top of the tarpaulin in dried-out creek beds. At Mataranka I was kept awake by possums throwing twigs and woke in the morning surrounded by the brilliant plumage of peacocks. Deep in the Outback, we woke at dawn to an unearthly orange sky, our bodies covered in a film of red dust. Around us we could see the footprints of small animals and, on one occasion, the trail of a large snake whose pathway had been interrupted by our sleeping bodies.

One night, we slept among one of the oldest religious sites in the world: the unearthly rock formations of Karlu Karlu (or the Devil's Marbles) which feature in many of the traditional Dreaming Stories. One of these tales tells of Arrange, the Devil Man, who, while travelling through the area, made a hair-string belt (a traditional adornment worn by initiated men). As he twirled the hair to make strings, he dropped clusters of hair on the ground which turned into the great red boulders of Karlu Karlu. We slept in their shadows and, as dawn broke, John tried to capture on film the essence of the charged atmosphere. I could understand why for 30,000 years, the Aboriginal peoples of Australia believed themselves 'owned' by this inhospitable land; left to their own devices, they would live in constant connection with the numinous.

The indigenous people claim that their physical world is connected to a subtle or psychic dimension and that this other dimension, or Dreamtime, actually exists beyond the speed of light. Their ancient belief system also has extraordinary parallels with monotheistic religions, including belief in a supreme intelligence called Baiame who dreamed or thought the world and mankind into being, much as the God of the Old Testament spoke the earth into creation. Baiame also laid down laws for living, purity and sacrifice, just as Yahweh did when he laid down the Ten Commandments through the medium of Moses. Their belief system also records a great flood, similar to that recorded in Genesis, and tales of a god becoming man. The Aboriginal people tell how, after the flood, Baiame manifested himself on the earth as a man to explain to his creation how best to live, telling them not to fear him for he was their creator and had come to instruct them and help them overcome their difficulties.

Yet these people, who embodied such an ancient wisdom, seemed to have been thrown on the scrapheap of life in Australia. Torn from the land which lay at the very core of their identity and connection with the eternal and their creator, they wandered like lost souls, living in burnt-out cars and shanties deep in the Outback, drinking themselves into prison cells and early deaths in dried-out creek beds – far from the eyes of the tourists sold on Dreamtime mythology and T-shirts featuring Aboriginal art work. It was heartbreaking and humbling.

In the early mornings I would wander into the wilderness and sit on a rock in the rising heat, listening to the rustle of life in the scrub. Occasionally the horizon would be broken by the magnificent lope of a kangaroo. Nothing had prepared me for the eerie emptiness of the Outback. Since childhood I had been fascinated by deserts. During my earliest wanderings among the fields and hillsides around Larkland, I had somehow recognized the need to escape human habitation and constructs in order to see clearly, and deserts, like mountain tops, seem to somehow bring you closer to the 'other', to the divine.

In that wilderness landscape, I struggled with the connections and chasms but knew that in the vast desolate emptiness, I had once again been touched by God.

15

The Turning Tide

We reached Darwin at the beginning of the wet season as the parched land began to spring into colourful life. We set out in a spirit of optimism to look for work but weren't prepared for the weather: the temperature was over thirty-five degrees centigrade and the humidity was so intense that the air felt like hot soup.

We shuffled, sweating profusely, down the main street, ducking into air-conditioned shops to cool down. By the time we arrived at the job centre, we both resembled drowned ducks. One look at the manual work on offer convinced us that Darwin was an unrealistic option for employment, so we headed for the nearest air-conditioned bar to drink ice-cold flasks of non-alcoholic beer and began to understand why Darwin had one of the highest rates for beer consumption in the world.

Back at the hostel, I used the receptionist's typewriter to finish off more articles to send back to publications in the UK while John went in search of a lift to Broome. When he eventually reappeared, it was in the company of a middle-aged wiry Englishman with a white Nissan van who offered to take us to Perth in exchange for petrol money. We were very glad to have transport but there was something about the man that disturbed me; he would not meet my eye and had a curious way of moving – a studied leisureliness that breathed tension. He seemed to be a man at war with himself.

On the first night out of Darwin, our driver turned off the road and we bounced our way down a dirt track several miles into the bush. As the sun set, our companion sat in silence by the campfire, his only contribution to the conversation being a caustic reference to the fact that we were in the middle of absolutely nowhere, followed by a slightly manic laugh. I was relieved to find our lift was still with us in the morning.

Around two hundred kilometres out of the Outback town of Katherine, we picked up a hitchhiker; a Japanese boy in his late teens who we found standing on the side of the road with a guitar in one hand and a loaf of white sliced bread in the other. He spoke little English but eventually managed to convey that he had hitched a lift with a jackaroo who worked on a nearby cattle station, in the mistaken belief that he would be taken to the next town. Instead he was left mercilessly on the side of the road with no water in blistering heat. After several hours, he was profoundly grateful to have been rescued.

Our hitchhiker had no money or food, other than the loaf of bread, so we fed him and in return he used mime and drawings to tell us about his life in his home town of Hiroshima. 'Many ghosts,' he told us, drawing wispy figures flying over rooftops on a beer mat. He also gave me a 'lucky' yen which I wore with a St Christopher on a chain around my neck.

In Kununurra, our driver told us of a change of plan; he now wanted to cross the Kimberleys via the Gibb River Road, an un-surfaced track which was likely to be impassable and was so remote that you were unlikely to see another vehicle for days or weeks. He also suggested that, as this was the last opportunity to visit a bank before Broome, we should take out as much of our cash as possible. Suspicious of his motives, I dug in my heels and insisted that we take the National Highway. So instead we travelled in uncomfortable silence, dodging buffalo, through the gaunt beauty of the Kimberleys, the Outback settlements of Halls Creek and Fitzroy Crossing, and finally on to Broome, where we laid out our swag tent on a deep red sandy beach.

For the first time, John and I began to talk of a future that lay beyond Australia. John wanted to travel to Europe but I was reluctant to think about returning home. I knew that my visa for Australia would run out in a few months but had wondered whether we might make a life together Down Under. I knew that at some point I would have to think about life beyond travelling but was reluctant to make any decisions. However, the implications obviously began to percolate through to my subconscious and, one night, I sat bolt upright in my sleep and exclaimed, 'Oh my God, I don't have a pension,' before lying back down and continuing to snore.

In Broome, John and I parted company with our driver and arranged a petrol share with a young couple in a converted school bus who were travelling Australia to get over the pain of losing their baby. I felt a pang of guilt over our transferred allegiance; no doubt our misanthropic chauffeur was also trying to escape some deep pain but he was not an easy travelling companion.

Together with the couple, we headed down the Great Northern Highway, washing-up rattling in the sink, curtains billowing out of the open windows with over 2,200 km of wilderness ahead of us. The days began to merge as we bore on through the vastness of Western Australia, the road running straight as a die through the scrubland. On a wooden board at the back of the bus, I sat with a thick notepad and pen crafting our journey into bite-size chunks for sale. Every couple of hundred kilometres we would come across a group of pre-fab shacks, a ramshackle pub and, if we were lucky, a petrol pump.

In Exmouth, we watched fish the size of men being hauled off weather-beaten deep-sea vessels; glittering Spanish mackerel, ominous-looking sharks, hideous hammerheads and green-and-yellow dolphin fish carried over broad shoulders. From thereon,

John would appear at mealtimes like a victorious hunter with assorted fish and spider crabs, which we fried over the campfire or boiled in a billy can.

It was in Exmouth that we parted company with the young couple. Having gone on the road in the hope of leaving behind their pain, it had finally caught up with them and they decided to stop running for a while. Our next lift was with a retiree who had left home with a caravan after his wife died of cancer. The road seemed littered with people trying to escape their past.

As we passed down through the Tropic of Capricorn, the weather changed and a bitter wind began to blow. We now had to sleep in, rather than on, the tent and borrowed a couple of tarpaulin sheets to set up a shelter in which we could cook. Then in Kalbarri, we were hit by the tail end of a hurricane. In the middle of the night, we were woken by a loud ripping sound, a blast of cold rain and an unexpected view of the night sky as the upper section of our tent separated from the ground sheet and blew away down the beach. The rain was bucketing down as we gathered up our belongings and ran for the cover of the ladies toilets, where we spent the remainder of the night.

I knew that I had a choice to make; my Australian visa was due to run out in a couple of weeks and my remaining planned flights were close to their sell-by-dates. I could rush past the remaining destinations on my round-the-world ticket to get home before it expired, or John and I could try to get to Perth as fast as possible to renew my visa (a process that required a certain level of liquidity) and stay in Australia until we could both afford to make our way to the UK.

'I could always follow you to the UK when I've earned enough money for a ticket,' John suggested forlornly. But I knew deep in my heart that I wasn't meant to leave him again, that we had been brought together for a reason. I had once turned away but now I listened to that still small voice that told me to simply trust and love.

So the decision was made: I would stay and forego those plans made in a previous lifetime and, instead, give my life to John. It was time to make new plans.

We celebrated by spending the last of our funds renting a dry caravan with a fridge, cooker, table and electric lights and purchasing a box of cheap red wine. A week later I walked into the immigration office in West Perth with just three dollars in my pocket and, by some miracle, persuaded the official to renew my Australian work visa. Later that night, I broke the news to my family that I would be extending my trip once again and would eventually be returning with a six-foot-six Australian souvenir. But first we needed to fund the journey.

We managed to secure work in the run up to Christmas for a Christian charity set up to help homeless and poverty stricken Australian families. We were picked up at our hostel early each morning and dropped off at various malls around Perth equipped with collectors' tins. We were occasionally the targets of mildly abusive comments such as 'don't you realize that you are giving Keating an excuse to phase out social security' and 'oh God, not more poor people' but in general the shoppers were kind and gave in abundance, particularly to John 'the tall man with the lovely grin'.

The Christians at the charity welcomed us with open arms. I still harboured a distrust of the 'church' and had a rather patronizing tendency to dismiss the gaucheness of some born-again Christians but I couldn't help but be touched by the disarming openness and warmth of my fellow workers who drew us enthusiastically into their community. Until that point, my journey had mainly involved letting go of the secure and the familiar, of places and people, but love now seemed to encircle me, and the more I allowed myself to be loved, the greater that circle seemed to become. The tide of my life was turning.

16

The Intruder in Their Midst

It is just over 3,840 bum-numbing kilometres from Perth to Canberra; hundreds of bus hours dominated by the vast empty expanse of the Nullarbor Plain (Nullarbor is Latin for 'no trees', a very apt description). When we arrived in Canberra, I felt as if I had landed in another country. It was only then that I truly understood that Jonas Kestutis Vilkaitis was as much Lithuanian as Australian.

John's family, like so many others, had migrated to Australia as refugees following the Second World War, having been passed like bloodied shuttlecocks between the Nazi and Soviet occupying forces. John's mother Marianna was born in 1946 in Feldkahal in Bavaria, after her mother and father left their farm in Lithuania to head to Germany. When Lithuania passed into Soviet hands after the war, they boarded the immigrant ship *Goya* bound for the migrants' camps of Australia.

John's father Norbertas was also born away from his parents' homeland in a refugee camp in Nymindegab, Denmark, after the remainder of his family were deported to Siberia (an estimated 12,000 enemies of the people were arrested during the 1941 Soviet deportation campaign, mostly formerly military officers, policemen, political figures but also intelligentsia and their families, under the policy of elimination of national elites).

By 1949 both had made their way separately to migrant camps in Australia: Marianne to Parkes and Norbertas to Camp Greta near Newcastle. Life was indescribably tough in the early days but both families found a place in their new homeland. They were hard workers and embraced the Australian dream, saving to buy land on which they first pitched tents, then built sheds and eventually temporary housing. The two families' paths finally intersected in Cabramatta on the outskirts of Sydney.

The immigrant Lithuanian community clung fiercely to what they could salvage of their heritage, meeting regularly to wear the colourful national dress and to dance. As president of the Lithuanian dancing group, Marianna was keen to involve more young men and encouraged Norbertas to join. Six months later they were married.

By the time I met Marianna (who by this time called herself Mary) and Norbertas, they were divorced and living in separate parts of Canberra. Life had not been easy on either of them and, somewhere down the line, the sheer hard graft of clawing their way back up the ladder of life had worn out their love. But what they still shared was a passion for their homeland and a vibrant cultural framework that even years of Australian living had not eroded.

I felt ill-prepared as I entered this new world. I knew next to nothing about Lithuania. The only reference I had seen to the country was on a beautiful hand-painted eighteenth-century map that hung on the walls back at home. For a reason he could never explain, my father had felt compelled as a student to buy the map which represented the great Lithuanian-Polish commonwealth (which in the sixteenth and seventeenth centuries was one of the largest and most populous states in Europe). He hung the map in his rooms at Oxford, on the walls of various flats in London and then, finally, in the sitting room at Larkland, without ever imagining a family connection to the country depicted.

As I was taken into Mary's and Nobertas's homes in Canberra, I felt as if I had entered a hybrid land that lay somewhere between the Asia Pacific and the Baltic. The walls of their classic Australian single-storey houses were covered with homages to the homeland: maps; yellow-green-and-red flags; coats of arms featuring King Vytautas the Great; distinctive two-barred crosses; amber ornaments from the Baltic and grainy black-and-white photographs of a hillside covered with a cloud of crosses. High shelves were filled with male and female dolls dressed in the distinctive woven linen national dress: ankle-length skirts with brightly coloured aprons and thin geometric woven ties or sashes. In amidst the colour, a wooden carving of Rūpintojėlis – the Jesus who cares for us – his head resting on his right arm, his left hand on his knee, a crown of thorns on his head showing drops of blood, and his face full of solicitude and sorrow.

As I was introduced to the family, I felt as if I had entered a land of giants: John's younger brother was even taller at six-foot-eight inches and Mary, who had once trained as a model, towered over me at a slim six foot. As the family piled into Mary's house, the Australian accents were peppered with a rich guttural dialect from the Baltic. I simply bathed in the chaos, as Australian and Lithuanian effortlessly interwove.

When it came to food, however, we were firmly in Lithuanian territory. Each of the families' houses came equipped with the typical gargantuan barbecue, large enough to bake half a cow, and there were plenty of opportunities for 'barbies' but the heart and soul of the hearth was truly Lithuanian. Despite the intense summer heat, Mary, Norbertas and others plied us with delicious and hearty meals featuring grated potato, pork and veal mince, fried onion and bacon and sour cream. John was in heaven and would beg for specialty Polish Kransky sausages which he ate with sauerkraut for breakfast, lunch and dinner. I began to realize that he had a whole relationship with pickled vegetables that I didn't really understand but this was nothing compared to the veneration afforded to the humble herring.

Lithuanians are not alone in affording herrings an almost mythical status. I once heard of a Dutch herring festival which involved not only eating but also composing odes to the fish. When I first met Marija, John's paternal grandmother, it was obvious that as a non-Lithuanian I was on thin ice. I was invited to lunch but she studiously avoided addressing me directly or speaking in English until, in imperious tones, she demanded of John, 'Does the English girl eat herring?' After I nodded enthusiastically and polished off platefuls of pickled fish, she finally deigned to look at me, and patted me on the arm as if to let me know I had passed the test.

My full initiation into the world of herrings came as the family prepared and shared their traditional Christmas meal of *Kūčios*. Like many Eastern European and Baltic peoples, they celebrated on Christmas Eve. Each family has slightly different traditions but the celebratory meal generally consists of thirteen dishes, thought to represent the twelve apostles plus Christ (or pre-Catholicism, the lunar cycle). No meat can be served and, in the Vilkaitis household, herring formed the basis for the majority of the dishes. The table was dressed with the best linen with wheat or hay laid underneath to represent the manger of Jesus's humble birth.

The meal began with a cold mushroom soup that tasted of the earth, followed by endless variations on herring marinated in vinegar, salt, sugar and other mild spices: herring with onions, herring with tomatoes, rollmops, herring pâté, herring salad, battered herring and *koldūnai* (delicate ravioli parcels made with forest mushrooms). Finally the meal came to a close with a rich fruit compote and *slizikai*, delicate little bread rolls served up in sweet poppy seed milk.

Traditionally, the Christmas tree is covered with a white cloth and a bell rung to signify when Christ joins the meal, when he leaves presents for the children and when he departs. After everyone has satiated themselves with herring, the cloth is then pulled from the tree and the giving of gifts commences.

I sat amidst the colour and laughter and felt overwhelmed by this wonderful family who had opened their arms to the intruder in their midst: the 'English girl' who was about to steal away their son. It would have been so easy to reject me, to freeze me out of the close circle they had created but instead they invited me in and showered me with gifts. When I called through to Larkland to wish my parents a merry Christmas, I felt a tug at the heart strings. My life would henceforth be divided between these two sides of the world.

Time was tight and I had just a few months left on my work visa for us to both make enough money to buy two one-way tickets to England. So after Christmas, we bid the family farewell and headed back to Sydney. We managed to secure some very cheap digs in the red-light district of Kings Cross and to find casual work telemarketing and data inputting.

Over the following couple of months, we were like ships in the night, communicating mainly through hastily written notes. I would often pass John on the stairs as I headed out for a day shift and he returned from a night shift. Even at seven o'clock in the morning, sallow hookers would be hanging around street corners in worn-down heels and thigh-length boots. As I walked down past Hyde Park and into the city, I would pray that there was still a way out for them.

Finally, we scraped together enough to buy two tickets to Heathrow with two brief stop-overs – one in Bangkok, the other in Delhi – plus a little 'start up' money for when we got back to the UK. On our last night, we ate oysters and drank white wine beneath the Opera House as the sun set over the Harbour Bridge. Uncertain when we would return, I felt a mixture of emotions: an intense love of this sun-filled city, a sense of guilt at my role in John's departure from the land of his birth but also excitement in the knowledge of the world that was about to unfold before him. Late at night, I put a couple of my last

Australian dollars into a phone box in Circular Quay and told my parents that John and I would be arriving in a couple of weeks' time.

On the first day of April, I woke in Bangkok to the familiar howl of temple dogs. My heart leapt as we tumbled out into the melee of tuk-tuks and carts selling fragrant squid, fish balls and noodle soup on Khao San Road. John's eyes widened in wonder at the pungent chaos. He was determined to absorb everything in his path, from the golden edifices to the teeming food markets lining the Chao Phraya River.

His fascination with the religious imagery of the Outback landscape now paled in comparison to his obsession with the minutiae of Buddhist iconography and ritual; his lens capturing everything from amulet markets to the verdant offerings at roadside shrines. A whole new world of colour and meaning opened up to him and he was unstoppable. It was obvious that a few days in Bangkok would never be enough to satisfy his curiosity, so my mother received the first of many phone calls and, taking her diary, crossed out the entry reading 'Kate and John arrive Heathrow'.

We initially headed south to the islands, then north to Chiang Rai and the hill tribes of the Mekong River, and finally east to an area called Nan which had only just opened up to tourists again after a period of unrest and banditry. We rolled into town on a motorbike and immediately attracted a following who guided us to an empty hostel where the owner seemed confounded by our presence.

We ventured out into the street in search of food and, as we walked down the lane, faced a phalanx of marching locals necking golden-coloured whisky from Mekhong bottles. Unsure whether we had come upon a party or a riot, we tried to meld into the shadows but were grabbed by a tangle of insistent arms. 'Mekhong,' a group of young men shouted, thrusting tumblers of whisky into our hands as they swept us along on the tide. John's height caused great amusement but did nothing to slow our progress as we surged down the main street and off into a labyrinth of lanes lined with teak houses on stilts.

Eventually, we came to a raucous halt outside a beautifully carved house, positioned high above a well-swept yard. We were pushed up a flight of steps and into a cool interior where we knelt with others before a distinguished middle-aged gentlemen and his wife, who obviously owned the house. A spokesperson from the group placed a colourfully wrapped gift and a silver bowl of water and lotus flowers before the couple and made an elegant speech before dousing the householder with the water.

Then it was our turn. We were formally introduced, doused with water and encouraged to do the same to our hosts. I tried to resist but my unwillingness seemed to be causing some unrest; so hoping for the best, I flung the water in the direction of various parties to rapturous cries of thanks, '*Khop khun kaa, khop khun kup.*' At the next house, I had a hose pipe turned on me.

Later, after several bowls of deep-fried frogs, a local English-speaking teacher told us that we were some of the first tourists to visit the town since the province re-opened and that we had arrived on the most auspicious day of Songkran, the Thai New Year. The evening ended with several rounds of 'Auld Lang Syne' in Thai.

It was six weeks before we could tear ourselves away from Thailand in order to continue our journey to the UK and, once we landed in India, it became once again clear that we were going to sacrifice future financial security for present experience. Sitting in a café in the old quarter of Delhi, we determined that we would hold out in India for as long as our visas and our joint finances would allow. Tomorrow would take care of itself.

From Delhi, we headed out west to the Thar Desert on the border of Pakistan. We steamed through the desert by night and were woken in darkness by the haunting cries of chai sellers at remote railway stations. We slept like disciples on the open flat roofs of the medieval sandstone city of Jaisalmer; its ancient walls looking out over the shifting desert sands which we crossed on camels to the border of Pakistan, curling up close to their pungent hides in the cold of the night.

From Rajasthan, we headed north into the verdant Punjab and to the Golden Temple of Amritsar. In the outer pilgrimage centre, we shared a small room with a gentle Sikh family, sleeping on simple charpoys. Each morning, I joined the women to wash before we walked into the ethereal beauty of the white marble temple complex, circumnavigating the Nectar Pool to line up outside the glittering golden temple to hear the sacred Sikh text, the Guru Granth Sahib, read aloud by voices that seem to resonate down the ages. From Amritsar, we headed north to the Himalayas and Rishikesh the 'home of the Beatless' (sic) where my former neighbour and the rest of the Fab Four had sat at the feet of their guru Maharishi Mahesh Yogi.

In Dharamsala, the seat of the Dalai Lama's Tibetan kingdom in exile, we slept in spartan monastery cells and were covered in bedbug bites. By day, we watched the burgundy-clothed monks slapping their palms and dancing in vigorous theological debate among the trees, and listened to the wounded-animal squeals of the elongated ceremonial trumpets of the monastic orders. Inside the temples, I felt as if I had entered a strange, dark and intoxicating world in which folklore, magic and religion merged amongst the incense. To try to understand the complex and heady brew, I signed up for classes on Mahayana Buddhism at the Centre for Tibetan Studies but the teachings only served to reinforce my increasing conviction that a world without God made no sense.

And then, hypnotized by the Himalayas, we headed to the fabled Shangri-La of Kashmir. It was not surprising that the company who organized our houseboat were so desperate for us to sign on the dotted line. The situation between Pakistan and India had been unstable for some time with terrorist attacks in both Calcutta and Bombay and the divided ownership of Kashmir remained a flashpoint. The Foreign Office had advised against travel to Kashmir at this time but, as a fairly seasoned traveller, I had come to regard the FO as over cautious, so we decided to proceed.

We left Jammu Tawi early one morning and began to wind our way up the precipitous mountain roads which were littered with ominous signs telling drivers 'don't be rash or you'll end up in a crash', 'your family are waiting please oblige' and 'drive on horse power not on rum power' – as well as the burnt-out shells of those who had not taken heed. Our naivety began to dawn on us when the bus driver stopped so that the passengers could get out and watch a raging gun battle in the valley below while he swigged rum. But even the sound of gunfire could not still my heart as we broke through the Jawahar Tunnel into the snow-rimmed valley of Kashmir, shrouded in mist and as beautiful and unspoiled as a pearl.

However, as we made our way down the mountainside to the lake below, it became clear that we were driving straight into serious trouble. Along the roadsides, muzzles of guns poked their way out of makeshift bunkers formed from sandbags and nets. Trucks carrying young soldiers with Kalashnikovs ran up and down the road to Srinagar. As we reached the outskirts of the city, we were diverted but when we finally made our way to the main marketplace we could no longer delude ourselves. We were surrounded by khaki green; armed forces dwarfing the civilian population.

The soldiers stood shoulder to shoulder down the middle of the road and, as the bus slowed, one asked angrily, 'Where have you come from?'

We passed through the market square and into an area of bombed-out buildings, burnt-out windows and blackened walls, where the bus stopped and we were told to get off. During the journey, John had got talking with his neighbour who now offered to help us, 'I will go all the way with you but you have to run. There is a curfew.'

So John and I tentatively stepped off the bus – a couple of lone Westerners out of their depth in a simmering war zone and, hoisting our backpacks, ran for our lives towards the lake. As we reached the shore, our rescuer, who said his name was Mohammed, pulled up at a small *shikara* in which we edged away from the armoury on the shoreline and towards the calm, still centre of the mountain-rimmed Dal Lake.

We never found out what happened to our original houseboat but we were taken to a rather small, faded boat on the eastern edges of the lake. We unloaded our backpacks and climbed onboard. As the sun went down, we sat in silence listening to the prayer calls from the mosques interspersed with scattered gunfire and the sustained whistle of rockets sailing through the air. I began to well up. Mohammed handed me a sweet tea saying, 'Please don't cry, you are in paradise,' before taking the shikara and leaving us stranded.

Later, Mohammed reappeared with his brother Mustapha and a pungent and delicious goat stew. Having spotted John's professional camera gear and my notepads, the brothers talked to us until late into the night, giving us their view – no doubt one-sided – of the atrocities that had apparently been committed against the mainly Muslim population by the Indian authorities. He told us about children whose arms were lopped off in retribution for rolling grenades under the wheels of army vehicles, before leaving us well fed but once again stranded.

As the days progressed, so did the violence and the visits to our houseboat. We were not permitted to leave but provided a captive audience for sellers of everything from local saffron to carpets and toilet paper to chocolate. Having finally secured some tourists, our host was determined to use us to benefit the local economy. I couldn't blame him but we were in a gilded cage with no way off the lake without his help.

Eventually, our rescuer came and told us that there would be one plane leaving Srinagar the following day and that, if we gave him our remaining rupees, he could secure us a place on it. It seemed like our best chance of getting out of Kashmir so, after hiding away an emergency reserve, we handed over the remainder of our funds. The next day came but no plane ticket. As the sun began to descend again, I felt overwhelmed by frustration at our situation. We had now lost our last bargaining chip and were increasingly unsure of our value to our 'hosts'. Finally, at nightfall, our rescuer reappeared and told us, 'Best you not on plane. Grenade thrown at bus going to the plane and many people were killed. I saved your life, see.'

Then the following morning, for no apparent reason, we were told to pack our things and were taken by *shikara* to the edge of the lake. Mohammed pointed to a bus standing close to the water's edge surrounded by guards, 'You be all right now. Go. Go.' So just over a week after blundering our way into Dante's inferno, we rolled out of Kashmir past the weary faces of soldiers and children bearing arms, back up into the silence of the mountains.

The end was nigh and we knew it. I had travelled for far longer than I ever intended and had been blessed beyond belief. I had been embraced by strangers and kept from harm. I had been guided on a path that had transformed my life by a force I didn't fully comprehend or understand but which I now respected enough to listen to. The time had come to go home, to engage with reality and to begin a new life in an old country with John. I was terrified and dearly wanted to continue to hold off the future but I could read the signs.

So on 29 June 1993, John and I took off from New Delhi airport and flew towards our future. As we descended into Heathrow, I gripped the arms of my seat so tightly that my hands turned pale and John turned to me grinning, 'You aren't going to keep this plane from landing, you know.'

Part Three

As You Pass Through the Waters

17

The Thinning of the Veil

The ancient Celtic Christians believed that there are in this world 'thin places'; places in time and space where the boundary between heaven and earth is thinner, where human beings experience the divine more readily; moments when the veil between ourselves and our creator seem to be drawn back, offering a glimpse of the eternal; transparent moments when we feel in touch with the 'other', the numinous; moments that exist between the *chronos* and the *kairos*; moments pregnant with meaning, which help us to see the random nature of our existence from a greater perspective.

Sometimes these moments are linked to the momentous events in our lives, those pivotal rites of passage, the boundary marks of our journey. Sometimes they come upon us, like a still small voice in the dead of night, speaking into our unconscious. Too often we fail to recognize those moments. Caught up in the busyness of living, we fail to stop, look, listen and wonder but if we are attentive we are rewarded with meaning.

John and I were married on a gloriously sunny day in July 1994. After exchanging vows in a registry office in Milton Keynes, we returned to Larkland in a vintage Ford that my father had hired especially for the day. As we disembarked, we were surrounded by confetti, family and friends. The afternoon passed in a champagne-filled haze. Mozart serenaded the bleating sheep in the fields beyond. I moved as if in slow motion, as sunlight bathed the garden and fields in a golden glow. The tendrils of love wove around me, wrapping me in happiness, and at the centre was John. The chances of us coming together to this place were so infinitesimally small and I knew, in a way that was hard to define, that there was meaning in the coincidences that had drawn us together.

I floated through the gathered assembly taking in the faces that represented so many stages in my life, understanding clearly for the first time the role that each of them had played in bringing me to this place: my father, whose face had been wreathed in joy as I had walked down our rickety stairs that morning, cloaked in ivory silk with flowers in my hair; my mother, who had taken a simple ceremony and turned it into a celebration of life; my sister, who had now matured into a woman; my mother-in-law from Australia; friends from school, university, London and even Sydney. I could read the story of my life in the guest list. Meaning unfolded before me like a map.

My parents had adored John from the moment they spotted this giant in Indian pyjamas wandering through the arrival doors at Heathrow. Untrammelled by convention, they immediately saw in him the qualities that I so loved. That night, my father took down the hand-painted map of Lithuania from the wall in Larkland and gave it to John saying, 'I know that I am meant to give this to you. I bought it long before you were even born but that's synchronicity.'

He told him, 'You were meant to come into our life and family.'

John was deeply loved by both my parents but particularly by my father. The day that John asked him for my hand in marriage was one of the happiest of my father's life. On my wedding day, he rose unsteadily to his feet and read out a jocular poem he had dedicated to John called 'Once a Jolly Swagman'. Later that day, I watched my father sleeping like a dormouse in an old rocking chair on the terrace as friends and family milled around drinking champagne in the sunset. He was satisfied; I had forsworn the trappings of materialism and hadn't settled for an accountant, lawyer or an upwardly mobile careerist. Instead, I had set sail for foreign shores and had brought home my soul mate. My father had done his part in shaping me for happiness.

We all failed to spot the signs: the slower faltering step, occasional slurring of words and blurred vision. On the fateful day, I was staying overnight at Larkland. The evening before, my parents had been to a party and came home glowing, my father in fine spirits. He flung open the door of the sitting room and came towards me arms outstretched, his tired eyes crinkled at the corner, his face wreathed in smiles and drew me into a great bear hug, 'My Katie, my Katie.'

That night, I curled up in the bed that I had slept in as a teenager, wrapped up against the October chills. There was no sense of my father's angst in the house, any sense of darkness had been chased away by my parents' bonhomie. God was in his heaven and all was right with the world.

The morning's rays were already stealing across the bedspread when I was woken by a crashing sound and a muffled cry from downstairs, 'Katie, Katie. Help me!'

I raced down the winding stairs and, hearing another crash, flung open the door to the sitting room. There was my father lying like a winged bird on the floor. His face was contorted with agony and he clutched his arm in pain. I wanted to hold him but instead ran for the telephone and dialled 999. On the floor, he moaned incoherently half in rage, half in pain, shouting in disbelief at his body that had failed him so.

My mother, who was asleep upstairs, looked so peaceful, like the young bride who had first slept in that bed surrounded by dust cloths and paint brushes, full of hope for the future. I hated to wake her, to see those frightened eyes. Her vulnerability as she sat immobile on the edge of the bed, unable to navigate her way forwards even to decide what clothes to wear, was unbearable. As tenderly as possible, I guided her, 'Mum, we have to go now. The ambulance is coming. We will follow.'

'But we were going out today.'

'I know, Mum. But we have to go to the hospital now.'

'My Dan. My Dan,' her face crumpled like a child's.

The flashing blue lights in the lane outside Larkland seemed out of place. And as my father was manoeuvred on a stretcher out through the French windows, I could almost visualize him looking on from his habitual spot on the terrace beneath the cherry blossoms, glass of wine in hand and a wry smile on his face. Inside the ambulance, I sat patting his hand until he withdrew it muttering, 'That's not going to do much good is it?'

We followed the ambulance up the leaf-covered lane and out onto the high road that my father and I so loved, with its views over the valley, and saw the spire of Olney church rising through the morning mist.

Once we reached the hospital, the day took on a more practical tone. It soon became clear that my father had suffered a massive stroke, the latest in a series of attacks, previously so subtle that they had passed unnoticed but which had slowly been robbing him of his eloquence and movement.

My mother sat with a friend in the waiting room while I accompanied my father into Accident and Emergency and then finally onto a ward, where a frighteningly efficient nurse barked out questions from a clipboard: name, date of birth, ethnic origin, religion? My father who was curled up in pain seemed unable to speak, so I answered for him but when we came to the question on religion, I was at a loss.

What was my father's religion? Was he a born-again Jungian? Was he a Buddhist? In recent years he had been studying the *I Ching* and *The Tibetan Book of the Living and Dying*. (He once told me that the book's colourful descriptions of near-death experiences corresponded with his own as he had lain in a restless coma following his near-fatal air crash.)

How could I answer on his behalf this foundational existential question, a question with eternal implications and one which I knew had occupied his waking thoughts for most of his life? I began to realize that despite his rhetoric on life and man's state that, when it came to this all-important question, he had been an intensely private man. I knew that this was a question that ultimately only he could answer.

Then out of his pain, my father mustered all his energy, opened his eyes wide and said in a voice as clear as a bell, 'I am a Christian.' And after a lifetime of words, these turned out to be his very last.

Time took on a new form of elasticity. The sister on the ward told us that he was stable at present, suggested we take some time away and reassured us that she would call us if anything changed. My mother, employing her characteristic survival tactic of denial, decided to go shopping. After I watched her depart, I got in the car.

Almost by instinct, I found myself on the road to Tyringham-cum-Filgrave. I passed beneath the archway and over the beautiful bridge that my father had first crossed over thirty-three years previously in search of a different life. I parked the car by the bridge and walked up into the quiet churchyard and stood in one of his favourite spots, looking out over the cattle grazing beside the River Ouse. I could imagine him there, elbows on the fence, cigarette in hand, smiling quietly to himself.

I sank down onto my knees in the long, damp grass, tears running down my face, hands pressed together and prayed as if my soul would burst, 'Lord, don't take him from us yet. Let us have him a little longer. Please don't take him.' I sobbed and prayed until I felt emptied of all emotion.

Exhausted, I made my way up through Filgrave and, from a phone box outside my old village school, I rang through to the ward.

'Mrs Vilkaitis, your father has had another stroke. A very big one. He stopped breathing. We resuscitated him but there is no brain function,' the sister explained.

My knees went weak beneath me, 'Is my mother there?'

'No, we don't know how to get hold of her. But we suggest you come to the hospital now.'

In desperation, I called the shopping centre but wasn't sure what kind of message to leave – Mrs Nicholas come to the hospital, your husband is dying? In the end I left off the final point.

At the hospital, I approached my father's bedside on tiptoe as if not to wake him. I had hoped he would look peaceful but, beneath his salt-and-ginger hair, his brow was wrinkled in agony.

'Why does he look so in pain? I thought you said he was brain dead,' I asked.

'Well there may be some brain function still.'

'So he might come to again.'

'No, he isn't going to come to.'

I sat beside him, patting and stroking the back of his hand. Every couple of minutes, his body jerked as if in pain and his brow would furrow. I kept looking up and down the corridor. Where was my mother?

The sun's rays were lengthening outside the window when the doctor materialized beside me. He nodded, checked my father's charts and then sat down facing me. 'You are Mr Nicholas's daughter?'

'Yes.'

'And you are the only next of kin?'

'Well, I am trying to find my mother. And I have a sister; she is on holiday in Devon.'

'I would suggest that you need to contact anyone else who might want to come and be with you.'

'Is he dying?'

The doctor's voice softened, 'He won't last the night. I think we have a matter of hours at most.'

He paused and then said, 'There's something I have to ask you now. This will not be easy.'

I heard the doctor's voice as if from a great distance saying, 'Your father seems to be in a great deal of pain. I am sure you can see that. We cannot change the outcome of this. He is dying, but we can make the experience more comfortable for him. We can give him some high doses of morphine. It will ease his pain but it will hasten the end.'

'And there is no turning back? He can't wake up again?'

'No, we are certain of that.'

I wanted to scream; how can you ask me this? Why do I have to be the one to make this decision? I had spent most of my life terrified that my father's depression would become too much for him and that he would take his own life. As a child I had willed him to stay alive but, in a cruel stroke of irony, I was being asked to give permission to end his life. God, this isn't what I asked you for. I watched impotent as my father wrenched again in pain beneath the bedclothes and then spoke.

Half an hour later, I spotted my mother walking unsteadily down the corridor on her walking sticks, her face full of optimism. I quickly intercepted her path and guided her into a side room. She looked confused and childlike again, so I wrapped my arms around her. 'Mum, I need to tell you something. Dad has taken a turn for the worst . . .' It took about five minutes for my mother to finally take in what I was telling her. 'Oh my Dan,' she wailed.

He looked so peaceful as she sat beside his bed. I had told her all but the final decision that I had made for my father. I never did tell her. I didn't want her to feel that she had, by her absence, left me to make that heartbreaking choice on her behalf. I also wasn't sure I could bear knowing if she would have made a different decision if she had been there.

I left her holding his hand and headed to a telephone box. John was already on his way. My sister was on a short break with her long-term boyfriend Mike in Salcombe but I had no idea of their address or phone number. In the end I contacted the local police and gave them a description of my sister, her boyfriend and their car in the vague hope that they might be able to track them down. Then I called Theresa in Corfu. Her voice sounded ragged as she took in the news. 'I will try to get a flight to Athens tonight and then on to you tomorrow,' she said. I had to point out that her brother was unlikely to still be with us by the time she arrived.

I didn't have the contact details for most of his friends but, one by one, they miraculously began to materialize by his bed. It was as if he had put out a last siren call that brought friends to his side. As the evening progressed, laughter rang out from his corner of the ward as they lovingly exchanged stories about this wonderful, eccentric, idiosyncratic, obdurate and brilliant man. The tales wound around us like comforting arms and then another miracle: my sister's voice on the phone, broken but determined. The local police had managed to track her down and delivered the awful news but now there was still a chance. 'Tell him to wait for me,' she pleaded.

The night bore on and friends flowed around the bedside, holding my mother, crying and laughing. I sat quietly holding his hand, talking to him, 'Oh Dad. I love you so much. I've always been so afraid of losing you. You are right. I am like you. Perhaps I am the last Nicholas. What will I do without you?'

After years of fighting the idea, I finally understood that one of the few people who saw the world as I did was about to leave the planet and the world would be a far lonelier place without him; such is the selfishness of grief.

The doctors and the nurses came and went, each time expecting the end to have come. But I knew he was waiting for Charlotte; he would never leave the world on anybody else's terms but his own.

Then she came and, in the low night-light of the ward, embraced her father. He had waited for her. He could now go in peace. We watched him expectantly but, as the minutes turned to hours, it appeared that he might defy all expectations and last the night. It seemed there still was unfinished business.

I was completely exhausted so John suggested that we step outside for a few minutes and get a hot drink. I didn't want to leave my father's side and clung to him, hugging his prone body before I could be persuaded to finally depart for a few minutes. We walked into the cool air of the corridor and, as the ward doors swung closed behind me, he drew his last breath. I was his unfinished business.

Later that night at Larkland, Charlotte and I slept at the foot of our mother's bed. Wrung out with grief, we fell asleep while our mother sat, as she had done every night for the last three decades, book in hand, illuminated by her rose-covered side light, waiting for sleep to overtake the words. As she slept, my father used to creep in and lovingly take the glasses from her face and book from her hands and place them on her side table, before turning off her light.

We slept like the dead and woke with aching backs. As Charlotte raised her head above the counterpane, I heard her sharp intake of breath. My mother lay sleeping peacefully, her glasses folded on top of her book which was closed on the bedside table, the light extinguished.

Over the next few days, I began to question my sanity. I reasoned that grief had made me forgetful and that I must have turned off the lights in the room I had left only seconds before without realizing it. The idea that my father was continuing his habitual mission to reduce our electricity consumption after his death was too ludicrous to entertain but, even when I deliberately set about to light up the entire house like Battersea Power Station, the lights just kept on going out.

One day, my mother ventured out for lunch with a friend and, before she left, turned on my father's old radio at full blast as he used to do when he left the house in an effort to convince potential burglars that Larkland was still occupied by deaf inhabitants. When the two of them returned a couple of hours later, the radio was silent, the switch having been moved from on to off.

My father's 'Heath Robinson'-like appliances also seemed to take on a life of their own in the days after his death. First his hybrid washing machine, made out of elements bought at second-hand auctions, decided to disgorge a flood of soapy suds throughout the ground-floor rooms. This was closely followed by the explosion of his temperamental dishwasher.

But the last straw came one dark November evening when I was alone in the house. John was in London and my mother, Charlotte and her boyfriend Mike had gone to the nearest neighbours for dinner but I wanted to be alone with my thoughts. In the quiet of the house, I began to talk to my father, telling him how much I missed him. I had no idea whether he could hear me or not but this one-sided dialogue made me feel better. As I wandered through the empty rooms, I began to hear a vague rumble in the walls which rose rapidly in decibels until it became a shrieking rattle that pervaded the whole house. Every single radiator in the house seemed to be shaking as if trying to peel itself away from its supporting wall.

Alarmed, I phoned our neighbours and within minutes a posse appeared and confirmed that I wasn't imagining things. My father's crazy central heating system seemed to be trying to shake the house apart. After a brief investigation, Mike and our neighbour managed to take the heat out of the system. They told me that the water in every radiator in the house had been boiling but no-one had put any fuel into my father's 'fires of hell' boiler for hours.

By that point, my mother became convinced that my father's spirit had somehow followed us home to Larkland. She had a theory, based on her previous research into her book on psychics and mystics, that when the deceased were taken without warning, they would sometimes hang around in the form of energy in household electrics until they felt they had finished communicating all they needed to. Perhaps my father was indignant at having been cut off mid-stream in one of his monologues.

After a few weeks, our electrics returned to normal and life began to take up a new rhythm minus my father's presence. However, he did seem determined to have the last word. One night, as I slept at the house, I was woken by a voice that seemed very familiar and frankly rather irascible, saying emphatically, 'I cannot change that which I am, in order to become.'

I sat bolt upright in bed and looked around me. The moonlight shone in through the windows casting shadows on the floor; I was alone and slightly shaken. Was it a dream? I didn't have a clue what this obscure statement meant but it sounded like the kind of pronouncement my father would make.

It wasn't until sometime later, while clearing out Larkland, that I found my father's copy of *The Tibetan Book of Living and Dying*. Flicking through the pages, I spotted a reference to the 'bardo', an often traumatic transition stage which the soul supposedly passes through before it goes on to the next stage of existence. I read that:

> During the first weeks of the bardo, we have the impression that we are a man or woman, just as in our previous life. We do not realize that we are dead. We return home to meet our family and loved ones. We try to talk to them, to touch them on the shoulder. But they do not reply, or even show they are aware we are there. As hard as we try, nothing can make them notice us. We watch, powerless, as they weep or sit stunned and heartbroken over our death. Fruitlessly we try to make use of our belongings. Our place is no longer laid at table, and arrangements are being made to dispose of our possessions. We feel angry, hurt, and frustrated, 'like a fish', says the *Tibetan Book of the Dead*, 'writhing in hot sand'.[1]

The book also claimed that on the forty-ninth day, the soul moves on or 'becomes'.

It was exactly forty-nine days after my father's death that I was awakened from my sleep by the voice in the night.

18

Rebuilding

We had never intended to stay in Britain. In fact, we only envisioned staying in the country long enough to earn enough money to travel in Russia, China and potentially Latin America but my father's death changed everything.

My mother was so vulnerable, living alone in a large crumbling house full of memories, surrounded only by fields and stranded by her inability to drive. She had always been a truly terrible driver (during her driving test she managed to get all four wheels on the pavement while trying to parallel park) but a few years before my father's death, she had backed into another vehicle in a supermarket car park only to discover, when dealing with the insurers, that her driving licence had expired fifteen years before. It was obvious that we couldn't leave her, or the country, for any length of time.

Mercifully, John had fallen in love with all things British and European. While I had returned home, John was, of course, still travelling. In recognition of this, we bought a tourist guide to the British Isles which proudly claimed on its cover that 'Britain is one of the most beautiful islands on earth'. I dismissed such a claim as rubbish but was forced to eat my words as we began to explore my homeland with the same fervour as we had Asia.

We bought ourselves a tent and on every possible occasion headed out to explore, making our way from Lands' End on the most south-westerly tip of Cornwall to the wilderness of Cape Wrath at the most northerly tip of Scotland. For our honeymoon, we toured the magnificent Scottish Highlands, camping beside the fabled Loch Lomond and beneath the glowering granite magnificence of the Cuillin mountains on the Isle of Skye.

We bought our transportation, a battered old Ford Fiesta, with £500 – the exact sum that we had left in our bank accounts to build a new life when we had finally landed at Heathrow. While my friends had all been buying houses, three-piece suites and four-wheel drives, all I had to show for my thirty-one years of existence were two boxes of books and the 'head in a grid' in my parent's attic as well as a life-changing set of experiences and encounters. But as I began to try slotting back into the rhythm of everyday life in the UK, I could not feel poorer for it.

During the initial summer months after our return we stayed at Larkland. These were halcyon days of long lunches under the apple trees, sipping wine and reminiscing as I introduced John to my childhood. John managed to get some casual work with a local company and I secured some freelance work with a local business magazine. The copy I churned out wasn't going to win me any Pulitzer prizes, but once again I was writing for a living. I felt it was important to start as I meant to go on.

John was loving every aspect of his new life; the lushness of the English countryside (he said he had never seen so much green before), the layers of history just waiting to be uncovered all around him, and English churches. Within days John had developed a fully-fledged obsession with ancient English 'high' churches and cathedrals and he embarked on a photographic odyssey which would shape much of his artistic output over the next few years.

The fact that John had been brought up as a Catholic hadn't really made much of an impression on me until this point. I had so little formal connection with the church that the fact that we sat on different sides of a divide that had fractured many countries including Ireland, land of my ancestry, had not really bothered me.

I knew from my father that the Irish side of my family had a somewhat antagonistic attitude towards the church. My great-great-grandfather Charles O'Conner was reputed to have hated Catholics. He wouldn't let a priest cross the threshold and refused to allow his wife Kate to practise her faith. My great-grandmother Lizzie Burridge was never baptized or given any religious education, and inherited this deep distrust of the Catholic Church. So it was somewhat ironic that both my sister – who had married her long-term boyfriend Mike – and I ended up wed to Catholics. John was not a practising Catholic but I found it hard to dismiss his obsession with religious iconography as purely aesthetic. I suspected that the lessons and reverence of his youth had embedded themselves somewhere deep in his psyche.

After a few months we made the inevitable and necessary move down to London. We were invited to stay with some friends in a housing association terraced house close to Arsenal football ground. We gratefully accepted as the rent was minimal, the location central, and our housemates congenial and passionately artistic, even if the house was so cold that your posterior stuck to the bottom of the bathtub in the middle of winter.

From this base of operations, we began the task of establishing a life in the UK. For both of us this meant starting from scratch; I was determined to try breaking into journalism this time round and John wanted to try carving out a career in photography.

By this stage, John had compiled a significant portfolio of beautiful and profound images which he used to secure a pitifully paid role as a photographer's assistant. He spent his days lugging around lighting equipment and setting up artful shots of consumer goods for advertising. I knew that we were made for each other when he, too, became disenchanted by the vacuous nature of the work. He also tried a couple of weddings but it was clear that John had more of an artistic than commercial vision and would have to find some other way to pursue his photography while earning a living. So instead he enrolled to study photography at Central Saint Martins College of Art and took a job at a photographic retailer in Oxford Street.

In the meantime, I spent my days touting my folio around various editorial offices trying to get my first step on the journalistic ladder, but changing career in your thirties, and breaking into the media, was not an easy task. I sent out over two hundred letters, tried out for subbing jobs with *Vogue* and assistant roles at the BBC in the hope of just getting a foot in the door, all the while trying to ignore the well-paid salaries being offered by consumer PR agencies.

Finally, one of our housemates told me that there had been a call from a magazine offering me an editorial assistant's job but that he had accidently wiped the message from the answerphone. I was in despair. Having made so many applications, I had no idea who the offer had come from. I was ready to throw in the towel when the phone rang again; the editor of *Artists and Illustrators* magazine had received my letter and copies of my student art reviews and offered me some freelance work. I was on my way.

Within weeks of starting work with *Artists and Illustrators,* I interviewed Sir Ernst Gombrich, one of the world's greatest art historians and author of the seminal book *The History of Art* which had formed the foundation of my university education. I sat in awe in his sitting room beside a polished grand piano piled high with manuscripts. 'The only thing I have in common with Leonardo is untidiness,' he told me.

I went on to interview a range of artistic grandees from the legendary pop artist Peter Blake (creator of the imagery for The Beatles' *Sergeant Pepper's Lonely Hearts Club Band* album) to the idiosyncratic Maggi Hambling and the Portuguese portraitist Dame Paula Rego. I felt as if I had been given the key to a world that I had previously only observed from afar. At the same time I also managed to get some work as a freelance theatre reviewer with the *Camden New Journal*, and the world of London theatre opened up to us both.

Having secured a foothold, the work began to flood in. I began to write art, theatre, film and restaurant reviews for a range of magazines including a regular *Great Art Buys* column in *Ideal Home*. I also used my experience of writing with the business magazine in Buckinghamshire, to get some freelance work with a couple of titles run by Haymarket, the publishing group owned by former Deputy Prime Minister Michael Heseltine.

It was my brother-in-law Mike who suggested that I make use of my previous experience in public relations and contact *PRWeek*, one of the Haymarket magazines. I was at first reluctant but met with the editor who asked me why I hadn't contacted the magazine before, given my background. I didn't tell him that I had been trying to distance myself from the world of PR.

PRWeek occupied a unique position in the world of journalism, sitting in that no-man's-land between journalists and those who make a living by influencing them. I had decided to plant my flag firmly on the side of journalism and was concerned about being drawn back to the 'other side', but as we talked I began to see a whole new realm of possibilities. As a journalist, I had to grudgingly admit the power of public relations; while the media were loath to admit it, anything up to 70 per cent of the news that reached viewers had its genesis in a call from a PR or communications professional.

I arranged to do a couple of news shifts at Haymarket's labyrinthine offices behind the Georgian facades of Lancaster Gate but within a couple of months was offered a part-time post as features editor. By that point, I was beginning to earn a decent income as a freelancer and had a range of work lined up, including a commission for a book on Pre-Raphaelite art. On one level, I was loath to give up the freedom and variety that this life afforded but, at the same time, we really did need somewhere of our own to live.

After a freezing winter in the by now almost derelict house in Arsenal, we had rented a one-bedroom, first-floor flat in Muswell Hill, a leafy and picturesque area of north London with views down over the city. But whenever we visited our friends' well-appointed (and mortgaged) residences, it became clear that, if we were not about to flee the country again, we had better invest in some bricks and mortar.

Freelance journalists are not regarded as good guarantors but for some reason my local bank manager in Buckinghamshire saw some potential in me. 'I may live to regret this, but I have a feeling that you are going to make good,' he told me. So in a stroke of synchronicity that my father would have appreciated, we bought a flat on the top floor of a Victorian terraced house on Cavendish Road, in the north London suburb of Haringey.

The flat was ranged across two levels; the sitting room was light and bright with a huge bay window and there were two bedrooms, one of which faced out over a garden and would become my office. Downstairs lived a jazz pianist who had once played with rock band Oasis. The area was mainly populated by Greek and Turkish immigrants who lived in an uneasy truce, which was occasionally broken on a Friday night when the pubs turned out. The main thoroughfare was lined with mouth-watering baklava shops and grocers selling freshly baked Turkish bread and rough red wine, day and night. When we couldn't sleep we would go and buy freshly baked loaves before dawn.

Life was good. We were enjoying all that London had to offer, taking in plays, cinema, exhibitions, eating and drinking with friends. I loved the time I spent working from home (I once conducted a telephone interview with Maggie Thatcher's ferocious press secretary Sir Bernard Ingham in my pyjamas) but it didn't take long for my part-time work for *PRWeek* to become all-consuming and eventually I bit the bullet and accepted a full-time post as deputy editor and, subsequently, editor, of the magazine.

From the outset I seemed to fall on my feet. In the early days, I secured an interview with Jane Atkinson who had just resigned as PR advisor to the iconic and increasingly controversial Princess of Wales. I had first met Jane when working in the advertising agency and we had kept in touch. She was already being pestered daily by various national newspapers for her side of the soap opera that was Princess Diana's life but, to my delight, she decided that she would give the story to me as a friend and editor of her trade magazine.

Jane had started working for the Princess at a turbulent time: Diana's former press officer Geoff Crawford had just resigned following her sensational *Panorama* interview a few months earlier. Her private secretary Patrick Jephson had also left and the Palace press office had been fielding enquiries.

In the corner of a restaurant near Buckingham Palace, she told me how the telephone had become a tyrant, with calls starting from breakfast programmes at 6.30 a.m. and continuing until as late as midnight from the morning papers. 'My brief was to be available twenty-four hours a day for the Princess of Wales and the media,' she told me. But Jane had been surprised to find out that the Princess set her own PR agenda, often without heeding her advice – sometimes with great success, at other times less so – and that the Princess's movements were shrouded in secrecy, but subject to leaks.

Jane also said that she resented the media intrusion into her own privacy and family life, including paparazzi shots of her out walking the dog, which no doubt fuelled her understandable reluctance to be interviewed. On the day she resigned, Jane returned to her house to find forty journalists camped on her doorstep. She was smuggled in through the garage while her husband George went out to tell the media she was staying with a friend. But the media stayed and the following day her children conducted an elaborate facade of carrying on as if their mother were not there while Jane hid from the lenses.

Eventually she gave them the slip and escaped the media glare by heading across the Channel.[1]

Leaving the restaurant with a full notepad, I felt as if I was carrying a state secret and, as we walked out into the sunlight, a photographer leapt out in front of us and fired off a couple of shots. I didn't envy her but the resulting article was picked up by the *Daily Express, The Daily Telegraph,* the *Daily Mirror* and the *Daily Mail.*

Later on, I scooped another royal exclusive with Sophie Rhys-Jones as she prepared for her marriage to Prince Edward. At the time, Sophie was a public relations practitioner with a stake in a PR company called R-JH based in west London. Once again, she had been pestered relentlessly by the media but after a couple of meetings agreed to a single interview with *PRWeek,* on the basis that we talked about her business interests which she planned to continue after her marriage into the British royal family.

Most of the interview was, fairly predictably, about the success of her business but my ears pricked up when she began to talk about the Palace's views on her business plans. She said that the family had been supportive but that she had already had to consult with the communications secretary at Buckingham Palace about the potential problems posed by her determination to be a working royal.

'I think the media would really like me to give up work and start appearing on a regular basis helping causes and charities. I have never pretended that I would do anything other than continue my work and obviously I have had a lot of approaches from organizations which I have been turning down,' she explained. 'But I think that once I physically start doing what I have promised to do, there will come a time when they [the media] will decide I am not appearing enough for them. All it would take is for a national newspaper to find a supposedly disgruntled charity which feels I have turned my back on good causes to make a story.'

She gave the impression of one already sorely stung by the media, who admittedly had not given her an easy ride, 'When I deal with the media, right from the word go, I have done so in what I hope is perceived as a professional manner and speaking the same language. But during the last five months there have been a number of incidents, when they have written things that are not only untrue but unfair and irresponsible. I have learnt that however close you are to the media business, when it is you they are writing about, it really hurts and won't stop hurting.'

She mentioned a letter she had received from the editor of a national newspaper who told her to 'carry on being nice to the media because, believe it or not, it works,' saying, 'I can positively say to you that after the last few weeks that I don't think it is true.'[2]

On publication of the story, I was subjected to a blitz of newspaper, radio and TV enquiries and interviews which did wonders for the magazine's circulation. In the aftermath, Sophie, who obviously saw me as a benign media ally, sent me the most spectacular display of flowers which I passed on to my uncharacteristically starry-eyed mother.

However, only two years later, I justified her scepticism about the media. Married to Prince Edward, the Countess of Wessex found herself at the centre of a media hurricane after being duped by the notorious *News of the World* reporter Mazher Mahmood, or the 'fake sheikh', into a series of indiscretions about members of the government and suggesting the potential for access to the royal family.

I knew this incident would fuel media cynicism and derision about public relations – a profession which I now realized had far greater depth and breadth than I had ever imagined. So, fired up with indignation, I penned a stinging leader column stating that, 'As a member of the Royal Family, there can be no such concept as an off-the-record comment to a mere acquaintance. And such naivety is incompatible with the role of a PR practitioner.' I also pointed out that, in her earlier interview with *PRWeek,* she had stated categorically that the only way she could continue to run her business was by eschewing any suggestion that she was trading on her royal status.[3] The column went to the subs on Wednesday night and I headed for home.

The following morning, I wandered blearily into the sitting room carrying a bowl of cereal which I promptly dropped on the floor as the words 'and Kate Nicholas, editor of *PRWeek*, has accused Sophie Wessex of selling the royal brand' emanated from the TV screen.

I threw on some clothes and drove to the train station, where I was horrified to see reference to *PRWeek* slating Sophie Wessex on the front page of the *Daily Mirror* and a double-page spread quoting extensively from my leader in the *Daily Mail.* The top story on BBC *News at One* featured Jennie Bond standing outside Buckingham Palace with an umbrella and a copy of the magazine. '*PRWeek* has written a very hard-hitting editorial,' Bond told viewers. As the news team huddled round the screen, a call came from Heseltine's office informing me that there were journalists outside the front of the building and I had better go and deal with it.

Feeling the need for some crisis PR advice, I rang Lord [Tim] Bell, former advisor to Margaret Thatcher and possibly the smoothest operator in the business. Bell, who was obviously amused, immediately dispatched one of his top advisors who turned out to be none other than Jane Atkinson.

Jane arrived in Hammersmith like a white knight and together we crafted a newswire announcement offering interviews, managed the deluge of calls and hit the studio circuit in a cab until late that night. I only realized that my contribution to the mounting story had gone worldwide when I received a call from *PRWeek*'s publisher who was in Singapore saying, 'I've just seen you on TV dissing the monarchy.'

In the end, my fit of pique garnered coverage as far afield as Australia and Japan. *The Independent on Sunday* summarized the situation, writing: '*PRWeek* magazine accuses Sophie of "naivety" for speaking so openly to the "sheikh". Its view is backed by Trade Secretary Stephen Byers.' Journalists had just been waiting for someone willing to speak out. The magazine sold out almost immediately, and we saw a satisfying spike in our subscriptions while our brand awareness reached new heights.

Closer to home, however, my outspoken opinions were not well received. In the doctor's surgery, the receptionist fixed me with a glassy stare and said indignantly, 'I saw you on television being nasty about that nice Sophie Wessex.' That weekend, I accompanied my mother to a ruby wedding anniversary celebration. She made her displeasure clearly known throughout the journey: 'You do know that you will be cut from their Christmas card list, don't you?'

But this was nothing in comparison to the reception I received from the gathering of monarchist pensioners at the party. None, it seemed, had failed to spot my television appearances. I was now *persona non grata*. So after being frozen out of every conversation, I grabbed a bottle of champagne and sat in the corner getting slowly sozzled.

But the royal gravy train just kept rolling on. In 2003, I secured the first on-the-record interview with Mark Bolland, the royal PR advisor who had played a key role in the rehabilitation of Prince Charles's image following the death of the Princess of Wales and securing the public acceptance of his relationship with Camilla Parker Bowles. Bolland spoke to me just after resigning his post to start up his own PR consultancy.

Unwittingly, I had established a reputation as a royal commentator. When *Panorama* contacted me to say that they wanted to interview me for a special on Charles and his soon-to-be-bride Camilla, I pleaded quite truthfully that I was ill in bed with flu. The producer was not, however, so easily put off and turned up with his equipment, setting up a studio in my living room. While the furniture was being moved, a kind Indian sound man fed me balls of turmeric and honey which successfully restored my voice long enough to complete the interview.

In addition to the royal entourage, I was meeting an extraordinary range of public figures from Chancellor of the Exchequer Gordon Brown to the fabulously successful entrepreneur Richard Branson; from British Airways Chief Executive Rod Eddington to Dame Anita Roddick, founder of the iconic ethical high street chain Body Shop.

I was also working with some great contributors including Sir Bernard Ingham whose weekly column was one of the magazine's highlights. I had approached our first face-to-face meeting with some trepidation, having heard so much about his fearsome reputation at Number 10, but found him to be a brilliant and slightly self-effacing man with a mesmerizing set of eyebrows. In fact, he reminded me so vividly of my father that I confided this fact, at which he blushed and replied, 'That is the first time anyone has ever compared me to a poet.' It was the beginning of a wonderful working relationship but, to ensure a balanced political agenda, I also brought in Charlie Whelan, the bullish and highly entertaining press secretary to Gordon Brown.

I attended a range of glittering events including the BAFTAs (British Academy of Film and Television Arts Awards) where I got talking with the humble but brilliant actor Pete Postlethwaite. At the Silver Clef music awards, I sat on a table with Roger Daltry and Pete Townsend of the legendary rock band The Who, and applauded U2 lead singer Bono's impassioned speech on his Jubilee debt campaign.

At singer Elton John's charity fundraising white tie and tiara ball, I encountered film stars Joan Collins, Sean Connery and Hugh Grant as well as music legends Mick Jagger, George Michael and Bob Geldof, the man behind the Live Aid fundraiser for Ethiopia. The whole event was held in an exquisitely decorated marquee in the garden of Elton John's Windsor mansion and felt like a surreal wedding at which all the guests were A-list celebrities. My disconnection with reality reached its apogee when the girl-band singer Geri Halliwell, who was ahead of me in a long queue for the loos, suggested that we 'go' behind the marquee. I could only stammer, 'I'm sorry, I don't think I could pee with a Spice Girl.'

Working for *PRWeek* also gave me access to previously distant, political spheres. I took over as deputy editor the year that the Labour Party won the election. Tony Blair had sashayed his way into Number 10 following the most extraordinarily sophisticated communications strategy engineered by former Labour Party Director of Communications Peter Mandelson and former *Daily Mirror* journalist Alastair Campbell, who went on to become Blair's chief press secretary. A tired and unelectable party had been completely rebranded; the age of spin was born and suddenly the influence of public relations on our society had become of interest to more than a small coterie of media and communications professionals.

Eventually, Campbell almost eclipsed Blair in terms of sheer column inches and *PRWeek* maintained a watching brief on the spin coming out of Number 10. By this point, just about every public-facing body, organization, political party, individual or army had its own communications or PR operation and, on a professional level, I wanted *PRWeek* to be able to provide an analysis of how every major news story had been managed by professional communicators – to provide the news behind the headlines. On a personal level, it was the closest I could come to following in my mother's footsteps.

So in addition to trade and domestic stories, we also ran in-depth analysis of the Kosovo crisis propaganda by NATO's Chief Spokesperson Jamie Shea, reports by an intrepid freelancer from Northern Alliance's 'press conferences' in the Afghan city of Mazar-e-Sharif and analysis from an embedded communicator on the front lines in Iraq. Our stories began to be picked up and repurposed by other national newspapers and were regularly featured in *The Editor, The Guardian*'s round up of the best of the week's media stories.

I began making so many appearances at BBC Broadcasting House as a commentator on BBC News, as well as Radio 4's *Today Programme, You and Yours, The World Tonight* and *Woman's Hour*, that I began to receive regular, if rather paltry cheques. I also made regular appearances on Sky, Channel 4 and ITV news as well as CNBC's *Media Talk*. I started writing for national newspapers including *The Independent, The Observer* and *The Business* on spin, reputation and branding. My mother told me I had made it as a journalist when the satirical current affairs magazine *Private Eye* pilloried me as the editor of '*PRWeakly*' (sic).

In many respects, I revelled in my low-level notoriety and the amazing access to public figures but I also felt a sense of disquiet. My rise from freelancer to editor and commentator had been so rapid that I had not been able to fully assimilate and process the implications. My airtime seemed to depend on the vociferousness of my critique. In my attempts to live up to the role, I had developed a 'persona' that I did not always recognize and, as a result, I found it hard to fully enjoy my success.

When I finally encountered the Queen at an event at St James's Palace, I was horrified when she seemed to smile in recognition and relieved when she looked past me to greet the news reader Nicholas Owen. At another press event, I bumped into Campbell who commented rather acidly, 'You make a rather good living out of me, don't you?'

19

Amazing Grace

With a salary in the bank account, we began travelling once again. At first John and I started to take shorter trips across the continent. In Western and Eastern Europe, John went into photographic rapture over the opulent Catholic architecture and iconography. In Egypt, we stood in awe among the colonnades of Karnak, rode at dawn into the Valley of the Kings, sheltered from sandstorms in an oasis deep in the Western Desert and snorkelled the wonders of the Red Sea, once parted by Moses.

I also travelled with work to Europe and beyond as Haymarket explored the potential for *PRWeek* to expand its footprint overseas (we eventually ended up with magazines in the US, Germany and Hong Kong with affiliates in Russia, Poland and Argentina). I also spoke at, and chaired, conferences in France, Germany, Brussels, Holland, Stockholm and South Africa, often accompanied by John who made the most of the opportunity to explore. At home, we were determined to squeeze every last ounce of cultural potential out of the capital but, no matter how full our lives were, something was missing.

I was very indignant when my doctor first described me as an elderly primigravida. At the tender age of thirty-four, I felt far from elderly but the National Health Service obviously felt I was irresponsible for not having found a father for my child at an earlier age.

But even the censure of the medical establishment and continuous morning sickness couldn't take away from our unbounded joy at the discovery that we were to be parents.

The fact that I was pregnant at all felt like a miracle. For eighteen months, I had suffered chronic pain and undergone extensive tests. Various theories were proposed and I was prescribed a drug which was also used to treat some cancers but the reality was that no-one seemed to know what was wrong with me. I was also warned, however, that it was highly unlikely that I would be able to have children.

I was distraught. I had always envisaged having a family and couldn't bear the thought that I had relegated John to a life without children. An exploratory operation rendered no further information but did confirm that my baby-making equipment was still intact. So I decided to come off all forms of medication and apply a mind-over-matter approach to the pain, which amazingly seemed to work. With a combination of exercise and acupuncture, the pain stayed at acceptable levels and disappeared completely when, to my joy, I finally became pregnant.

Perhaps women have a sixth sense because within days I knew that I was carrying a new life within me. I would lie on the floor of our sitting room with my hands on my belly, gazing at the sky out of our bay window, wondering at the miracle of life. I felt such love for this person to be, such a sense of responsibility and an overwhelming desire to protect against all odds.

At our dating scan, John was quite overwhelmed and, with tears running down his face, announced 'It's a human bean,' and, from thereon, the new life I carried within me became known as The Bean.

I also felt so grossly inadequate to the task. There's nothing like first-time motherhood to make a fully grown professional woman feel like a blithering idiot. Whatever I had achieved, I was a complete novice when it came to the business of bringing a new life into the world. I was a marketer's dream; so easily convinced that our child would die for want of an electric in-car bottle warmer or an automated rocker device covered in pictures of giraffes, that I lost count of the contraptions that we invested in but never used.

My sense of inadequacy also meant that I allowed myself to be bullied into countless tests for abnormalities including a risky amniocentesis, knowing full well that nothing on earth would make me agree to terminate this child. I already knew that my love would be sufficient for any quirks of nature that my child may suffer as a result of my tardiness in becoming a mother.

I worked until two weeks before my due date and then spent four weeks like a stranded whale on the sofa, waiting and praying for my baby to come. When I was two weeks overdue, I was taken into hospital to be induced.

At first I was reassured to be in hospital, even if I was the oldest on the ward by at least a decade and the girl opposite me had to be given methadone injections on a regular basis. But the warm blanket of reassurance faded over the following fifty-seven hours of labour, in which I was repeatedly induced to no avail.

I had entered the hospital with a birth plan that consisted mainly of aromatherapy candles and whale music but by the second day I wanted every drug known to mankind. I was in such pain that I ended up wrestling with a nurse when she tried to take away the gas and air. On day three I was given a drug to speed up labour and I began to climb the walls. In the early hours of the morning, the doctors finally realized my baby was in distress and I was rushed to the operating theatre.

Our beautiful daughter was born at 6.50 a.m. on 7 April 1998. Despite being one of the most oft-repeated scenes in the world, it was for the two of us, quite simply, the most extraordinary moment of our lives. Bellowing encouragingly, our daughter was wrapped in a shawl and placed in her father's arms; his face beaming with adoration. We kept repeating, 'Hello, Alyssa, our little Aly-Bean.'

In the recovery room, I was finally allowed to hold my precious daughter with her mop of dark hair, long legs, delicate fingers splayed like starfish and grey-blue eyes which already blinked at the world. Back on the ward, I gazed at her in wonder as she slept. When she didn't cry as much as I expected, I woke her to check that she was still breathing. I could not believe that we could have produced something so beautiful. She was not a small baby but when John held her little body against his chest, she seemed so vulnerable and he so protective. I could hardly believe it when the staff allowed us to walk out of the hospital with her.

Back at home, the days and nights merged as I fed, changed and bathed and then spent hours gazing at my baby in adoration. Within weeks, she started smiling at us in recognition and, having discovered her feet, would spend hours trying to catch them. With the absence of adult company, my vocabulary regressed into a stream of baby nonsense. I would carry her around the house singing badly constructed songs on the subject of being an Aly-Bean (apparently this tendency to sing is instinctual and helps with a child's language development, no matter how appalling the lyrics).

John took to fatherhood like a duck to water despite a last-minute panic attack a couple of months prior to my due date. 'I am going to make a terrible father,' he had told me over a romantic Valentine's dinner in a local restaurant. In a slight panic, I pointed to my enormous stomach and told him it was a little late to be having doubts. It turned out that he was afraid of having a boy in case they were keen on football, which he just didn't understand, and was so relieved when the midwife told us, 'It's a perfect little girl.'

The birth of a granddaughter also seemed to inject new life into my mother. We began to drive up to see her every second weekend and, when she held this tiny baby, I could see a younger woman in her eyes.

When Aly was five weeks old we took her to the local parish church thanksgiving service in preparation for her baptism. It was very important to me that my daughter was baptized; I still felt uncertain about the institution of the church but sensed that her immortal soul was at stake, and didn't want her to suffer because of my own inner conflict.

Over the previous few years, I had attended, mainly out of curiosity, services at a range of churches including a giant charismatic black majority church in Finsbury Park. I still had some deep-seated reservations and didn't feel comfortable going back to the Baptist Church, so instead decided to take our child to the local Anglican Church, a beautiful thirteenth-century edifice made famous by its former curate John Newton who wrote the iconic hymn 'Amazing Grace'. Newton was a reformed slave trader who had been buying and selling slaves in the area now known as Sierra Leone when he was caught in a near shipwreck off the West African coast, an experience that led to his conversion to Christianity and inspired the world-famous hymn written in 1772.

As I stepped through the ancient portal of the church I wondered if I would be hit by a thunderbolt, but instead was greeted effusively by the vicar and the lay minister, a rather idiosyncratic former Church Missionary Society (CMS) missionary who told me she had worked in Nigeria and India. I was also particularly struck by the fact that my daughter's baptism would take place during Christian Aid week and that the prayers for her soul would be intermingled with those for people in the far-off land of Ethiopia.

As we prepared for Aly's baptism, I found myself in the pews in Olney on a regular basis, sometimes with John and, on occasions, my mother. I felt almost irresistibly drawn to the place. There was something about the liturgy of the Church of England that resonated deeply within me and conjured up a sense of mystery that had been missing in the church experience of my youth. Holding my darling daughter in my arms, I had a dawning comprehension of the sheer unconditional breadth and depth of the love of God. I would do anything to protect and nurture this child; how much more must my creator love me?

Aly was christened on 27 September wearing a beautiful white lace christening gown we had bought for her in Bruges during her first European tour (at just four months old she had surveyed the delights of Holland and Belgium perched high above John's head in a special baby backpack). Aly had evidently inherited the Vilkaitis genes and had grown so fast that, by the time of the christening, it was a tight squeeze to get her into her exquisite gown.

Her father was moving from strength to strength artistically. A couple of months after Aly's birth, John took part in a joint show called *The Outsiders* which featured his wonderfully idiosyncratic photographic records of British life. He had also joined a local artists' co-operative and had started studying ceramics. I was at a loss, though, to see how he could work in clay in our first-floor London flat. The time had come to re-assess our living arrangements.

In 1995, my mother had finally admitted defeat and left Larkland. At the time, it felt as though we were losing a part of ourselves. As we dismantled each room, and wrapped our past in newspaper, we had retold the tales of our family; memory becoming myth as we wove our oral history. On the last night, we sat on packing cases eating fish and chips out of vinegar-soaked paper, drinking champagne out of old mugs.

On the day of our departure, I woke before dawn and for the last time watched the sun slowly steal its way down the fields, over the cherry tree and into my bedroom. As the day began, we wandered in a dazed state, bidding farewell to each room before closing the door on each chapter of our lives. Then, huddled together like figures from a Chekhovian drama, we walked with our arms entwined out through the rose-filled garden and drove away from Larkland.

My mother had moved into a compact but pretty cottage on the market square of the local town of Olney. The move seemed to inject new life into her and she had begun to create a future without my father. But her health had begun to fail and, as we became increasingly aware of her vulnerability, we spent an increasing amount of time driving up the motorway from London.

At the same time, John and I had begun to see how having a child changed your relationship with the city. I was becoming more concerned with how to manoeuvre a buggy onto a busy bus than the latest exhibitions in town and, when I walked through Finsbury Park, I noticed the used hypodermic needles in the grass rather than the colours of the trees. As I contemplated the thought of Aly going to school on the London underground, I realized that I wanted a different kind of childhood for her.

We found our family home en route to Northumberland. It was early in the morning and we were bickering over the industrial quantity of nappies required on a camping trip, when my mother called; 'A house has come on the market in the next village of Weston Underwood. Nothing ever comes up there. You need to go and see it.'

'Mum, we are going on holiday today.'

'Well I'm just telling you, I can't promise it will be there when you get back.'

I knew Weston Underwood well; an exquisite seventeenth-century village of thatch and stone situated very close to the village where I was brought up. Weston was every Australian's idea of what rural England should look like. The opportunity seemed too good to miss, so we broke our journey to view the property and fell in love at first sight.

We put in our offer on the house while heading north in the car up the motorway and had the mortgage papers sent to a campsite in Northumberland. Six weeks later, Aly was climbing in and out of packing cases in our flat in London, sticking colour-coded dots on her forehead to ensure that she was taken with us to our new home.

So after all my travels, I found myself living just five miles from Larkland. If I walked to the end of our lane and leant on the wooden cross bar gate, I could look out over the valley, wistful in the knowledge that just on the other side of the tree-covered hills lay my childhood home. In the mornings, I could once again walk out over the fields, striding through the morning mist and copper autumn leaves, bathing in the beauty of the sunrise. From the edge of the village, I could look down on the town of Olney where my mother lived and the spire of St Peter's and St Paul's, the church where I had been so welcomed and where Aly had been christened. I had come home.

The familiarity of my surroundings was like a balm to my soul but it soon became clear that much had changed in the time I had been away. Childhood friends had all moved away and it was only on rare occasions that I recognized anyone from my school days. It was as if I had the chance to begin again, to make all things new against this comfortingly familiar backdrop.

Like my parents before us, we soon began to receive visits from our city friends who gloried in the novelty of our rural idyll. The village was so small that it did not have a shop, the only community centres being an atmospheric pub with timber beams and a roaring log fire, and a beautiful and ancient church dedicated to St Laurence, whose bells would wake us in the morning and lull us to sleep in the evening. I loved to go and sit in the churchyard, listen to the birds and look out over the fields towards Filgrave. It reminded me of the village church of Tyringham where I had knelt and prayed for my father – but attending was a different matter. The church had a very small congregation who were not really prepared for the intrusion of a middle-aged mother and a crying baby in their midst.

So, instead, I set my sights on the spire of St Peter's and St Paul's, the home of 'Amazing Grace', which I knew from earlier visits attracted young families. I felt a certain sense of trepidation as I returned to the church as a parishioner as opposed to visitor. At first

I thought I could creep into the back of the church unnoticed but was greeted with open arms, like a prodigal daughter returning to the fold. Once again I was amazed by the unguarded and unconditional welcome given by the community to a comparative stranger. No questions were asked; I was simply accepted as I came, baby and all.

I would sit in the crèche in the back of the church, straining to hear the sermons over the clatter of Thomas the Tank engines bashed against doll's houses but, even if the substance of the word of God often escaped my comprehension, I rapidly found a deep sense of belonging among this new community and the church became for me an oasis of calm. As the sun shone through the exquisite stained-glass windows, casting coloured patterns on the ancient floor, and voices swelled the tune of familiar hymns, I simply bathed in a sense of God's presence; a sense that I had hitherto found only out in the open fields, in a far horizon or the emptiness of the desert. In the liturgy, I felt a sense of awe at the concept of being so fully exposed to my creator and gained perspective in viewing the vicissitudes of my life. It was as if he was saying to me personally, 'Be still and know that I am God.'

Despite being regularly late for work after getting stuck be-hind tractors on the way to the train station, my career continued to progress. After my return, we launched a magazine website and moved increasingly online, publishing a twice-daily worldwire which drew news from *PRWeek*'s international magazines and stringers in twenty-eight countries.

I was also becoming increasingly comfortable with my role as the public face of the magazine. I chaired our own numerous conferences and forums and worked with our events department on the *PRWeek* Awards, an annual glitter-fest at the Grosvenor House Hotel on Park Lane which attracted 1,400 of the great and the good of the PR and media world. As editor, I had to open the event, working with a range of presenters including news anchor Jon Snow and comedians Stephen Fry, Rory Bremner, Jack Dee and Jonathon Ross. I was astounded by how much work they put in but, despite their professionalism, it wasn't always possible to prevent creative improvisation. On the night, I would watch Michael Heseltine's face with trepidation as various unsavoury jokes rolled out.

I also seemed to have to attend a bewildering array of industry functions, lunches and receptions, which created its own challenges. I wanted to be fully present for my Aly-Bean – to play with her, read to her, laugh with her and cuddle her – which mainly meant giving up sleep. At bedtime, I would sing songs I had made up for her and at night she would often sleep curled up on my chest in her penguin pyjamas. On wakeful nights, I would stand in the dark in her bedroom with her in my arms playing 'Where is moon?' as it drifted behind the clouds. At the weekends, I would hardly let her out of my sight.

I bounced from one day to the next, overcoming lack of sleep with caffeine. I prided myself on my almost preternatural energy levels (my father always used to say that my spirit was too big for my body). When I felt under the weather, which seemed to be increasingly frequently, I simply pushed on through, willing my body to overcome any weakness. But a month after our move to Weston Underwood, my body fought back.

John and I were due to attend the British Society of Magazine Editors Awards at The London Hilton on Park Lane. Once again I was suffering from a flu-like virus but I had been shortlisted, and was determined not to miss my moment of glory. As the night progressed, I began to feel faint and by the time I was beaten to the award by the editor of *Building* magazine, I hardly cared, despite the protestations of my boss that I had been 'robbed'. Somehow John and I made our way home on the last train and I collapsed into bed.

The following morning, I was so tired I could not even stand up. For once I had no option but to give in and to stay in bed until I recovered. Three weeks later I was still so exhausted that if I got out of bed to make a cup of tea, I would have to sleep deeply for four or five hours to recover. Finally, I gave in and saw a doctor who told me in no uncertain terms what I had done to my body by not allowing it to recover from recurrent viral infections. I was diagnosed with chronic fatigue syndrome (ME) which I was told could be debilitating for the long term if I didn't manage myself better. 'This whole situation is much more complex than a simple mind-over-matter approach,' he admonished me.

As I lay in bed for weeks on end, Aly-Bean took advantage of my presence. Surrounded by my pillows she would hold tea parties for her 'Bippo' and present me with various toys, items of clothing and shoes, utilizing her tiny vocabulary to explain their significance. When I became too tired, she would use her little fingers to force open my eyelids.

On dark days, I became afraid that my life would be limited to that one room; that my body would never recover its former energy and I would be destined to limp my way feebly through the rest of my existence. I would pray with wordless groans.

On good days, I would walk up the lane opposite our house and watch birds and rabbits as they nibbled their way along the hedge-rows. At night, I dreamt of being in an elevator that ascended so many floors that, when the doors opened, I looked out on a beautiful landscape high above the clouds, with rolling hills and valleys leading to a glittering light-filled city. I felt glorious, light and unencumbered and, even though I could see no other human in sight, I knew I was not alone. On those mornings, I woke filled with hope.

I was one of the lucky ones. Slowly but surely my body began to function again. Day by day I grew stronger, able to walk further and play with my beautiful daughter and, after several months, I managed to pick up the reins of work again. But I had been forced to recognize the truth of my father's theory about the relative size of my 'spirit' and body. I would need to pace myself if I intended to last the course.

20

Meant to Be

John had rapidly adapted to rural life. He loved the sense of space and the verdant countryside which was such a contrast to the sun-burnt, dusty hills of his home in Australia. When not working in the new city of Milton Keynes – which he said was 'like Canberra without the sun' – he would walk for hours across the fields and woodlands that surrounded our village, photographing the plentiful wildlife and fauna. His portfolio began to be filled with surreal close-up photographs of fungi and sunlit glimpses of wild deer.

He also began utilising the ceramic skills he had acquired in London. We built a small wooden studio in the back garden, complete with a potter's wheel and table, and set up a kiln in the garage. In winter it was freezing but in summer it provided a welcome escape. Gradually, the house began to fill up with beautifully glazed pots and mixed-media shrines filled with garish Catholic, Hindu or Buddhist memorabilia and offerings.

Every trip we went on became a material-gathering mission for his artwork. Driving along winding Greek mountain roads, he would stop on hairpin bends to photograph the moving roadside shrines to victims of the Greeks' idiosyncratic approach to road rules. We made our way across Europe exploring Catholic, Orthodox and various shades of Protestant churches built in Gothic, Baroque and Romanesque style. One of Aly's first words was 'church' and, as she grew up, one of her most common backseat complaints became, 'Oh Dad, not another church.'

John also began to read voraciously on religious imagery, absorbing enormous detail on everything from Mexican votive retablos to European amulets. Our house began to fill up with tomes on various religions and, as my husband spent hours wandering around churches taking photographs, I sat in the pews with Aly gazing on centuries of religious artwork, reflecting, listening and increasingly praying.

At home, I began to leaf through John's burgeoning library and every now and then I would delve into our crumbling family Bible, an ancient leather-bound tome in which the names of generations of children had been recorded. Then on a trip to Durham Cathedral, I bought myself a rather funky Living Translation Bible with a metal cover featuring a ring-pull can adorned with the word 'Thirsty'. I began at page one of Genesis and what I found was sheer poetry which spoke about the mystery of existence.

I began to look for time to read and reflect and, as such, my commute proved a true blessing. I came to value this time of transition between my role as wife and mother to that of professional; a time when I could simply be. I would buy myself a cappuccino on the station platform, fight my way through the crowds to a hard-won seat and then settle myself down to read. None of the other commuters seemed to notice that I was reading the Bible as opposed to the latest John Grisham until, one evening, a scruffy girl with long dreadlocks, a leather jacket and colourful striped socks, came and sat opposite me. I buried my head in Isaiah but became aware of her eyes on me. I could sense she was watching me and I felt threatened. As we neared Tring station, she rose up and loomed over me and said, 'I've got that one; it's great, innit?'

As she jumped off the train, my jaw hung open; God had taught me a valuable lesson. The 'Dreadlock Girl' had blown apart my preconceived image of Christians. Like most journalists, I had harboured suspicions that Christians' other worldliness and willingness to trust rendered them too naive for this world. It was this that made many journalists so unwilling to admit their faith in case they were considered lacking in sufficient analytical abilities to comment on current affairs. As far as I was concerned, Christians still generally fell into two brackets: octogenarians who clung fiercely to outdated church traditions or born-again fanatics whose gaucheness was not only embarrassing but vaguely dangerous. Dreadlock Girl made me think again.

I began to expand my train reading material and became like a sponge for information, interpretation and historical evidence about Christ. I wanted to know that he existed and to understand who he was. I was fascinated by the accounts of Jesus's life and death by the Roman historian Josephus, and loved the honesty with which novelist and theologian C.S. Lewis addressed many of the issues that still caused me doubts. Like many before, I was particularly struck by his argument outlined in *Mere Christianity* that you can't just regard Christ as a great man or a moral teacher, on the basis that any man who made the claims that he had done would have to be seen as either mad, a liar or a purveyor of a truth too great to ignore. And as Christ was so evidently rational and good, I was left with no other alternative than to agree that he is indeed the son of the living God.

My approach, however, was one of the head rather than the heart. I still didn't really *know* Christ. It was as if I had read his biography, heard the evidence of witnesses, but hadn't actually met him yet.

At weekends, I started to take Aly to Sunday school which she threw herself into with abandon, revelling in cotton-wool sheep and sticky-back-plastic shepherds. The only problem was that, as she was so young, I had to stay with her, and could only look on wistfully at the more adult service below as I joined in with the hand movements to 'My God is so big, so strong and so mighty'. Eventually I was cajoled into joining the Sunday school leadership team.

At first I was dismissive of lolly-stick theology, but was soon humbled by the piercing questions of a group of pre-schoolers. But possibly the scariest public speaking experience of my life came when I had to explain the Holy Trinity to a group of four- and five-year-olds. John came up with the brilliant idea of using water, steam and ice to explain the concept of the Trinity being three in one; different manifestations but of the same divine substance – a concept that many adults still find hard to grasp. But I was stumped by the profundity of their questions and the whole experience proved far more intimidating than being in the spotlight at the *PRWeek* Awards.

By this point, Aly was five years old and blooming. She seemed to be a very happy and well-adjusted child, despite the *Daily Mail's* dire warnings about the psychological damage that working mothers inflicted on their children. She had plenty of friends but I continued to worry about her being lonely. I had always imagined us having more than one child. I remembered how solitary I had been before Charlotte came along and, even if I hadn't initially welcomed her birth with open arms, I knew how much I adored her as she grew up and how close we had become as adults.

But on this one issue, John and I had reached an impasse. I was implacably opposed to the idea of testing the validity of a child. Somewhere deep down inside, I believed utterly in the sanctity of life from the moment of conception. I would never again consider having tests to determine the potential chromosomal abnormalities that I knew were a risk when giving birth later in life. John respected my qualms but also felt that it would be unfair to Aly to risk bringing a child with severe disabilities into the family, as so much attention would be diverted away from her. So, as my biological clock wound down, we found ourselves in complete deadlock.

The year that I turned forty, I sadly accepted that Aly was going to be an only child and reluctantly began the task of giving away all the baby clothes that I kept, so hopefully, in the attic. It was there that John crumpled after finding me weeping uncontrollably, hugging a new-born's Babygro. 'If it matters to you that much, then let's try for another child,' he told me.

I fell pregnant almost immediately and saw this as a sign that this child had been waiting in the wings. Everything seemed to be going so well, I wasn't even suffering from the debilitating morning sickness that had been such a nightmare when I was pregnant with Aly.

When I passed the three-month mark and the baby began to show, I began organizing my maternity leave. It was agreed that it was time to give my talented deputy editor a chance to shine and that I would return to the magazine after my maternity leave as editor-in-chief with responsibility of growing the *PRWeek* brand portfolio.

I was thrilled. Everything seemed to be going according to plan. I felt ridiculously well, so we felt relaxed when we went for our four-month scan at the local hospital but, as the nurse passed the ultra-sound scanner over my belly, I noticed her frown.

'How many weeks did you think you were?' she enquired.

'Between sixteen and eighteen.'

'It's just that the foetus doesn't seem large enough to be sixteen weeks. Are you sure you got your dates right?'

I began to tense and then wondered why it was so quiet. Why couldn't I hear a heartbeat?

'Well it is possible that the baby has not developed properly, and it is no longer viable.'

'No longer viable!' I wanted to scream.

'I can't confirm it yet, but it is possible that the baby has died in the womb.'

The room began to swim.

She continued, 'It is likely to be a chromosomal abnormality. You are forty years old, aren't you?'

Time slowed down as she told me that the foetus couldn't be aborted yet, as they would need to confirm that the baby's heartbeat had in fact stopped. 'The best thing you can do is to go home and let nature take its course,' she told me.

So I went home and waited to find out if I was carrying a dead child.

I prayed and read, manically, everything from the Bible to Jilly Cooper novels. One morning, a well-meaning neighbour invited me round for a coffee. I roused myself and walked down the road only to find that the other guest was a new mother and her delightful three-week-old baby girl. I made my apologies and ran up the lane in tears.

On the 11 May 2003, I began to feel pain and was taken back into hospital where I gave birth to a baby girl who we called 'The Littlest Vilkaitis'. Before I left the hospital, I met with the chaplain in the light and bright hospital chapel. We lit a candle and I wrote a dedication for the 'Littlest' in the book of remembrance.

I finally admitted defeat. I was obviously too old to have another child. As I cuddled my little Aly-Bean, I just told myself I was so grateful to have had the opportunity to be a mother at all, and vowed we would surround Aly with so much love that she would never feel the lack of a sibling.

I returned to work as editor-in-chief for *PRWeek* and installed my deputy as the new editor. To numb the pain, I threw myself back into work, planning a redesign and relaunch of the magazine, a portfolio of new supplements and events including a major summit on brand and reputation run jointly by *PRWeek* and the International Communications Consultancy Organization (ICCO). I worked with our editors in the UK, US, Germany and Hong Kong to bring together a stellar line-up of global speakers including the former US Assistant Secretary of State for Public Affairs James Rubin, the Queen's press secretary and communications heads from global giants such as Shell, Starbucks, Nike and IBM.

I also began working on a business plan for a new international title called *Reputation,* capitalizing on an increasing recognition among companies of the value of their reputation to the bottom line and the need to be ethically and environmentally responsible. I flew out to our New York office and met with senior partners at law firms, management consultants and accountants to assess the advertising potential.

I realized that I was enjoying the new role which brought me into increasing contact with a new breed of 'campaigning' business experts who were just as concerned about ethical practices and sustainability as they were about profit – as well as with international non-governmental organizations or NGOs. I began to see the potential for convergence between my early passion for social justice, my flirtation with the not-for-profit sector, and my experience in business journalism and communications. A new column slot in the magazine also gave me ample opportunity to air my many opinions.

However, I still couldn't shake my sadness or the sense of incompleteness. So John and I took the money that we had optimistically saved to fund my maternity leave and blew it all on a trip down the Romantische Strasse and into Bavaria. We took Aly to see Schloss Neuschwanstein, the iconic castle featured in the film *Chitty Chitty Bang Bang*, and danced at a beer festival surrounded by lederhosen-wearing Bavarians.

On our return home, I still felt unable to shake the ennui so we headed to Wales with a tent and spent a week combing rock pools around the tiny cathedral town of St David's. One day, walking along the coastal path, we came on the tiny chapel of St Non's which marks the place where St David was born in the midst of a terrible storm. It was said that as his mother gave birth, a well opened up in the ground and a ray of light shone down illuminating the spot. The well had become the site of a sad little shrine adorned with baby shoes and socks. We all cupped our hands and drank deeply, before spotting a woman washing her dogs in the waters.

Boarding the train down to London again, I began to feel an overpowering sense of nausea. The only thing that seemed to quell the desire to vomit was a diet of Cornish pasties. Three or four times a day I would head down to the café below the Haymarket offices to buy yet another fatty snack. After four days, the motherly owner came round the other side of the glass counter and patted me on the arm saying, 'I buy in extra pasties for you now,' – which is how the Turkish owner of a Hammersmith café became the first person to know that I was pregnant again.

This time I wasn't holding out too much hope but, according to the doctor, the fact that I felt in an almost constant state of nausea, unlike the previous pregnancy, was a good sign. In October, I flew out to Berlin for the global summit, spending most of the flight in the aeroplane toilets. Despite my sickness, I was excited and had made sure that I was chairing panels that I felt particularly passionate about, including one on the rising power of the NGOs which featured the UK CEO of Greenpeace and the global communications head from the World Wildlife Fund.

I felt inexorably drawn towards this different breed of professionals employed in the international charity sector and was keen to spend time with them but as the debate progressed I turned increasingly green and my comments and questions became more perfunctory. The moment that the debate closed with audience applause, I shot off the podium and headed for the nearest exit. In the end I disappeared to throw up so frequently during the event that my boss nicknamed me 'David Blaine' after the American magician and illusionist who had recently suspended himself in a Plexiglas box over the Thames and gone without food for forty-four days.

When a twelve-week ultrasound revealed a perfect little human being with all fingers and toes intact, I made a decision that would set me on a collision course with the NHS. If God had granted me the opportunity once again to bring a life into this world, I would not do anything to jeopardise that life that I had prayed for. At my first meeting with the obstetrician, he told me that I should have an amniocentesis and, when I refused, intimated that I was being irresponsible given my age and that if I had a Down's syndrome child that I would be putting an unacceptable burden on the NHS. We ended up locked in battle over his desk.

In the end, I paid privately for a non-invasive nuchal translucency scan at an expensive London clinic. I was still implacably opposed to a termination but felt this would provide some reassurance for the doctor as much as ourselves. To our relief, we were told that the baby had a lovely straight back and a well-developed nose bone. In fact, my tests were so good that the doctor told me to 'go home and enjoy your pregnancy'.

John and I floated out of the clinic. We needed to celebrate, so went to see the Gothic exhibition at the Victoria and Albert Museum and, afterwards, sat on a bench outside eating sandwiches. It reminded me of when we were first together in Sydney, broke and falling in love. And when we went to pick up Aly from my mother's, we were able to finally tell her that she was going to have a little sister or brother. She hugged my tummy and said, 'I will call it Dot.'

During my pregnancy, the workload was frantic as we geared up for the relaunch of the magazine and began to churn out supplements; on occasions I was still in the office at midnight. Despite my burgeoning bump and habit of disappearing from the 'green room' to be sick, I was still regularly called on as a broadcast commentator. On one occasion, I was asked to do a remote interview with the *World at One* from the BBC headquarters at White City. At reception, I was given the key to a tiny sound room and a set of instructions for patching myself into the programme. All went according to plan until the last couple of minutes when I was overtaken by a wave of nausea. The moment I went off air, I threw up in the waste paper bin and then wandered the corridors of White City looking for somewhere to clean up my mess.

As time progressed, my journey to work became increasingly taxing. I observed with some amusement and irritation the way in which professional women in particular would dive behind their newspapers when they saw me enter the train carriage like a galleon in full sail. Invariably it would be the drunk with a can of Special Brew who would get up and offer me his seat with a hearty, 'Come on, love, and get off your feet.' In the end I lost all sense of shame and would stand at the head of the carriage and demand in a loud voice, 'Who is going to give me their seat today?' But before I left on maternity leave I was told that I would be returning to a publishing role; once again pregnancy had resulted in a promotion.

In the early hours of 18 May 2004, we wrapped a sleeping Aly in a big pink blanket and took her down to her grandmother's, and at 9.35 a.m. I gave birth. Given the calamity of my first delivery and my age, I had been told that a natural birth would be too risky and that I would have to have an elective caesarean. In the end it was all ridiculously civilized and I realized why celebrities were often too posh to push. I felt a tugging sensation, heard a loud cry and the midwife saying, 'That's a loud baby,' followed by the magic words, 'It's a girl,' and 'What a head of hair.'

Our prayers had been answered: we had a lovely healthy baby girl and a sister for Aly. My daughter was passed directly to me and I lay behind the green screen gazing down at the lovely little bundle in a blanket. She had a head of ginger hair and Aly's mouth. I whispered, 'Hello, little Emily. Welcome to the world. Welcome to the family,' and then passed her to her father who looked ecstatic with the same radiant look of love as when he held Aly for the first time. Back on the ward, the sun streamed through the window as I lay on the bed,

Emily's face close to mine. Already so curious about the world, she struggled to open her eyes, and I felt I was looking into her soul.

Aly initially approached her new sibling with carefully composed nonchalance but was won over by the fact that Emily had come bearing a present for her: a lurid pink and green Barbie mermaid which she had been coveting. Mercifully Aly was too young to question where her sister had been keeping it for the last nine months. She simply gazed at her in amazement and peered over the cot to kiss her with a goofy grin on her face.

I spent three days in the hospital in a state of bliss, watching my little Emily sleep beside me. I kept thanking God for another miracle child, the second child that I had believed was beyond my reach. Before we left the hospital we went to pay our respects to the Littlest Vilkaitis. I still mourned but realized that if this lost child had survived, the extraordinary little human I now held in my arms would not have had the chance of life and I already couldn't imagine a world without Emily. God has his plans even if we don't understand them. What I was sure of was that Emily was meant to be.

21

Encounters

For some time, I had been unhappy about the fact that, with both parents working, Aly had to reluctantly attend an after-school club and I really didn't want to put Emily into a nursery for eight hours a day. It wasn't that there is anything wrong with either option but it seemed ludicrous to work only for someone else to enjoy our children.

I loved my job, but John was fairly half-hearted about his and would rather devote time to his art work. He also wanted to take a degree. As an undiagnosed dyslexic, he had failed to get the necessary qualifications at school but, as a mature student, was able to enrol in the Open University to study part-time for a BA degree in Religious Studies. So the decision was made and John became a student and house husband.

Aly really began to appreciate having a sibling when we told her she no longer had to go to after-school club and could instead spend the afternoons in the paddling pool, while her sister played with her toes under a sun shade. One day I found a piece of paper on which she had written, 'I love Emily.'

Emily was a very tactile child. While Aly was happy to play in-dependently, Emily needed to be constantly melded to my body. So I ended up carrying her around the house in a sling like a Balinese child, her feet rarely touching the floor. The only way I could prepare or eat food was with her strapped to my front and, on various occasions, she ended up with lettuce or ham on her head as I tried to intake sustenance between feeds. She also didn't sleep as much as Aly, and in the first few months I made the fatal mistake of using the car as a sleep aid, strapping her little body into a car seat and driving the country lanes in the early hours of the morning. I became nearly psychotic from lack of sleep but once again came to treasure watching the world come to life and the summer sun rising up over the fields, as I did in my childhood.

Emily's first articulation was 'Ning', which led to her being called 'Ning Ning' and later 'Pea Pod', 'Pumpkin' or 'Pickle' – an apt moniker, given the fact that as soon as she could move she was getting herself into trouble. Within weeks, she could roll into a ball like a tiny hedgehog and rock her way off our double bed. You couldn't take your eyes off her for a minute.

I had arranged to take six months' maternity leave; having waited so long to complete our family, I wanted to have unadulterated time with my children but reality, as ever, was waiting around the corner. One glorious summer's day, John was down working at his allotment tending to his vegetable garden, Aly was at a Holiday Bible Club in Olney and I was spending the day on a rug under a parasol in the garden rubbing Emily's tummy as she giggled uncontrollably. I didn't hear the phone ring and it was only when I walked into the darkness of the house that I saw the flashing light on the answerphone. My sister's voice was cracked with emotion as she explained that our mother had suffered massive heart failure and oedema of the lungs and was in intensive care in Nuneaton, a rather non-descript town in the Midlands.

I tried to call back but got no response. So in a state of shock, I threw Emily into the back of the car with a pack of nappies and raced down to collect Aly and then John. It was only when we were half way up the motorway that John asked, 'What on earth was she doing in Nuneaton?'

The children weren't allowed into intensive care, so I went onto the ward alone. I hardly recognized my mother who was deathly pale, barely conscious and surrounded by tubes and monitors. I sat beside my sister holding my mother's hand, listening to her laboured breathing. Charlotte told me how she had collapsed at a nearby service station on the way back from a visit to her in-laws in the Wirrall.

The doctor told us it could go either way and advised us to stay close by. So we waited, caught between the need to care for the old and the young. At one point, as we rested our heads on her bed, I heard her whisper, 'My guardian angels.'

My mother's grip on life was tenacious and over the following twenty-four hours her oxygen levels began to rise, but the doctor was brutally frank. Her unhealthily emotional relationship with food had finally caught up with her and she would need to be hooked up to oxygen for at least sixteen hours a day for the remainder of her life, which would not be long unless she changed her ways – a harsh reality he left us to share with her. As Charlotte and I walked back onto the ward, we caught our mother slipping a chocolate under her oxygen mask from a secret stash she had in her handbag. I felt despair wash over me; I now had three children to look after.

I began to drive up and down the motorway on a daily basis with a two-month-old in the back seat. I also had to prepare for my mother's homecoming, organizing social services, home help, commodes, wheelchairs and wiring the house for oxygen. Working on the basis that every cloud has a silver lining, Charlotte and I conspired to use my mother's immobility to replace her high fat, sugar and salt diet with home deliveries of salmon, broccoli and new potatoes – much to her fury. We later discovered she would send out the carers we had organized to go and buy her fish and chips to supplement her diet.

It was, however, the combination of her sheer stubbornness and her love of life that enabled her to defy the odds. By the time I returned to work in October, her heart was recovering, her oxygen reliance was reduced to night time hours and she was able to totter with a tri-walker to the local 'chippy' to buy her own unhealthy diet supplements.

On my return to work, John and I both entered new worlds. John was understandably nervous on the day he handed in his resignation and began his new life. Emily turned out to need almost constant attention but he soon became adept at studying with a book in one hand and a rattle in the other. The girls thrived on the unadulterated attention, healthy food and his endless imagination. It turned out that John had a real way with children. Within months, he was doing craft sessions at the church pre-school group, and helping out at Aly's primary school. The children loved this giant bear of a man who had materialized in their midst like Arnold Schwarzenegger in the film *Kindergarten Cop.*

Back at Haymarket, it began to sink in how much my role had changed. I had been promoted to associate publisher with responsibility for growing the profitability of *PRWeek* and its various offshoots. Having hired a new editor, I had to give him room to make the key day-to-day editorial decisions and I felt cut off from the news agenda. My days were taken up with spreadsheets and, as Heseltine ran a very tight financial ship, I started memorizing the net contribution figures in case I bumped into him in the lift. It was a baptism of fire but the company generously paid for me to study for an MBA-based publishing diploma which gave me the necessary grounding in financial and business management. So I swallowed any misgivings and tried to focus on commercial strategy.

That Christmas was a memorable one. On Boxing Day an 8.9 magnitude earthquake under the sea near Aceh in north Indonesia generated a wall of water that fanned out across the Indian Ocean at high speed, slamming into coastal areas with little or no warning. We watched our television screen in horror as the tsunami swept away hundreds of thousands of lives.

As the days went by, watching the news reports became almost unbearable. I cried uncontrollably as I watched a Muslim couple carrying their children to be buried. The suffering was on such a scale that it almost seemed unreal. I remembered some of the pristine beaches before they were torn to shreds. But there were also stories of extraordinary generosity: a homeless man emptying out his pockets in a bank saying he wanted to do his bit; an impoverished pensioner giving her weeks' pension saying she could live without it. At midnight on New Year's Eve, we joined the two-minute silence. On New Year's Day we drove to St Alban's cathedral and placed our candles in a shrine to the victims. We rang the Disasters Emergency Committee fundraising line – but it all felt like a drop in the ocean.

Back at work, I found it hard to concentrate on the figures while the reporters talked to international charities involved in helping those affected by the crisis. It finally hit home that my divorce from the news agenda was final; a new editor had taken my place and I had to move on. I knew I was being unreasonable and ungrateful but I felt impotent and irrelevant in the face of such suffering.

Surely I hadn't been given such blessings – my health, happiness, security – for my own edification. I began to pray for ways in which I could use these blessings, to put my growing faith into action. So when an agency asked if we wanted to join forces with them to run a celebrity auction to raise funds for the victims, it seemed like a God-given opportunity.

The event, which was scrambled together in a couple of weeks, took place in a marquee which had just been vacated by London Fashion Week. The driving force was Sara Pearson, CEO of an agency called The SPA Way, who, together with *PRWeek* readers, came up with a bewildering range of items for auction: use of the 'Shaguar' car from the Austin Powers film, a cricket bat signed by the English cricket team, signed DVDs, CDs and books as well as tickets to West End shows.

Liz McClarnon from girl band Atomic Kitten opened the event and, after being mobbed by photographers on arrival, accepted a styrofoam cup of lukewarm coffee, rolled up her sleeves and began to serve on a stall. In the back room the Disasters Emergency Committee counted the cash. It certainly didn't help drive up company profits but, for the first time in months, I felt a sense of congruence. It seemed that God was actually listening and I began to take prayer more seriously.

Every morning, as I trudged the pavements from Kensington Olympia station to our offices, I would talk to God and sometimes even listen. One spring morning, as I strode down the road silently praying, I spotted an old woman bent double over a shopping trolley, clutching on to a hedge by the side of the pavement. The street was empty apart from the two of us. I groaned inwardly as I thought about the meeting for which I was already late, but I was the only Good Samaritan on offer. So I crossed the road to ask if she needed help.

Her name was Lydia and she was eighty-six years old, fiercely independent but accepted my arm. As I walked her to the shop at the end of the road, she began to tell me her story. A Czech Jewess, she had managed to escape with her parents from Prague during the war due to the kindness of strangers and had lived in London ever since. She lived alone but had family in Oxford who would visit her. Over the next few months, I became regularly late for work. As we shopped, she talked about her past and I told her about my husband's family and their escape from Lithuania. She said with sadness but not rancour, 'Hitler and Stalin, they were both the same.' I had the distinctly eerie feeling that Lydia was somehow also an answer to my prayer.

It was becoming increasingly clear to me that I did not want to be a person who walked by on the other side of the road, whatever the cost. The seeds of this conviction had been sown long ago in my childhood when I first learnt of the suffering of the Dalits of India, had been nurtured as I came face to face with poverty in Asia, and had really taken root at UNICEF where I had been given a glimpse of a different way to make my life count. Suddenly, everywhere I looked, I seemed to be able to see God at work in those around me and I became almost preternaturally alert to the encounters he seemed to be engineering.

At this time I was befriended by the ex-CMS missionary who had been involved with Aly's baptism. Rena was an extraordinary and often forceful character, so when she invited me for tea at her house, I could tell that she wouldn't take no for an answer.

It was a beautiful spring afternoon and I was just relaxing into the moment with a cup of tea when Rena launched her attack: 'God has a job for you to do.'

I nearly choked on my biscuit. 'Does he?'

'Yes, and I can tell you what it is.' She had my attention. 'You know about media. We need someone who knows about media to help the Olney Newton Link.'

The Olney Newton Link was a small local charity which aimed to improve education and relieve poverty in Newton, Sierra Leone. The unlikely link between the small market town in Buckinghamshire and the war-ravaged community in West Africa was a legacy of the church's former curate John Newton. When Newton was caught in the shipwreck that inspired 'Amazing Grace' he had been buying and selling slaves in the area now known as Sierra Leone. After his conversion, he went on to help the British abolition of the slave trade, providing much of the information on the functioning of the trade that William Wilberforce required to bring the practice to an end. For this reason, a settlement for returned slaves near Freetown in Sierra Leone was named after Newton.

After the end of the terrible civil war in Sierra Leone, the townspeople of Olney started to raise funds and goods to help the people of Newton rebuild homes and lives shattered by rebels during the hostilities. What Rena wanted me to do was to bring the work of the Link to a broader public and to increase the funds available.

It seemed like another God-given opportunity and I threw all the energy I had left after the day job into pro bono work for the charity. There was a great story to tell and we managed to get regional TV, radio and newspaper coverage including interviews with visitors from Sierra Leone such as the Pastor Brima James Kabia, who told reporters that Newton was a model of much needed Muslim/Christian harmony. When the community said they needed to equip a lost generation with the skills to make a living, we galvanized a town full of small businesses, artists and craftspeople to open up their doors and teach skills to raise funds for a skills centre. I loved the work with the charity and became a trustee.

Although it seemed somewhat counter-cultural in my secular work environment, I was also becoming more open about my growing faith and even wrote about religious issues in my regular *PRWeek* column (the last vestiges of my career as a journalist). There was plenty to write about; after the materialistic excesses of the 1980s, people were more given to soul searching but the church, which seemed to be at war with itself, was mired in its own PR challenges and, as the influence of fundamentalist Islam made itself felt, people were left pondering their own spirituality with mixed results.

In one column, I expressed my sadness about a Channel 4 television programme in which viewers voted on a new set of commandments which actually excluded the love of God. In another, I lambasted Birmingham City Council's decision to re-brand Christmas as 'Winterval' as political correctness gone mad, pointing out that even most Muslims, whom the council were trying so desperately not to offend, recognized the importance of the birth of Jesus if not his divinity. I received letters of support from both a bishop and an imam.

I also began to receive letters from some of the few Christian professionals working in public relations. Some were funny and encouraging; others expressed how difficult it was for them to admit their faith in the workplace. Among the correspondence was a message from the head of communications for the Church of England, Peter Crumpler, a holy, humble but highly skilled PR practitioner who had previously headed up communications for British Gas.

We met for a coffee in a café near my office and Peter told me that it was obvious that I was on a profound spiritual journey and that he wanted to encourage me to step out in faith, as he had done. A couple of days later I received a gift, a book called *Prayers for Work*. And a few weeks after that he arranged for me to attend a thought-provoking session at Lambeth Palace by the Archbishop of Canterbury, Rowan Williams, on the responsibility of the media in society.

Through *PRWeek*, I also came into contact with Business in the Community, a charity set up by Prince Charles to engage corporates in securing a fairer society and more sustainable future. Inspired by the business leaders involved, I started to write a column on corporate responsibility for *Ethical Corporation* magazine. A few months later, I was invited to chair part of the World Public Relations Festival in Trieste which was focused on diversity. The festival opened with an impassioned message from Desmond Tutu who said that in a global context, organizations needed to build strong and respectful relationships and to embrace the difference in attitudes, values and expectations, including faith.

I could see that something was happening in the business world; a new ethos was emerging that prioritized not just profits but people, and this new breed of leaders seemed to be finally shaking off the rampant corporate greed of the 1980s and realigning the business world to a greater moral code. On a personal level, it was as if the scales had fallen from my eyes and for the first time I began to see potential for a greater connection, or at least for less separation, between my growing faith and work.

To my frustration, the proposed launch of *Reputation* magazine hadn't come to fruition. There just wasn't enough of a worldwide market. Instead, I began to work with Business in the Community on a joint venture, a *Responsible Business Yearbook* which would provide up-to-date thinking on legislation, developments and contact details of the myriad of professionals and companies now working in the area of corporate social responsibility in the UK. It was to be my first new launch as a publisher and an opportunity to create something in an area that I felt passionately about.

I felt I had found a way forwards that gave me greater internal coherence and enabled me to put my faith into action more overtly, without a wholesale revolution in my life . . . but God had other plans.

22

The Call in the Night

Our little family was blossoming. Aly was emerging as a complex mix of vulnerability and attitude, a sensitive child full of contradictions who cried but also laughed easily. One moment she would appear so grown up but at other times displayed all the self-control of a belligerent toddler. It was obvious that she was reaching out in every direction, testing her boundaries and seeing who she could become.

We shared a love of horses and on crisp mornings would ride together across the fields and through woodlands. As I watched her cantering ahead, I was filled with a mother's apprehension and wonder at the young woman she was becoming, and the prospect of her growing away from me hurt like a hole in my soul.

Her sister Emily was growing into a ball of fearless energy who ran around the house enthusiastically pointing at various objects shouting, 'This. This.' She had two great obsessions in life: animals and boxes. Her favourite animals were giraffes (which she called 'Too Talls') and 'Bish' which she chased around tanks in the local garden centre aquarium. When it came to boxes, she would put them on her head and run around the house or spin to music until she fell over.

Everything was 'more' with Emily: 'More book. More animal. More honey (on anything).' She also fiercely resented any infringement on her freedom. After her first day at pre-school she came home complaining that 'Sandy Dinosaur lady said sit down'. When told she was a girl, she protested emphatically, 'No, Emily a boy.'

Both children had become well known at St Peter's and St Paul's. Aly sang in the church choir, was thoughtful and would ask profound questions such as 'Why was God born?', 'What was there before God?' and 'Why did Jesus have to die such a horrible death?' Emily was best known for her regular Sunday-morning dash down the aisle to the altar and for getting her head stuck behind a two-hundred-year-old font.

My youngest definitely marched to the beat of her own drum and I could already see signs of the Nicholas family non-conformity emerging. Like my father before me, I recognized myself in my daughter.

I counted each precious moment with the children like petals; I could so easily crush them and carried them with utmost care. I knew that each apparently transitory moment would leave a permanent impression; every kiss and kindness was an investment in their future. Every smile, every moment taken to listen to their questions and ideas would shape their attitude towards life and act as a lightning rod for their faith.

I was also surrounded by a loving church family but I still felt like a pretender. As an errant Baptist, I had not been confirmed in the Church of England and was therefore unable to take communion. Instead, when it came to the Eucharist, I would bow my head to be blessed alongside my children.

One Sunday morning, as I knelt beneath the beatific gaze of the stained-glass Christ, I was overcome by an inpouring of warmth and light running through me like electricity. As the vicar laid his hand on my head and spoke the blessing I was filled with a sense of pure joy, as if God had surrounded me and suffused my whole being with his love. Shaking, I rose to my feet and as I walked back down the aisle I could sense him beside me. As I sat down Aly asked me, 'Mum, why are you crying?'

God had been so patient with me, leading me gently, speaking in his still small voice but it was as if he finally had said, 'Enough is enough,' and used a megaphone to speak into my soul. I felt blasted with love and light.

Up until that point I had thought of God as a mystic entity, the numinous that I had experienced as a child and in the deserts of Australia, but suddenly he felt so close. When I read the Bible he now leapt off the page for me in the person of Jesus. I finally grasped that God had become one of us, that he had lived our lives, felt our fears, cried and laughed, died and then defeated death. It was as if the scales had fallen from my eyes enabling me to finally see that, in Christ, I had come face to face with God; that in his amazing compassion, wisdom and love, Jesus revealed no less than the mind of our Creator.

The words of the Bible seemed to take on a life of their own. Whatever situation or conundrum I faced, I seemed to find the answer in those ancient pages. It was as if the word of God was speaking directly into my heart, helping me to understand, giving me the peace or challenge that I needed to grow in faith.

I finally understood what Jesus meant when he told Nicodemus, 'I tell you the truth, no-one can see the kingdom of God unless he is born again . . . no-one can enter the kingdom of God unless he is born of water and the Spirit' (John 3:3,5). I felt that I had been somehow born again, created afresh and I wanted to commit myself to him utterly.

I was confirmed in the Church of England on Mother's Day by the Right Revd Alan Wilson, Bishop of Buckingham, who told the assembled group of middle-aged men, women and teenagers, 'Love is not a feeling but a decision. A decision to look differently at one's fellow man and woman and see them as God sees them, not just their imperfections but to see what they may become, to see them in hope.' In response, I uttered the immortal words, 'I turn to Christ,' and pledged to use my life to promote peace and the lives of others.

As the Bishop placed one hand on my shoulder and the other firmly on my head and spoke the confirmation, he brought his face close to mine. In those eyes there was so much goodness and understanding. It was as if he was looking into the very depths of my being and, for the first time, I put out my hands to accept the body and blood of Christ. I had been washed clean.

I knew that I had been blessed with a mountain-top experience. After a lifetime of searching, God had finally made himself known to me in a way that had blown away my doubts and misconceptions. But I was conscious that the real test of faith was not how you respond to such heady experiences, but how your faith and reliance on God shapes your everyday existence. I instinctively felt that I could not just pick up where I left off, to simply return to business as usual at work or at home but I struggled with what this looked like in practical terms.

However, events conspired to force my hand. At work, I was told that it was time I expanded my horizons and was asked to take on the role of publisher of *Horticulture Week*, a highly profitable magazine and a favourite of the horticulturist Heseltine. I was conscious that this was a very good and potentially lucrative offer but all I could think was, 'Oh Lord, I am going to end up selling supplements to garden centres.' Once again, I had the conviction that, while I really didn't know what God actually wanted me to do with my life, this wasn't it. So to the amazement and frustration of my boss, I politely expressed my gratitude and turned down the offer.

I wasn't, however, naive enough to think that this would be the end of the matter. Haymarket had invested substantially in my training and clearly had other plans for the management of *PRWeek*. It was unlikely that they would simply let me sit tight, so I began to pray – very hard – for guidance.

I was pouring over cromalins of advertising pages, when my eye fell on a full-page advertisement for a head of communications at an international development agency called World Vision. As I read the copy, I could hardly believe my eyes. World Vision, it turned out, was a Christian organization focused on alleviating poverty for the world's most vulnerable children, whose UK office was located about ten miles from Weston Underwood. In my office, I cast my eyes heavenward and simply said, 'Thank you, Lord.'

When the head-hunter answered the phone, we went through the usual banter. She obviously thought I was calling her to offer another advertising deal, so I took a deep breath and launched in, 'You know that ad you have just placed for an organization called World Vision?'

'Yes.'

'Well I'd like to apply for it.'

There was a long silence at the end of the phone and then she replied, 'That wasn't what I expected you to say.'

The head-hunter explained that they had had a lot of interest but as this was a key leadership role the charity were really looking for a Christian as well as a PR professional. I told her that she'd found one.

The following day, we met up in a café at Euston Station to run through my credentials. The head-hunter again expressed her surprise that I was a Christian working in the media but I pointed out that this wasn't as paradoxical as it might appear, as journalists after all are seekers after the truth, or at least this is how they start out before they are corrupted by circulation figures and ratings.

A couple of weeks later, I sat in the bright and airy reception of the charity's offices in Milton Keynes, the walls covered with brilliantly coloured photographs of children in the Bolivian mountains. Above the reception desk were emblazoned words of pure poetry: 'Our vision for every child, life in all its fullness. Our prayer for every heart, the will to make it so.' I knew deep in my soul that I wanted to be part of creating the will to make it so for these children.

However, it was soon obvious that getting the job would be no walk over. The panel was led by a beautiful and charismatic Zimbabwean with a voice like melted wisdom and the ability to cut to the core of any issue. I was given a case study and asked how I would deal with the kind of appalling reputation crisis that no NGO would ever want to suffer. I was also asked about my faith journey and, to my surprise, I found myself pouring out the story of my search and enlightenment. Forty-eight hours later, on the Saturday morning, I received a call inviting me to meet the CEO and to talk about strategic direction for the next five years.

Everything seemed to be moving so quickly. We were just a few days away from the launch of the *Responsible Business Yearbook* and that year's *PRWeek* Awards judging. I had too little time to take in the implications of the events that were unfolding or to think about World Vision and its strategy. A majority of the preparation for the second interview was carried out squatting on the floor of a packed evening commuter train and sitting-up in bed in the early hours of the morning.

I was exhausted and, as I became overwhelmed with tiredness, doubts crept in. As the main breadwinner for the family, was I being fair to my husband and children? I knew that this was a path I desperately wanted to follow but the role didn't come with the kind of remuneration that we had become used to. John, however, was adamant that I should follow my heart. We drew up a budget and with some judicious surgery balanced the books; it looked as if we would have to draw in our belts but could manage.

But as one fear was assuaged another reared its head. Despite the punishing commuting schedule, I began to feel a creeping sense of claustrophobia as I contemplated working locally every day, my horizons diminished to a fifteen-mile radius around Weston Underwood. I began to wonder if I would ever again operate at the centre of the political and media landscape and to question if I was really ready to embrace what I feared would be a more parochial lifestyle.

I had almost talked myself into withdrawing the application when I was picked up by a chatty cab driver at Milton Keynes station. As we drove towards Weston, we somehow got on to the subject of charities and he piped up, 'That World Vision has an office in Milton Keynes. Always taking those guys to the station to go down to London and Heathrow.' It seemed as if God wasn't going to let me off the hook so easily.

Suddenly, I seemed to encounter World Vision everywhere I looked. At a Chartered Institute of Public Relations Awards ceremony, I noticed that World Vision was nominated for a 'gong'. When I met up with my former deputy editor, he told me he had recently shared a cab with the charismatic Zimbabwean at the Labour Party Conference and been duly impressed.

At church it transpired that my friend Rena was acquainted with the celebrity co-ordinator of World Vision who also sat on the Heritage Lottery committee for the Cowper and Newton Museum (of which my mother was a leading light). There were so many connections but, even so, I continued to wrestle with the decision, questioning whether I was on some kind of colossal ego trip. Why would God call on me? Was I deluding myself?

On the Sunday before my second interview, the service at St Peter's and St Paul's was centred on the call to feed the hungry and the words of the first hymn, 'Here I Am, Lord' by Dan Schutte, seemed to reach into my soul.

> *I, the Lord of wind and flame,*
> *I will tend the poor and lame.*
> *I will set a feast for them.*
> *My hand will save.*
> *Finest bread I will provide*
> *'til their hearts be satisfied.*
> *I will give my life to them.*
> *Whom shall I send?*

Here I am, Lord.
Is it I, Lord?
I have heard you calling in the night.
I will go, Lord,
if you lead me.
I will hold your people in my heart.[1]

The next day on the train into work, I glanced up just as a woman carrying a large carrier bag walked past along the platform. The bag was plastered with one word – Faith. I had to laugh; it was like a scene in a bad romantic comedy. By the time I walked back into the Milton Keynes office for my second interview, I felt at peace; and when I was offered the job a few days later, I simply replied, 'I think I am meant to do this.'

I handed in my resignation on the same day as the *Responsible Business Yearbook* launch at the Business in the Community Excellence Awards. My colleagues were shocked but supportive; I was moved when my boss told me he had seen how important my faith had become to me, and that he couldn't offer anything to compete with such an opportunity.

At the launch and awards ceremony later that evening, members of the International Youth Parliament spoke about ongoing issues in Sierra Leone, and I felt something shift inside me. I realized that from this point onwards, I would no longer have the luxury of being an observer but would be called upon to play my part in preventing such poverty and injustice. I felt daunted by the responsibility but profoundly grateful.

The response to my decision from *PRWeek* readers was overwhelming. Some in the public relations industry were puzzled as to why I hadn't capitalized on my bulging 'black book' of contacts to set up a highly profitable consultancy but I also received countless messages of goodwill as well as offers of support. The announcement also gave me an unprecedented opportunity to speak and write openly about my faith and the reasons for my decision.

The morning of my departure from Haymarket, I set off early in order to finish my handover to the new publisher. I was already quite tense when the train ground to a halt in the middle of the English countryside. Rail delays had been a regular feature of my life for the past seven years but I still felt my blood pressure rise as the minutes ticked by.

After half an hour, the stress began to show and I heard a soft voice ask, 'Are you okay?'

Looking up, I noticed that the commuter sitting opposite was a vicar complete with dog collar.

I don't know why but I blurted out, 'Sort of. It's my last day at work, I am about to make a huge change in my career. I'm excited but I am also so nervous; I just hope I am doing the right thing.'

'Do you mind me asking, where is your new job?'

'It's a Christian aid agency called World Vision?'

'Oh, I know them well. What are you going to be doing there?'

'I am going to head up their communications.'

To my astonishment he then said, 'The previous head of communications is an old friend of mine. I know a lot about them.'

Over the following two hours, as we sat immobile in a siding, the vicar painted a wonderful picture of the opportunities laid out before me and before we parted company he prayed for me and my new life. It felt like a final sign from God that this was the path I was meant to follow.

I joined World Vision UK in 2006 on the charity's Day of Prayer – a day on which all 45,000 staff around the world stopped their frantic round of activity to pray for God's guidance and for the world's children. As I joined the crowd thronging into Milton Keynes' airy ecumenical church, I had no idea what to expect but as the Holy

Trinity Brompton Band (house band for Alpha Course founder the Revd Nicky Gumbel) launched into a soft rock rendition of 'How Great is My God', I realized that this was going to be a far cry from my church experiences to date.

As the day progressed, we heard from staff around the world about what it meant to be a Christian in the workplace with moving accounts of how God had used World Vision to transform the lives of some of the most vulnerable people on the planet. I was surrounded by inspiring people dedicated to putting their faith into action and I was blown away by the experience. By the time we sang a rock version of 'Amazing Grace', I had my hands in the air along with everyone else, singing away as tears ran down my cheeks.

In the months and years ahead, as I met staff from around the world, I would be exposed to a wide range of denominations and styles of worship, from Orthodox to Vineyard, Pentecostal to Catholic. I would attend services with congregations of thousands in the US. I would worship at the vast Yoido Full Gospel Church in Seoul (which has over 800,000 members) and on the top of a shopping mall in Manila. I relished the sense that I was part of a worldwide family, united in faith despite our differences.

In the UK office, I enthusiastically joined in the weekly in-house services and special prayer groups. I loved the fact that we started meetings with prayer, especially when visiting staff prayed in their own languages. I found the experience completely liberating.

I nearly fell over the first time someone told me to go and pray instead of getting stressed out but it was good advice. It soon became obvious that the workload was enormous and outstripped the resources available. Most charities run a very tight ship to ensure that the maximum amount of funding gets to those in need and World Vision was no exception. I had inherited a small but talented and highly committed team. It was obvious that the one thing that was not in short supply was passion. My challenge was to harness this and steer it in the right direction, while also coping with the tyranny of the urgent.

In the office, the first task to cross my desk was an announcement that Pakistan's President Musharraf had thanked World Vision for its work during the recent devastating earthquake – a far cry from publishing garden centre supplements. In fact, I would go on to work on a tragically large number of humanitarian emergencies, including the response after Cyclone Nargis hit Myanmar in 2008, the 2009 hostilities in Gaza and the devastating earthquake in Haiti in 2010; working with media and digital channels to try to get as much information out about the crises as soon as possible.

The experience was always humbling and shocking. Humbling, in that public appeals were fuelled by photographs, videos and stories gathered by dedicated staff on the ground whose own lives and families were often impacted by the disaster they were reporting on. The fact that these staff were local and often lived and worked with the communities affected meant that we had very early access to information and to spokespeople, something the media knew and valued.

Shocking, in that the scale and nature of the suffering was beyond anything I had witnessed from the other side of the fence. In the aftermath of the Haiti earthquake, I was shaken as we surveyed images too horrific and disturbing to ever make their way into mainstream media. British editors knew too well that the giving public like their suffering to be relatively sanitized.

No matter how great the suffering, it was critical that we conveyed a sense of hope and reassured the public that their generosity could affect a difference in these shattered lives. And once again I found myself touring London TV studios as a spokesperson, this time not as a commentator or an observer but as an advocate for those whose voice was too often ignored.

It wasn't easy. Alleviating poverty turned out to be an overwhelmingly complex task. You couldn't just build a school, children also needed to be adequately nourished for them to be well enough to attend. This meant working with parents to help them ensure a livelihood, perhaps through agricultural training or start-up loans for small businesses. And before you could get children into a classroom, you needed to work with health authorities to make sure that they were free from disease and that there were trained teachers available. Water needed to be provided to prevent kids being taken out of school to walk miles to the nearest water source and, sadly, it was often necessary to challenge deeply ingrained beliefs that excuse child neglect or abuse. All of which was very hard to fully convey in a thirty-second TV advertisement or a two-minute television interview.

The story became even more complex when you introduced politics and conflict, as the chaos of war dissuades many from giving even when the lives of children are at risk. I also found that it was equally difficult to engage the public and the media around those emergencies that crept up on a country; the chronic food shortages or the slowly developing diseases of poverty. Slow grinding death wasn't sufficiently dramatic or photogenic for the media.

The challenges were enormous but so were the opportunities. Just before I joined the charity, ITV announced it was to relaunch the iconic *Challenge Anneka* programme to coincide with the second anniversary of the tsunami and had chosen to partner with World Vision UK. Earlier in the year, celebrity presenter Anneka Rice and a fifty-strong crew of staff and volunteers had flown out to Kalutara in Sri Lanka to work with local people and World Vision staff to help rebuild and equip a maternity clinic, a centre for children and a cricket pavilion. They were accompanied by the UK office's emergency communications officer who steered the volunteers towards producing something that would benefit the community for the long term.

The programme was all but in the can by the time I joined the organization but the devil was in the detail of the editing. The emergencies officer and I made numerous trips down to the production company in London in order to ensure that the community were represented in all their courageous glory and not as hapless recipients of Western charity.

On Boxing Day evening, the communications team gathered around a TV screen in the Milton Keynes office while the customer support staff sat poised by the phones. As the programme came to a close, the World Vision telephone number flashed onto the screen and the continuity announcer encouraged viewers to call in. The office fell silent as we all held our breath and then the phone lines exploded. In the end, over 3.34 million people watched the programme despite it being scheduled at the same time as the blockbuster film *The Pirates of the Caribbean.*

We then went on to work with another production company on a four-part prime-time Channel 4 documentary called *Millionaire's Mission* which took a radical reality TV approach to engaging the public with the complexities of poverty. In the programme, eight business leaders were challenged to use their entrepreneurial skills to help combat poverty, living and working with a Ugandan village community. Cameras followed their every move as they faced the challenge of working in a hugely different environment far from home and with one another. The entrepreneurs were mentored on screen by our charismatic Zimbabwean spokesperson.

One morning I picked up the phone to hear a broad Yorkshire accent: 'Kate Nicholas, what on earth have you got me into?' It turned out that one of the entrepreneurs was Deidre Bounds, a fellow backpacker who I had befriended at the hostel in Sydney. At the time, she had been toying with a new business idea and I had helped out by writing a press announcement. In the intervening years, the business had taken off turning her into a multi-millionaire and prime fodder for our reality TV show, a coincidence that my father would no doubt have relished.

When the show finally went out, it attracted over a million viewers and was deemed sufficiently unusual to be chosen as 'Pick of the Day' by a number of national newspapers and TV listings magazines. That autumn we held a packed Labour Party fringe event featuring Channel 4 News' Faisal Islam plus characters from the show including my Yorkshire friend.

The disparate strands of my life continued to collide. A year into the job, I ended up working with Julia Hobsbawm, an old friend from *PRWeek,* on a debate about the role of faith-based organizations in development, ranging from Christian charities to mosques. The debate was chaired by the evocatively named *Newsweek* bureau chief Stryker McGuire, and involved representatives from the Department for International Development, Islamic Relief, *The Guardian*, and the CEO of World Vison's Indian Office who argued persuasively that, while the UK's world view may be increasingly secular, the rest of the world was not – a fact you ignored at your peril.

At the One World Media Awards, I handed out a 'gong' together with Jon Snow, who had once fronted up *PRWeek*'s event and now told me, 'You've gone straight.' And my life seemed to turn full circle on the night that my World Vision colleagues and I stepped on stage at the Grosvenor House Hotel to receive the *PRWeek* Award for Broadcast Innovation for *Millionaire's Mission.*

At home, Aly was becoming increasingly involved in my campaigning activities. In 2007, we both joined an Abolitionists march organized by the Lifeline Experience group who had been traversing the world in chains in penance for the evils of slavery. In Olney market square, Aly waved an Olney Newton Link banner as I spoke about modern-day slavery and World Vision's work.

A couple of years later, she joined me on the Put People First march ahead of the G20 Summit in London. She lined up in front of the Houses of Parliament together with other World Vision staff's offspring for a freezing Press Association photo call (and ended up on the front page of the BBC website and in the *Daily Mirror*) before going on to a service in Westminster.

Aly seemed overwhelmed by the sheer number of people crammed into the Central Methodist Hall and her eyes opened wide when the modern worship band began to play. She was particularly struck by one of the speakers who ripped all the passages that contain the word poverty out of the Bible, until there was little left but an empty cover and a couple of fluttering pages.

Along with the thousands of others, my daughter bowed her head and spoke words of hope: 'May we see the dawning of a new world, with your values at its heart; a world of justice, mercy and humility. May the poor not be forgotten in the midst of the crisis. As your church worldwide, let us rise up in prayer.'

It was as if a light had switched on inside the precious child by my side. She had found an expression of Christianity that seemed young, relevant, impassioned and connected to contemporary social justice issues. Fired up and clutching a copy of *The Poverty and Justice Bible*, she joined the crowds that thronged out onto the streets. She later wrote, 'It has been one of the most thrilling but worrying days of my life.'

23

The Refining Fire

Whenever I fill out the kind of multiple choice psychometric tests which are used by companies to check out the mental health of potential employees, I always fall into the category described as 'driven'.

I dislike the moniker but find it hard to argue with the analysis as, the reality is, that I have always sought to extract every last ounce out of life. At work, I set a punishing pace which earned me the nickname 'The Energiser Bunny'. Outside of work, I was attracted to high-octane activities like horse riding and, occasionally, paragliding. When a friend's husband baulked at the helicopter flying lessons she had bought him for his fiftieth birthday, I took up the challenge in his stead.

It was as if I had to push myself to the limits of what I was capable of in order to feel fully alive. It wasn't that I wanted power, money or even status but rather to be able to live life to the very fullest. My mother's theory was that I was driven by a need to be 'fully Kate, whatever that may mean'.

I never truly believed that I had done enough or was enough, which is probably why I continued to crave external affirmation in different shapes and forms. When I was listed in the *PRWeek Power Book* as one of the most influential figures in communications, the recognition of my peers gave me a temporary glow of satisfaction which soon wore off. I still hadn't got it. I still didn't grasp that the only opinion that really mattered was that of God and that he really didn't care how many awards I notched up or how many column inches were devoted to me in a trade magazine – that he didn't need me to earn his favour.

I had been so eager to work as part of a Christian organization but hadn't really known what to expect. I had a rather idealized concept about what life would be like as part of a working Christian community and saw my move to World Vision as a retreat from the harsh, grasping and uncaring secular world and into the soft embracing unity of the body of Christ.

One morning, as I listened to the Radio 4 *Today* programme in the car on the way to work, I felt myself almost physically recoiling as the combative journalist eviscerated Deputy Prime Minister John Prescott on air. I felt his verbal assault like a physical pain but comforted myself with the thought that I was no longer part of that world; that I had entered a purer, fairer, less harsh plane of existence as part of a Christian community. But no sooner had the thought entered my head than it was pushed aside by another more insistent and authoritative voice saying, 'I did not take you out of this world so that you could retreat.' It was as if God was pointing out to me that World Vision wasn't some kind of spiritual spa for weary journalists and that the life experiences I had been given were to equip me for the work in hand.

The working model of a Christian NGO was certainly different from anything I had experienced previously. I was surrounded by passionate and committed people who, having invested their lives in doing God's work, wanted a say in what that work would look like. Goals and plans were agreed and actioned through collaboration, if not always consensus, in stark contrast to the world of media which can't really function as a democracy. (When a front page is due someone has to make a decision and run the show.) It quickly became obvious that while I had learnt all of the skills required to run a business, I had never learnt to be a leader in the true sense of the word.

I had arrived at the charity with big ideas. While media outlets scaled back their operations, World Vision had staff on the ground who had a deep understanding of the context and could provide breaking news about humanitarian need in some of the world's hardest places. (A majority of the staff were hired in their country of origin, including dedicated communicators, often ex-journalists, who would brave extraordinary conditions to deliver stories of need and hope.)

As the European bureau chief of Al Jazeera pointed out to me, 'What you have is gold dust. Correspondents are now parachuted in and out and have no knowledge of the situation. They fly in and spend four or five days, and pretend to know the ins and outs. We need to work more closely with organizations such as World Vision who are there on the ground and know what is going on.'

However, World Vision UK was only one of nearly 100 offices in a vast global federated partnership. It didn't matter how much potential I could see globally, my remit was domestic – and I wasn't even making great headway with aligning the UK team around a strategy. As the chief executive pointed out to me one day, 'A leader without followers is just taking a walk.'

The tension between the dreams I had nurtured and the reality I was faced with began to get the better of me and one day my Irish temper asserted itself in a tidal wave of frustration. Dismayed at myself, I grabbed my keys and headed for the car park.

In the local Starbucks, I nursed a cappuccino and began to see the situation more clearly. It was my own fault. I had set myself up for disappointment with unrealistic expectations. I also hadn't really thought through the implications of downsizing; while I had worked out what it meant for our domestic budget, I hadn't factored into my calculations how I would feel about giving up the enormous autonomy I had been granted when running *PRWeek*. Accepting that I was a cog in the machine wasn't easy when what I really wanted to do was to drive the engine.

As I sat in the coffee shop, I recalled my boss's words before I left Haymarket, 'Just remember, if you feel you have done the wrong thing, you can come back. All you need to do is call.' It wasn't too late. I could go back and admit the error of my ways and recommit to a career in publishing. I eyed my phone on the table but, as I contemplated my volte-face, I heard that voice again, low, clear and resonant, 'I never told you it would be easy.'

I felt the hairs stand up on the back of my neck. Obediently, I drank the last of the cappuccino, picked up my car keys and headed back to World Vision.

I thought I had been brought into the charity to transform its communications but it appeared that God first planned to transform me. He was refining me and I wasn't exactly enjoying the process. I felt exposed, as if all my protective layers had been stripped away, but I recognized that if this was to work I had to start again and find a new way to lead; to learn how to be a Christian leader. Jesus's words rung in my ears, 'Whoever wants to become great among you must be your servant, and whoever wants to be first must be your slave – just as the Son of Man did not come to be served, but to serve, and to give his life as a ransom for many' (Matthew 20:26–28).

I had spent all my life leading from the front, and had enjoyed the resulting recognition, but I realized that I had to start thinking differently about my team: to understand that my role was to help my staff be all that they could be; to root out the weeds that choked their progress and to give them space to grow. I had to turn my ideas of leadership upside down, to learn to lead from the back, but I had to get on a plane to truly understand what God was calling me to do.

It was in Malawi that I first came face to face with the reality that I was communicating. I descended into Lilongwe on an overnight flight from Johannesburg and was met by the local head of food security. As we emerged from the airport, I spotted a range of four-wheel drives sporting various aid agencies' logos – Concern, US Aid and World Vision. When our vehicle wouldn't start, the driver paid a group of men who hung aimlessly around the airport to give us a push start. Underneath a jacaranda tree, an old man stood completely motionless, watching the events unfold.

We drove through a landscape painted as deep terracotta as the Australian Outback, men and children wandering barefoot in the dust of the kerbside. The poverty was immediate and almost archetypal.

I stayed in a compound on the outskirts of the capital Lilongwe. The lodge was surrounded by high walls with razor wire and a guarded security gate, beyond which lay a beautiful, lush, well-tended garden. From beyond the walls, I could hear a cacophony of truck horns and clucking chickens. By night, the whole town plunged into darkness. Even in the very centre of town, figures merged into the blackness. I had lived most of my life in illuminated cultures and the environment felt alien.

In the morning, we set off along a dusty red road through Lilongwe, lined with amateur-looking shop signs and formidable security grills. It resembled the beginnings of a town but hardly a city. The roads out into the countryside, however, were good. And as we left the outskirts we passed huge churches under construction and a giant UNICEF sign featuring a picture of a young girl with tears on her face above the words 'Protect Malawi's children. Give them a birth certificate.'

Eventually, we left the tarmac and moved onto a dirt road so rough that it was immediately obvious why we needed the four-wheel drive. The only other vehicles on the track were bicycles, some laden high with boxes, and carts pulled by donkey and oxen. The earth was stirred up by any movement and women carrying baskets of food, washing and pots of water on their heads appeared, and disappeared, in the dust.

Down the side of the track, men and children sat breaking rocks in the burning sun. A woman scooped water from a dark hole, scum floating on the surface. At one point, we passed a man with a pretty child on his shoulders in a ragged but colourful dress. It struck me as such a gesture of love: to carry a child this high; to enable them to see the way ahead and to make them feel empowered. Every now and then we passed through a cluster of square or circular houses built with sun-baked red bricks and rushes with simple openings for a door. Everywhere men and women stood in the shade, immobile, as if they had not worked out what purpose movement would fulfil.

After a few hours of bouncing along the dirt tracks, we stopped in a sizeable village of mud huts and enclosures for livestock. As soon as the four-wheel drive stopped, we were surrounded by children and I struggled to squeeze out of the door. We were greeted by a man with a gentle face called Joseph, who parted the children like the Red Sea and introduced himself as a dairy farmer. Chairs were brought out and placed beside the animal enclosure and we were greeted by the head man who came and sat beside us under a tree.

When we were all settled, Joseph explained that World Vision had given him a cow and how it had transformed his life. With the milk he had been able to improve the nutrition of his four surviving children. He had also been able to sell the remainder milk at market and this, in turn, had enabled him to buy a bicycle. Beaming with pride he said, 'I was the poorest man in the village. Now I am the happiest man on earth.'

As he and his wife stood together with their bicycle in the cow pen to be photographed, I felt so humbled. I didn't want to leave that grace-filled place and quiet, dignified man and his wife. I would never have believed that such richness could exist in one of the poorest villages on the planet if I had not stood there in the sun, shaking hands with one of the happiest men on earth.

In another village, a group of young men clustered outside a low-slung concrete hut which had the words Kalolo CBO painted roughly above the door (CBO stands for community based organization; a group set up by villagers to improve living standards, who are in turn supported by agencies like World Vision). Two young men who looked no more than nineteen introduced themselves as Semu and Khisimini, the secretary and the director of the CBO, and took us inside their tiny headquarters, its walls piled high with sacks of maize. In the centre stood a tiny wooden table, littered with donated American maths and geography text books.

Taking out a set of notes, Semu stood and explained, without any trace of pride, how he and his friend had devoted themselves to caring for the children orphaned by HIV in the area, many of whom were living without adults. We heard how the two of them had initially fed, paid school fees and worked with the villagers to ensure protection for the children, and how the group had grown to twenty volunteers who were now looking after thirty-nine child-headed households.

As I watched these incredible young men talk, I felt humbled again. They seemed to embody the essence of selflessness; they had so little but gave of themselves to ensure the well-being of the very poorest members of their community. As I watched them I felt overwhelmed by the sense that God so loved them, that these were God's people at work. The tiny darkened room in which we listened to them speak felt like a holy place with an intensity akin to the incense-filled Orthodox chapels of Corfu. As I came out blinking into the sunlight, I felt transformed.

Later on, as I stood on a small inhospitable patch of land talking with a quietly spoken farmer about his tiny paprika crop, I couldn't help but wonder how on earth my journey had taken me from a swanky London advertising agency to discussing subsistence farming methods in Malawi. But with the sun beating on my back and my feet rooted in the earth, I also knew that this was exactly where I was supposed to be.

When I had travelled previously, I had never been more than just a tourist passing through, but I now felt that my future was entwined with that of these inspirational people. I felt utterly sure that what God wanted me to do with my life was to tell the stories of these people, to lift up their voices and to communicate the reality of their hardship, courage, sense of community, joy and hope.

In 2008 I flew to the Dominican Republic to attend a meeting of the global communications network. We drove out into the lush green interior of the island, up through multi-coloured villages and groves of cassava and banana plants. The country was not poor in the same way as Malawi but the inequality between the capital and the rural communities was evident.

At a hospital in the El Seibo region, we met with a group of young men and women who were impacted by HIV. Some had the AIDs virus, some had children who were HIV positive, and even the counsellors were infected. One woman told me that she had been fired when her employer found out that she had tested positive, that she had two children, the youngest of whom was six, and that the funding for her medication was running out. One man simply said, 'I am living with the condition. I am not afraid of death. It will be a gift from Jesus.'

During the subsequent communications meeting, I went down with what appeared to be the latest bout of a recurring virus. In habitual fashion I tried to ignore the headaches, stomach pains and shakiness. After witnessing the bravery of those living with HIV, I felt ashamed to even raise the issue of my own health but I could not ignore the way the room span or that my legs gave way beneath me every time I tried to stand up. Eventually I gave in and called a doctor who arrived late at night together with a translator.

After examining me, the doctor asked what I thought the problem was. When I said that I thought it was probably a 'woman thing' and related to my age, he snorted. The translator relayed his response, 'Lady, look around you. Other ladies your age, they are not falling over.' It began to dawn on me that there might be something wrong.

The doctor gave me an injection which got me on my feet long enough to get me through the last couple of days of the meeting and back on a plane. But back in the UK the symptoms returned with a vengeance and included periods of fainting. Increasingly I would disappear to lie down in the office first aid room and, on one occasion, ended up in the local Accident and Emergency department. I felt increasingly ineffectual and frustrated and that my body was letting me down.

After a few weeks, my doctor referred me to a consultant who said that my problems were indeed related in part to me being a woman of a certain age. His interim solution was to put me back on to the same 'cancer' drug that I had been prescribed a decade before for chronic pain, but, as the drug prevented production of oestrogen, he insisted that I also had to take hormone replacement therapy to prevent the horrors of osteoporosis, heart disease and strokes.

Two days later, I had my first injection and within two weeks I felt as if I had been given my life back. Within a month, I felt better than I had done for years with a renewed sense of energy and optimism. I was thrilled, until I was given the oestrogen booster whereupon the fainting, shakiness and pain came flooding back.

When I told the consultant that the symptoms had returned, he simply refused to believe me, 'The symptoms you describe are impossible. No-one has that reaction to oestrogen.' He added, 'Anyway I am not willing to keep you on the drug without the oestrogen add-back – it isn't safe. You have two options: live with the symptoms or we remove your ovaries. It will significantly reduce your life expectancy, of course, and you will have to self-inject with heparin to prevent blood clots. So you decide.'

John and I were in shock. We felt sure that there must be another option but only God knew what it was. So that night I got down on my knees and I prayed like never before . . . and then I went on Google and input my symptoms.

The first search result that came up was for a patient group related to hormone issues. I posted my story in a chat room and within minutes received a response from a woman who gave me the email address of a consultant in Harley Street. Relieved that there might be another avenue, I emailed the consultant who came back almost immediately offering me an appointment the following week. He also indicated that he might have an idea what was wrong with me.

That Sunday, a visiting preacher held a healing service at the church. I joined in the prayers, 'Lord, I am not worthy to receive you but only say the word and I shall be healed.' I knelt at the altar rail and, as the minister laid her hands on me and asked God to make me whole in mind, body and spirit, I felt a warmth coursing through me, as if I was a vessel filling with the Spirit.

Early the next day, I set off for London filled with hope and anticipation. After numerous tests, the consultant told me that the reaction to oestrogen I had experienced was fairly rare but that he had seen it once or twice. For the first time, I felt as if someone was looking at my symptoms rather than blaming my body for not working to rule.

What was clear was that the culprit was oestrogen; the tests showed that my system was literally flooded with the hormone, and it seemed my body hated it and was treating it like a virus, hence the viral symptoms. In fact it became clear that this unusual reaction to oestrogen had been causing problems for many years and probably lay behind my chronic fatigue nearly a decade before. However, the consultant told me that the good news was that with this much oestrogen flowing round my system, it would be safe for me to keep on taking the wonder drug that had restored my life, without taking an add-back. I could hold on to my ovaries and the prospect of reaching old age. I felt as if I had been given a new lease of life.

24

Crossroads

In 2010 I was reminded that change is a constant facet of life as a new CEO set about reorganizing World Vision's UK operation. As one of the executive team, I found myself in the curious position of shaping a new structure in which I might not have a place. I had always prided myself on my ability to deal with change; the explorer within me revelled in the new and unfamiliar and I recognized that it was only in change that we grow. However, I couldn't help feeling a little like a turkey voting for Christmas.

The whole exercise brought home to me how much my work at World Vision had come to mean to me and how heartbroken I would be to leave. There were also practical considerations; as the main breadwinner in the family, I was responsible for keeping a roof over our heads.

John was in the last year of study for his degree. His first solo exhibition *Pilgrim's Eye: Sacred Sights* featuring his eclectic mix of photographs and multi-media reflections on religion had also been well received and, once Emily started school, he had taken a part-time job at the local infant academy but he certainly didn't bring in enough to cover our bills.

In the midst of the restructure process, however, something happened which put everything into perspective. Early one morning in March, a group of militants attacked World Vision's office in north-west Pakistan killing six people. The victims, including two women, were all Pakistani nationals who worked for World Vision in the Mansehra district. An office administrator told the AFP news agency that about ten men, all wearing masks, had kicked the doors down, taken everyone out of their offices and started shooting. A locally-made pressure-cooker bomb, left on the scene, was detonated remotely.

I knew that there were ever-present risks for aid agency staff. One of my first tasks on joining the charity had been to handle media relations around an attack on a humanitarian convoy in South Darfur in which World Vision staff were wounded; two were shot in the head, a third in the arm, while five others received minor injuries from glass and shrapnel. But the latest incident reminded me how high the stakes were and of the courage of the staff in the field. By contrast, concerns about my own future seemed self-serving and unwarranted. If God wanted me to do this work, he would guide me.

What I found confusing, however, was that he seemed to be steering me away from World Vision. It was becoming increasingly clear that my role would change. The CEO had told me, 'It isn't that you won't have a job, it is whether you will have one that you want to do.' I knew I should start to look for alternatives but, despite all evidence to the contrary, I believed that God had brought me to World Vision for a reason and I couldn't stand the idea of ending up back where I started.

In the midst of my confusion, I was contacted by a friend who said that she 'had a word for me' and quoted Henri Nouwen:

> The word 'patience' means the willingness to stay where we are and live the situation out to the full in the belief that something hidden there will manifest itself to us.[1]

I decided to wait, be patient and trust that God would point me in the right direction.

A few days later I received an email announcing that the global office for the World Vision International partnership would be moving from Los Angeles to London. Some staff would be relocating but the vice president of global communications had made the decision to retire rather than move across the pond, which meant that the international office would be looking for someone to run global communications from the UK. I took a deep breath and submitted my application.

When the UK CEO announced the new structure, it turned out that I was one of the leaders least affected. Three of the directors' roles had been made redundant but I merely lost my place on the executive team as well as my responsibility for the digital staff who were hived off to another part of the organization. Others faced a far more uncertain future and I tried not to be ungrateful but I suspected my new role would prove frustrating.

In the midst of the resulting fall out, I flew out to Los Angeles where the outgoing global communications leader was running his last international meeting. The communications network met in Mater Dolorosa, a Passionist retreat centre in Sierra Madre, high on a hill overlooking the city. I woke at dawn each day and walked the Stations of the Cross, meditating and praying for direction – should I stay or should I go?

As the meeting progressed, a number of colleagues asked if I had applied for the global role and gave me encouragement. I was rather overawed by the communicators in the network and the opportunity of working with such talent was enticing but daunting. I felt part of a great global family but wasn't sure that I had what it took to head it up. Was I a good enough leader? Had God taught me enough over the previous four years? I also harboured concerns about whether the role, which would involve considerable international travel, would be compatible with motherhood. In the chapel I prayed, 'Your will be done.'

After the meeting, I joined a group travelling down through San Diego into Mexico. I needed to reconnect with our work in the field to remind myself why I had made the decision to join World Vision in the first place. The drive down from Sierra Madre was beautiful, the highway slicing through the desert and gently undulating hills. Over the border, we wove our way through the heady mix of chaotic traffic and roadside break dancers, parked and walked through a bustling market, selling tacos and Day of the Dead decorated skulls, to get to the immigration office. We queued for an hour and a half to get the necessary forms, were then sent to another office to pay our entry and then back again to the original office to get our passports stamped, by which time the immigration official had run out of ink.

Having been semi-officially sanctioned (I never actually received a Mexican visa stamp), we drove on through Tijuana until we reached a dirt track which cut through ochre-coloured hills littered with new government developments. Our destination was a desolate 'village' clinging to the dusty slopes beyond the purview of any government help.

We parked by a dirt track and then walked between homes made out of abandoned containers and discarded corrugated iron and wood. At the very top of the hill, we found a rudimentary concrete structure painted bright pink which served as a community centre. We were greeted by open smiles and guided inside to view a rainbow display of crafts – colourful piñatas, cakes decorated with carefully crafted marshmallow flowers and gaudy star-shaped decorations that I remembered from the market in Tijuana – all of which spoke silently of their makers' hope of a brighter future.

We went through a series of formal greetings as, with love and pride, the men and women pushed each other forward to be introduced. Everyone in the community had come to the border hoping to cross into the promised land of America but as the days turned to weeks, and weeks turned to months and years, they resigned themselves to the idea that this place was home. The government, however, had different ideas and refused to extend water or electricity to this place of stalled expectations. From their high vantage point, the inhabitants could only look out on the sparkling lights of the city below and wonder if they would ever be allowed to resume their journey.

In the meantime, everyone in the community looked out for each other. One marvellously colourful character told me that she was the 'dinner lady' and ensured that the children in the camp received at least one good meal a day at the community centre. Before we left, I was approached by a ten-year-old girl called Nineveh who proudly gave me a painted plaster cast of the cartoon character Dora the Explorer and told me she wanted to be an artist when she grew up. I clutched the doll tightly in my arms and tried not to cry.

I had seen once again the huge difference that could be made when a community, no matter how challenged, was given a hand up rather than just a hand out. I felt a renewed sense of conviction that there was more work for me to do with World Vision; more stories to be told and more supporters enabled to see communities not just as needy cases but as groups of vibrant, entrepreneurial and caring people who just need a little help to be all they can be, and to care for their children in the way they longed to be able to.

Back in the UK, I was called to an interview panel which included the former UK CEO who had first hired me into the organization and now worked for the global office of the federated partnership. I talked to the interviewers about harnessing the power of our grassroots presence to amplify the voices of not only our experts around the world but also the children and communities we worked with, and about utilizing digital technology to create life-changing connections with our supporters. At the end of the interview, I turned to my former CEO and said, 'You may be suffering a slight sense of déjà vu at this point, but the difference is that, in this job, I might actually be able to make it happen.'

A few weeks later I was called in to meet the chief operating officer, a tall American with a brain the size of a planet and a generous, infectious laugh. He told me that I was the preferred candidate but that he wanted to know how I would turn my vision into reality. He also advised me to talk to my family to ensure that they were comfortable with the amount of travel that would be involved.

During the following weeks, I worked on an operating plan. As I got to grips with the complexity of the global organization, I began to see a potential way forward. I talked to John about my excitement as well as my fears but he firmly told me, 'We have come on this journey with you because you wanted to make a difference; God has given you one of the biggest opportunities in your profession to do this. What will you think when you look back on your life and realize you were too chicken to take it?'

The girls also jumped at the idea that I could do some work from home, pointing out that they hadn't seen a great deal of me while I was working in London and Milton Keynes. The only caveat they imposed was that I could never be away on their birthdays. As the global head of communications, I knew I would be required to attend and record the international board meetings which took place twice a year. To my dismay, I found that the first of these fell on the same date as Emily's seventh birthday. The choice was clear: if I had to attend this meeting, I could not accept the job.

I prayed hard before the second telephone interview with the COO. All proceeded well and he liked my plan. I waited until the last few moments to share my family's parameters for my working life. The line went quiet for a moment, then came an emphatic, 'Of course you have to be with your daughter. When you look back, do you want to think you were in a dusty old boardroom or celebrating your daughter's birthday? These things matter. Family matters.' I felt like Gideon who, unsure of whether to proceed, had asked God for a sign. I had been given a green light. A few days later when offered the role, I accepted with a sense of total peace and certainty. I knew that the challenge ahead was enormous but that God would equip me.

Before I boarded a plane to meet my new team, I went on retreat to Launde Abbey in rural Leicestershire. One of the lessons I had learnt was to follow Jesus's example and to spend time in solitude and prayer before striking out in a new direction. The resident chaplain, a passionate hillwalker, told me, 'If you hillwalk it is very likely that you will find yourself on a summit surrounded by fog unable to see your way forwards or backwards. But this does not stop the resolute hillwalker. Through the fog you see emerging cairns or rocks by which you can navigate your way using a compass – and looking back at the cairns you have passed and to those you can spy through the mist, you can work out your direction.'

So I spent two days in silence walking, praying and looking back over the cairns in my life, and it became clear how the different paths I had travelled had brought me to this point. All the elements of my eclectic life to date seemed to converge in this new role: my early passion for social justice; my experience of advertising, public relations, journalism and even the business of publishing; the exposure to different cultures and poverty, as well as time spent with UNICEF Australia and World Vision UK. Looking back, I could see the signposts that God had laid out for me and recognized the gentle nudges he had given me to keep me on the right track.

I could even see that, if things had worked out differently at World Vision UK and I had retained a director's role, I probably wouldn't have had the courage to leave that safe harbour to set sail into the unknown. I understood that sometimes God uses the uncomfortable circumstances of our lives to make sure that we step out and take that leap of faith.

25

Distant Lives

In the early hours of the morning, I kissed my sleeping children goodbye, quietly closed the door and headed into the night, bound for Los Angeles. I was on my way to meet my new team who had gathered at the old international headquarters in Monrovia, beneath the San Gabriel Mountains.

In the darkness, I watched the motorway lights slide past and felt once again like that tiny child bound for Larkland and I recalled, with a pang of guilt, that no matter how chaotic my young life had sometimes been, my mother had been ever present.

It wasn't that I hadn't left the children before but I knew that in taking this job I had committed myself to a more transitory lifestyle and that this would be the first of many trips abroad. I couldn't help wondering if I was mad, leaving my husband and two beautiful daughters to go and spend time working on the other side of the world. But I had nailed my colours well and truly to the mast, so all I could do was to reassure myself that they had a wonderful father to look after them when I was away.

The impact of my decision was reinforced on arrival as I was shown the desk I had been allocated in the Los Angeles office. In fact, I subsequently ended up 'commuting' to the States on a fairly regular basis and Los Angeles became familiar in a way that I could never have imagined when our family had passed through on the way to Australia a couple of years previously.

I had inherited a remarkably talented international and senior team of communications directors, all of whom I had known and admired individually from afar. As chief communications officer, as I was now dubbed, I was responsible for guiding a network of around five hundred communications staff located in nearly a hundred countries – including some of the most fragile and insecure places in the world such as South Sudan and Afghanistan.

The network included extraordinary characters including an ex-journalist who had been one of the first to break news of atrocities in Rwanda, as well as the World Vision communicator who helped break the Ethiopia Famine story to the BBC in 1984 and helped introduce rock star Bono and his wife Alison to the relief work in that suffering country (a move inspired by his involvement in the Live Aid concert that made such an impression on me as a student). My peer group of partnership leaders were also mind-blowingly impressive; not only global leaders in their fields but humble, warm and open-hearted people.

I found that I routinely spent around ten days out of the UK per month and, with all the long-haul flights, my passport soon bulged with exotic-looking visas. One of my first trips was to Zimbabwe. I had no idea what to expect as the country had become something of a mystery over the past few decades. Flying from Johannesburg to Victoria Falls airport, I crossed a landscape that seemed almost devoid of population: a vast wilderness dotted with villages of neatly thatched roundevels joined by roads that bore through the bush straight as a die. Mist rose high into the sky as we flew down over the great crashing falls that straddle the nations of Zimbabwe and Zambia.

In the city of Bulawayo, I attended a meeting with the Rt Hon Vice President Joice Majuru, who at the time was seen as a potential successor to Robert Mugabe. In her speech, she commended World Vision for the work it had done over thirty-three years in areas such as health, sanitation and HIV/AIDS interventions but also made clear that international interference in internal politics was unwelcome. Deputy Prime Minister Thokozani Khuphe, Vice President of the MDC, also talked about her dreams for Zimbabwe and told us, 'When you go back to your offices, go back with your stories. You are God's instruments and I pray that you continue to focus on the women and children of this country.'

In the spring of 2011, I gathered leaders from across the World Vision partnership in Bangkok to create a global communications strategy. I had never expected to see the city again but it turned out to be one of the most cost-effective hubs for meetings of international staff and, before the meeting began, I stole a few hours to revisit my past.

Speeding through the streets in a tuk-tuk, I revelled in the familiarity of the pungent pavement cafés, smoke-stained buildings whose ramshackle balconies hung with laundry, the gleaming golden pinnacles and brilliant white temple walls. I disembarked at the bottom of Khao San Road and wandered through the labyrinth of wooden houses and small alleys that lay beyond the main tourist strip.

At the end of the road, I wandered through the grounds of the *wat* that I had once looked down on from my window many years before. Saffron-clad monks still bent double to sweep the grounds, but the scabrous dogs and paper-thin cows had been replaced by four-wheel drives. In the old wall, a door stood ajar providing a glimpse of a previous life and, as I stepped through, I felt like a young backpacker again. Filled with memories, I made my way to the market beside the Chao Phraya River where John and I used to eat, ordered a Pad Thai and watched the world go by. I couldn't believe that my path had led me back to this city that I loved so much.

In fact, my new life led me back not only to Bangkok but also took me repeatedly to Kuala Lumpur, Johannesburg and Delhi as well as other major hubs such as Nairobi and Chennai. Within a few months, I was getting on and off planes like buses and, as I passed through major airports, would often bump into colleagues who would exchange flight plans, 'Just come in from Delhi and I am going on to Harare and then up to Addis Ababa. Where are you off to?'

The fact that I rapidly regarded none of this as out of the ordinary was odd in itself. It was the little differences that I continued to delight in. In a hotel room in South Korea, I took photos of the high-tech toilet which glowed ultraviolet while it warmed and massaged your buttocks. I was definitely my father's daughter.

As I travelled, I became increasingly aware of the sheer tenacity, ingenuity, humour and creativity of the children and communities that we served. Their faith, optimism and selflessness were inspiring. In a slum along a tributary of the Ciliwung River in Jakarta, I met an amazing group of Muslim women. We accessed the slum through a narrow rain-drenched alleyway between two shops; the pathway barely wide enough for one person to walk with an umbrella. The narrow two-storey houses crowded in on each other, some barely standing, all clustered around a brightly painted mosque. Behind the buildings, the river flowed sluggishly by, its banks piled high with rotting rubbish, all the while threatening to rise and overflow into the lives of the slum dwellers.

A group of us were invited into the house of the village leader. The rain beat a percussion on the roof and walls and our faces were illuminated by the electrical storms as we were greeted by the local health volunteers: Sutihat, who as a single mother sewed to keep her family; Damilat, who had seven children; and Saidah whose six children lived in two rooms, three-metres square. She pointed to the rain washing over the doorstep and said, 'The river comes up every year to two metres and every five years to six metres. Sometimes the Government moves us but sometimes not. Then we take our things to the upstairs room.'

Despite their own struggles, these women managed health posts throughout the slum on just 700,000 rupiah a month (about £70). In Indonesia, 526 children under the age of five were dying every day and preventing these deaths often involved tackling ingrained beliefs in order to help mothers to provide better lives for their children.

'There was a man who had heard about breastfeeding and decided that his wife should do this,' Sutihat told us. 'But his mother-in-law kept trying to come in and give the baby coffee. So he slept across the door to protect the child. She has now grown up strong and healthy.'

I was amazed by their fortitude and calm, given the inevitability that their lives would be turned upside down. They were confident, proud women of humour and resilience with a deep love for each other and their communities. If they had been born into different circumstances, they would have been running a hospital.

As I showed them pictures of my girls and told them about how my youngest Emily was starting middle school, I felt the painful dissonance of the different circumstances in which our children were being raised. The slum itself seemed sadly familiar; I had seen so many as I had backpacked through Asia but then I had seen the residents as ciphers, symbols of poverty and could never have imagined such richness within these crumbling alleyways. These were not passive, hapless recipients of charity, but courageous people who had carved out lives of dignity in one of the hardest places in the world. They deserved a voice of their own and digital technology could give them that voice.

Many communities were already beginning to use social media as a means of establishing an identity and connection. In Asia, use of smartphones was ubiquitous even among the most deprived communities and mobile usage in Africa was the fastest growing in the world. In Manila, I heard about a small boy who had managed to track down his child sponsor on Facebook from a makeshift internet café on a landfill site, and in Latin America I heard about how young people were using YouTube to collectively express their outrage at injustice.

In a slum in Delhi, I met with a 'club' of child journalists. In a tiny poster-lined room, deep in the slum, a young man called Mosddipu explained how he had been trained to use film equipment by World Vision. The group said they wanted to make films on issues that affected them including gambling and addiction, education and violence against children. They saw these films as a means of changing their destinies, a powerful tool which would enable them to talk to those in power. They told me how they had managed to get the local police to tackle illegal alcohol retailers in the slum and had a case coming to court against a teacher for cruelty. One of the most moving testimonies came from a fourteen-year-old girl who confidently addressed the group saying, 'I was so shy that I never spoke. My family thought I was good for nothing. But when my mother saw the film I made, it was different. My brother told my mother that I had potential.'

On the Universal Day of the Child, two of the child journalists joined UN, government and NGO representatives on stage at a rally in Delhi calling for an end to the preventable deaths of children under the age of five. One of the children confronted the journalists and politicians present and asked, 'Why won't you pay attention to the plight of children?' The Indian MP's response was that, 'No child, brother, sister or daughter should die of preventable causes before the age of five and no woman should die giving life.' He told the children, 'The most precious thing a family can have is a child, and for our nation, our children are our wealth.'

As I travelled and met with communications staff around the world, I became increasingly conscious of the fact that I was merely the conductor of an extraordinary international orchestra. I was frequently awed by the bravery of the staff, many of whom lived and worked close to the communities and were often affected by the same conditions. When Typhoon Haiyan hit the coast of the Philippines, our staff were among those caught up in the chaos and one of the communicators went missing for a few days, presumed dead. They frequently took their lives in their hands to capture pictures and videos in an attempt to garner international support.

I came to the conclusion that in order to lead these remarkably dedicated staff, I needed to understand their world, to walk in their shoes for a mile or so. So in the summer of 2013, I arranged to spend a week at the Kenya office working as a national office communicator, one of the frontline staff responsible for capturing the stories, photos and videos that fuelled our marketing, campaigning and media work. Together with some of the real field communications staff, I set out for the Rift Valley.

Giraffe grazed on acacia trees as we drove across pale green plains, and baboons and warthogs wandered across our path as we ascended the hillsides and looked down from the dormant volcano of Mount Longmont on the glittering Lake Naivasha. Turning off the tarmac, we made our way along dirt tracks into the Ndabibi ADP, where I was set to work with the community to record videos for our child sponsors.

At a low-slung corrugated-iron-clad school house, we filmed children enthusiastically chattering about their hopes for their lives and their community. At a nearby water facility, the chairman of the project played shamelessly to the camera, determined to ensure his fifteen minutes of fame – and a new solar-powered pump.

By night, we stayed at the Elsamere environmental centre, the former home of Joy and George Adamson and the lioness Elsa, star of the film *Born Free*. We sat in the Adamson's old sitting room until the early hours sending video over flimsy broadband connections, watched over by Adamson's drawings of Elsa, and then ran at top speed across the grass to our rooms to avoid attack by curious hippos which had recently charged and killed a hapless visitor.

During the day, we drove out to a medical centre where women sat patiently with their children on the grass, having walked miles to see the doctor. In a field below the clinic, women in brightly coloured skirts hoed cabbages (this combination of medical facility and farm was part of the battle against malnutrition that affected so many of the waiting children). The women agreed that I could film them but only if I was willing to come and till the land with them. So I picked up a hoe and set to work.

Back in Nairobi, I was sent to interview and capture the stories of some of the women who lived in Korogocho, the giant slum on the eastern edge of the city. I had previously ventured into the slum accompanied by an armed guard (a skinny young boy with a rifle) and been shocked. Over 45,000 people lived in each square kilometre of the slum built on the edge of the Dandora dumpsite – thirty solid acres of domestic, industrial, biological and pharmaceutical garbage which grew at the rate of 2,400 tonnes of waste per day. The slum dwellers existed primarily off the detritus of the lives of the rich of Nairobi, collecting and trading the rubbish. The trade in drugs and guns was lucrative. Life was grim, particularly for women who lived there, 50 per cent of whom had been victims of rape.

We drove on to an area of the slum called Baba Ndogo and stopped at a small concrete café with peeling bright blue paint and a sign emblazoned with the words Cool Breeze Hotel. We were greeted by a tall, smiling woman who introduced herself as Beatrice. She had a self-confidence and easy manner that seemed incongruous in this place. Children swarmed round us as we were led inside a room which was about nine-foot by nine-foot square, the walls stained that indiscriminate smoke colour that seems to invade any built structure in a slum.

Along two of the walls were flimsy looking shelves for customers to lean on to eat and a group of faded plastic chairs. Above one of the shelves was a giant poster with the words Cool Breeze Hotel and pictures of sandwiches (I wondered which had come first: the poster or the establishment). Against the back wall stood a brown 1970s-style cooker, above which perched two cake stands and a blackboard menu. Beyond I could see a narrow corridor in which a small face would occasionally appear and then retreat.

Beatrice told us of a childhood of abject poverty even by slum standards; how the local church had paid for her to complete her education and how she had set up the 'hotel' with the aid of World Vision. She said she now employed five friends from the slum, two of whom slept in the 'hotel' with their children (which explained the mystery face in the corridor). With the proceeds, she had also opened a small shop in a nearby street for her mother, was paying for her youngest brother to finish his schooling and saving money to buy some land in order to construct a house for her family.

She told us that she planned to put a roof over the head of two women sleeping rough with their children in the street outside. 'I will build a house for them and give it to them,' she said simply and gracefully, with no consciousness of the enormity of her generosity of spirit. I got the sense from her that this was simply what she would expect any human to do for another. 'I haven't told them, it will be a surprise. World Vision has made a difference in my life, so now I want to make a difference in the lives of others.'

When we finished talking, Beatrice asked me if I would come and meet her mother. I was overwhelmed but followed her down through the slum, followed by a raggle-taggle parade of children, to the tiny wooden shop that her mother now ran. I stood outside in the rubble as the children touched my clothes and held my hands, until a late-middle-aged woman emerged on her daughter's arm.

The hardship of life was etched on her face but she had the shy smile of a child. We greeted each other and then she signalled to her daughter who emerged carrying two wrapped packages. As a crowd gathered, I was presented with a picture of an elephant and a plastic memento emblazoned with the words 'All the pleasures it has in store and because I appreciate you, I hope you have many more.' I choked with emotion as I stood clutching the treasures that I had been given. I had never encountered such utter dignity.

From Baba Ndogo, we made our way deeper into the slum and, accompanied by an armed guard, I made my way through the corrugated-iron maze, down through alleys so narrow that my shoulders grazed the rusting walls. I tried not to step in the fetid water and sewage that flowed along what passed for a path. I had spent time in many urban slums but, even so, the conditions in Korogocho were unspeakably depressing.

As we made our way deeper into the sordid labyrinth, I heard the incongruous sound of voices raised in songs of praise and, turning a corner, came upon a mass of smiling, singing women and children. In contrast to the surroundings, the alley way where they stood was swept clean and painted green.

A slight young woman, who introduced herself as Rosemary, invited me into a dark interior hung with swathes of coloured cloth and beads. She told me that this was the headquarters of Tuinuke na Tuendelee Mbele (Arise and Prosper), a group she had set up of HIV positive women who were creating products out of the waste on the Dandora landfill site. Beautiful bags were woven from discarded plastic, bead necklaces created from recycled paper, and charcoal briquettes formed for heating, which in turn funded a thriving community health network, a young mother's club for young girls who were pregnant (usually as a result of rape or being forced into prostitution) and a children's club which provided a safe space for the children to simply be kids.

Afraid of the implications, she had initially tried to hide the fact that she was HIV positive, but when this became impossible she turned into and embraced her situation with courage and determination. She told me, 'When God gave me an opportunity to live, I said I will live my life.'

Her energy seemed boundless, a light burned within her so brightly that she illuminated and transformed her surroundings. With passion she told me, 'I want to be a mother that people refer to and girls can come to whenever they want to get counselling and skills.'

As we made our way back out from this oasis of light into the stinking labyrinth, I felt as if I had glimpsed the divine at work. Surely if Jesus walked the earth today, it would be in places like Korogocho that we would find him – and perhaps still could.

On my return to Britain, I could not shake my disquiet at the insularity of our privileged lives and the comparative lack of compassion or community. I found it hard to imagine a parallel in my own society to the extraordinary selflessness I had witnessed in some of the harshest environments in the world.

I became convinced that we have profound lessons to learn from people like Sutihat, Beatrice and Rosemary. The poverty and the inequity they endure is inexcusable in a world of plenty and the injustices meted out on the most vulnerable are heartbreaking but somehow, in the midst of suffering, they seem to have discovered something that we have lost in the 'North'; a deep-seated understanding that we are all part of one body and that if one person is left behind, the whole community suffers as a result.

It was in the slums of Jakarta, Delhi and Nairobi and in the remote villages in Africa and Asia that I finally understood Christ's exhortation to love your neighbour as you love yourself.

Part Four

Homecoming

26

Through the Valley

When heading home, I always tried to take an overnight flight so that I would arrive in our village as the sun came up and the children tumbled out of bed. As I put down my bags, I would be greeted by two bleary-eyed children who, after hugging me, hurried to rip open precious packages containing eclectic gifts: Rosemary's brightly coloured necklaces, Zimbabwean million-dollar notes, ebony elephants from Kenya, mbira thumb pianos from Tanzania and artwork made by landfill dwellers in Manila. Then, fuelled by caffeine, I would enter the day; go shopping, take Emily to ballet lessons, visit my mother and try to readjust the settings on my sense of normality.

The children adjusted surprisingly well to their mother's globe-trotting. They were well travelled in their own right and had by this time circumnavigated the globe twice, stopping off in Asia and America en route to see their grandparents in Australia, as well as having undertaken various forays into Europe. In contrast to many of their contemporaries, who seemed to live on a diet of fish fingers and chips, they had reassuringly international palates; at the age of five Emily declared that her favourite food was sushi and Aly's favourite restaurant was a ramen house. But they certainly knew how to play on my sense of guilt about my frequent absence and embarked on a merciless campaign for pets.

Both had been given fish at one time or another; when Emily was a toddler she would pester us to go to the local garden centre where she would press her face up against the illuminated fish tanks and terrify the inhabitants by shouting 'bish, bish' at the top of her voice until we finally caved in and bought her one. However, we had held out on buying any larger or warm-blooded animals as we felt that our frequent and extended absences on family trips would be unfair.

Emily's book shelves, however, were crammed with factual tomes on animal, insect and marine life, and she would spend hours sharing her encyclopaedic knowledge of wildlife. Her favourite bedtime 'story' was a gruesome illustrated book about giant squid. One day I discovered numerous worms and woodlice in her bed – while I had been away, she had created a 'farm' for them in a plastic container of earth and had been surreptitiously taking it into bed with her. When John caught a couple of crayfish in the river, we were forbidden from eating them. Instead they were kept and fed in the bath until nature took its course. But the *coup de grâce* was delivered by Aly who, after one of my trips abroad, greeted me at the door with a snail climbing up either arm. 'These are my snail pets, I found them in the garden,' she smiled innocently. Two weeks later, two guinea pigs called Crystal and Chocolate were installed in a hutch in the garden.

Every time I returned home, I became increasingly conscious of how frail my mother had become. Her spirit was as vibrant as ever so I had pushed to the back of my mind the fact that her health was failing. But, as time went on, I often ended up spending the night at her house, sleeping in the spare bedroom, my ear attuned to any change in her heavy breathing. In the dark of the night, I would wake, wonder where I was and yearn for my children. Unable to sleep, I would wander into the next room and watch my mother, who looked young again – the years having slipped away with sleep.

In the middle of the night, I felt her presence so keenly but knew that it could not be for much longer. In the early hours, I would work downstairs until I heard her stirring and then help her dress. We would sit and drink tea together in the morning sun and she would tell me, 'It is so lovely to have someone in the house again.'

I could not imagine what it felt like spending a lifetime with someone you loved so dearly and then living another seventeen years without them. The thought of living on without John was unbearable. 'You get used to it,' she told me wistfully.

When I was at home, I took to wandering into my daughters' bedrooms at night to watch them sleeping. They, too, looked so much younger, their baby features visible as sleep stripped away the burgeoning sophistication – only the innocence remaining. I knew that such moments were precious. I sensed that my mother would be leaving soon and that my children were growing up and away from me. I accepted that this was the natural order of things but it didn't make it any easier.

A couple of months into my new role, I was called out of a meeting in Kuala Lumpur to take a phone call from my sister; my mother was in hospital again. It wasn't looking good and I needed to return home. With a sinking feeling in my stomach, I made my excuses and caught the monorail to the airline office in central KL. As I passed over the temple-littered skyline, I spotted the bus station where I had alighted so perilously in the middle of the night so many years before.

I landed at Heathrow before dawn and, as daylight broke, I made my way blearily onto the ward, only to be greeted by the sight of my mother tucking into tea and toast. Once again, she had kicked the Grim Reaper into the long grass and would live to fight another day. But my mother's condition was serious. She was contending not only with heart disease but also chronic obstructive pulmonary disease (COPD).

A few weeks later, in the midst of Christmas preparations, I found her frail, confined to her chair and hardly able to breathe. Once again, she was taken to hospital where the nurses prepared us for the worst but, once again, to our relief she rallied. But I had become one of the 'sandwich' generation, struggling to be all things to all people: a good daughter, a devoted wife and mother, and an international employee. I would lie awake at night, working the problem of time like a Chinese puzzle.

It seemed so hard to watch my mother dying by degrees but, in retrospect, I realize what an incredible blessing it was for her to be able to prepare herself – to die a good death. As she became more disabled, she wasn't able to get to the Baptist church which had been such a big part of her life but the pastor and elders visited her regularly and administered communion. I also spent an increasing amount of time with her reading Scripture, debating points of theology and praying. She had a fine mind and was plagued by questions. In particular, she was deeply bothered by the problem of pain and said that the most frightening words ever spoken were Christ's last utterance on the cross, 'My God, my God, why have you forsaken me.'

At first, I prayed for my mother's physical health. I lost count of the number of times that I sat in the critical dependence unit at the hospital pleading with God for yet another recovery, for another chance to be her daughter. But as time went on and the visits to hospital became more frequent and times at home more fraught with anxiety, I prayed increasingly for her spiritual health; that God would provide her enquiring mind with the reassuring knowledge of his presence and his eternal promise. My greatest fear became that my mother would also feel forsaken as the time came for her to leave us and my prayers became more fervent as her health continued to fail.

Then in March 2012 she went into hospital for the last time. Once again, my sister and I followed the ambulance to Accident and Emergency but both of us recognized that this time was different. The doctor was sure that the end was coming but said, 'It could be two hours, two days, two weeks or two months.'

It was as if my mother were in flight, circling an airport in a holding pattern waiting for instructions as she neared the end of her journey. There was nothing we could do but be by her side. Only the great air controller knew when she would finally come in to land. So we put the pressures of work, family and life on hold and simply accepted that God had her in his hands.

My mother, however, remained convinced that this was a temporary setback and none of us were willing to raise the prospect that she might not be returning home. And, incredibly, in the second week of her hospital stay she began to stabilize, at which point a stream of visitors started to appear at her bedside, including some of the great and the good of the newspaper world. That Sunday, as we celebrated Mother's Day, she sat beaming, surrounded by her children and grandchildren but, as I kissed her farewell that evening and wished her a good night, I had the distinct feeling that she had been somehow holding out for that special day.

Early the following morning, I received a call from the hospital; she could no longer breathe on her own and the doctor wanted my permission to put her on a ventilator. I could have said no but selfishly wanted time to say goodbye, so I agreed but only if the chaplain could be with her.

By the time I arrived at the hospital, my mother was delirious and fighting the doctors and nurses with all the strength she could muster. I placed in her hand a Bethlehem cross that I had given her a few years before and it seemed to calm her. Her doctor said that he would give her twenty-four hours on the ventilator to see if she responded.

During this time, she drifted in and out of consciousness and became increasingly delirious, but the next day a different doctor said, 'Give it another twenty-four hours.' My sister and I kept on asking why? The medics had made it clear that our mother was suffering multiple organ failure and that we were only buying time. We told them that she was a woman of faith who wouldn't want to be kept alive artificially, without hope of recovery, but we were facing the might of the National Health Service, the Hippocratic Oath and the medic's professional pride in maintaining life at all costs. So we sat by her side through the day and night listening to her mechanical breathing.

On the third morning, a Muslim doctor we had not met before came to see us. We spoke to him about her faith, the futility of the present course of action and her distress. He responded in gentle tones, 'I understand; the time has come to let her go on the last phase of her journey.' I felt overwhelmed with relief, gratitude and sadness.

My mother was taken off the ventilator and within the hour was once again lucid. Moved from the main observation ward into a side room, she lay peacefully in the sunlight that streamed through a picture window. We talked and held hands but at times she seemed to be looking at something beyond and, at one point, said in a rapturous voice, 'Oh it's beautiful . . . oh, wonderful, oh, joyous,' and with a look of almost child-like wonder on her face, she asked us, 'Is it real?'

In the following hours, she seemed to recognize those who had gone before her and spoke first to her mother saying, 'Ma, oh Ma,' and then to my father. 'Dan, oh my Dan, there you are,' she said with such warmth and love in her voice. Then to our amazement, she whispered in wonder, 'Jesus, Jesus, is that really you?' and then more clearly said, 'Oh, Jesus, yes, I am coming.'

It was as if, in those twilight hours, a veil had been drawn back, that we stood on the border between the natural and the supernatural. I whispered to her, 'Now we are seeing through a glass darkly but you are seeing face to face.'

As the last light left the sky, she began to talk directly to God, nodding her head as if in agreement, saying, 'Thank you, Lord, for a peaceful death. Thank you, Lord, for a wonderful life.' Then as she became weaker, she repeated the words 'yo-yo'.

At first, I had no idea what she was referring to but eventually understood that she was trying to tell us that, like the child's toy, she was being drawn back repeatedly from the new reality she was experiencing. Just before she finally lost consciousness, she called for a Bible which she clutched tightly, and spoke for the last time. Clearly and emphatically, as if she was drawing the last energy from the depths of her soul, she declared, 'Richard Dawkins [the arch secularist] was wrong. There *is* a God.'

Having spent so much of her life telling others' stories, she was able to convey so vividly the last chapter of her own on earth and reassure us of the fulfilment of Christ's promise: 'I will come back and take you to be with me that you also may be where I am' (John 14:3).

As the night wore on, her friends slipped away one by one, until only my sister and I remained in the room. We held her and told her, 'It's okay, you can go on now. He's waiting for you.'

She didn't leave us at the last breath. The change was not immediate; rather it was as if we were watching a gradual transition, her movement along a continuum from this life to another, from the corporeal to the spiritual, until finally she was gone.

After her death, a friend sent me an extraordinary book written by a colleague in World Vision, Rob Moll, who was also editor at large of the magazine *Christianity Today*. The book called *The Art of Dying: Living Fully into the Life to Come* recounted vivid and profound experiences similar to that of my mother's; deathbed visions of heavenly places, Jesus, and family, experienced over centuries.

It became clear to me that, while these days we spend most of our lives trying to delay or deny the inevitable, at one time Christians actively lived their death, following time-honoured rituals. I discovered that in medieval times, Christians learned the *ars moriendi* (Martin Luther's sermon on preparing to die) which urged people to be actively and spiritually involved as they transition from one life to the next. And that as recently as the nineteenth century, death was a community event; friends, family and neighbours would sit and watch the dying hoping for evidence of their eternal destiny.

The manner of death was often recorded by family and friends and shared so that others could draw 'comfort and encouragement from the reports of those who crossed over in peace and hope'.[1]

Moll had drawn on a wide range of sources and I read with amazement Dallas Willard's reference to how those dying often begin 'to speak to those who have gone before. They come to meet us while we are still in touch with those left behind. The curtains part for us briefly before we go through,'[2] and Stephen Kiernan's observation that 'people near the end appear to go back and forth, showing not anxiety, but ease and welcoming of what is to come'.[3] And I became convinced that it is only the modern medicalization – and often sedation – of death that prevents so many people from fully living into their own transition, and providing compelling final witness.

In many ways, my mother had a perfect death. Her experiences on a ventilator were distressing but, thanks to the kindness and wisdom of the Muslim doctor, she did have time to prepare herself for her journey. She was able to tell those she loved how much they meant to her and how grateful she was for the love that surrounded her. She was able to pray and to gently make the passage from this life to the next, together with those loved ones who had passed on before, and with her Saviour.

We commemorated her life in Holy Week, the week in which we remember Christ's death and resurrection, and as we laid her to rest, the earth seemed to spring into life.

For my mother, there was no sense of unfinished business and, in the days after her death, as I spent time alone in her house going through her things, I felt great sadness but no sense of her lingering presence. She had moved on and was at peace.

Over the following months, my sister and I worked side by side, sorting out her house which was packed from floor to rafter. We discovered missing pieces of our past, faded reflections in black and white: photographs of Charlotte during her dyed-black punk era, dated images of myself with 1980s shoulder pads and crimped bouffant hair, and shots of John and I arriving in Heathrow, wrapped in a mother's arms. We also found twenty-five years' worth of Christmas cards, itemized in bags, as well as every letter she had received over five decades, concert tickets, stately home brochures and recipe cards. I had never known she was such a magpie.

As life resumed, I repeatedly found myself in chance encounters with friends, neighbours or colleagues who were recently bereaved, facing the death of a loved one or even their own demise. And each time it was as if God said to me, 'Okay, I have shown you what this means, now tell them your mother's story.' Even when I was afraid that I didn't have the right words to comfort, it was as if God pressed a play button and the story of my mother's last hours, and the message of hope that it conveyed, came pouring out of me.

Eventually, I commemorated her death by recording a YouTube video of her story. Sitting in her empty and echoing house, I spoke of the gift that she had given us – a final and profound *Report from the Edge.*[4]

27

The Approaching Storm

After four years working with World Vision International, I knew instinctively that I was in the right place, at the right time, doing the right work. For the first time, I felt truly in sync with the rhythm of the world. I was using my God-given skills and was surrounded by people who were open, honest and stimulating but I still had a persistent, nagging feeling that there was more that God wanted me to do.

I was already working long hours, and the unpredictable nature of natural disasters meant that, more than once, I had sat on a beach poring over emails while on holiday with the family. I wasn't sure how many more hours I could work but I was hounded by a conviction that my personal experience as a communicator, broadcaster, journalist and columnist had been in preparation for a further task: that I was meant to use these skills to share his word, to preach.

I enjoyed public speaking and was undaunted by a conference room or even the 1,000 plus guests at the *PRWeek* Awards but, when it came to sharing God's word, I had felt inadequate to address even a room of Sunday school five-year-olds. As one of the executives of World Vision, I had preached and led devotions and retreats for staff all over the world but I always found it a nerve-wracking experience. God's words have an inherent power and when spoken can effect changes in hearts, minds and even bodies. Who was I to speak such words?

A few years previously, the curate at St Peter's and St Paul's had told me that she believed that I should pursue ordination, to work full-time in the church, but I had scoffed at such an idea. I had been such a reluctant and slow disciple, how could I be responsible for bringing others to Christ? But with her encouragement I had explored the idea of licensed lay ministry (LLM); a part-time, unpaid commitment to the church which seemed slightly less scary than full ordination. I began by attending a course on preaching but my transition to a global role, with its long hours and travel, had made even this commitment untenable.

I reasoned to myself that I was off the hook; that God obviously wanted me to focus on serving him through my work with World Vision. I focused on his exhortation to 'share your food with the hungry and to provide the poor wanderer with shelter' (Isaiah 58:7). So when the Diocese organized a vocations morning at our local church hall, I went along mainly seeking confirmation of the path I was following.

As I listened to the speakers talk, I mentally crossed the various options off the list: as the main breadwinner of the family, I could not even begin to consider giving up my job for a Church of England stipend and there was no way on earth that I could carve out the twenty hours a week study required for licensed lay ministry. As I chatted with the organizer over coffee, I explained that I had thought that I was called to preach but was obviously mistaken, as the various options available to me were impractical at this stage in my life. But as I prepared to take my leave, I heard her say, 'Wait a moment, there's a new scheme that we are running in the Diocese which might be for you. It's a lot less of a commitment than the LLM but means that you will be authorized to preach.' Once again, I felt the hairs stand up on the back of my neck.

I sought out our local vicar, who confirmed that she was supporting candidates from our church and told me that the first training course would take place over two weekends in November. There was no guarantee that the course would be repeated, so my timing was perfect . . . except that in November I was scheduled to attend a key international meeting in Tanzania and would be flying back on the first day of the course. I felt disappointed but reasoned that, once again, I was off the hook and this obviously wasn't a path I was meant to follow.

The following day, I was scheduled to read in church, and could hardly believe my eyes when I saw the passage from 2 Timothy:

> In the presence of God and of Christ Jesus, who will judge the living and the dead, and in view of his appearing and his kingdom, I give you this charge: Preach the Word; be prepared in season and out of season; correct, rebuke and encourage – with great patience and careful instruction.
>
> 2 Timothy 4:1–2

As I read to the congregation that day, I caught the eye of our vicar who was smiling at me knowingly. That night I tossed and turned until, at about three o'clock in the morning, I made a decision: I would see what I could do about attending the course and, if it proved impossible, then I would know that this path was truly closed.

First I had to see if it was possible to change my flight so that I could get back in time for the Saturday morning course, even if in a very jetlagged state. The news wasn't good; there were no flights available on the Friday night but the airline offered to hold a seat on the Thursday night flight. This would mean leaving the meeting early and I didn't hold out a lot of hope. I suspected that the World Vision president Kevin Jenkins, who was running the meeting, would not be keen on senior staff members leaving early, especially as I was leading a session on communications after lunch on Thursday.

Even then, in the unlikely event that the meeting ran to schedule, I would be very pushed to make the airport in time but I felt that I should at least try. So, with some trepidation, I emailed the president explaining the situation. Almost immediately, he responded saying, 'This is such an important reason, of course you have my permission to go.' Chastened, I booked the flight.

In Tanzania, I watched the clock, and as soon as my session on communications finished, leapt into a cab together with World Vision's director of prayer and drove down through the lush highlands. In the tiny Kilimanjaro airport, I told my prayerful companion about the hurdles that I had already overcome to attend this training session and expressed my continued scepticism about whether I would actually get to Nairobi in time to catch my connection (bearing in mind the additional challenge of fire damage at Nairobi airport which was causing significant delays in processing passengers). But, as I spoke, a voice came over the loudspeaker system: 'Precision Air flight to Nairobi. Good news. All our members are present, so we are leaving early.'

I turned to my companion and admitted, 'Okay, perhaps I am meant to do this.'

'I think that may be so,' she replied, smiling beatifically.

A few months later, I stood up in front of our local congregation to preach for the first time. My inaugural sermon was on Philippians 2:1–8, Paul's great homily on unity and community, in which he counsels the early Christians to 'in humility consider others better than yourselves' and to look not only 'to your own interests, but also to the interests of others'.

I had spent weeks studying and preparing but still felt terrified as I rose to speak. I silently prayed to God to help me, to put the right words in my mouth and, as I began, felt a warm wave of confidence wash over me.

As I told the story of Semu and Khisimini, the two young men from Malawi who had given all they had to help local children who had lost their parents to HIV and AIDs, I had a sense that this is what God had been preparing me for; to be a conduit for the lessons that we, who live in comparative security, could learn from those who lived out their faith in extremis.

However, even for those who lived in such security, the first few months of 2014 felt almost apocalyptic. Large swathes of the country were under water, hurricane winds battled our shores and freak fatal accidents included an elderly man who died on a cruise ship when a wave punched through a window and a woman killed by masonry as she sat in a stationary taxi outside a London restaurant. As the wind whipped around our house by night, I dreamt that I was handed a set of Tibetan handbells, similar to those I had seen in Dharamsala – a subconscious symbol for a warning or alarm.

The following months were some of the most intensive of my working life. The situation in Syria worsened by the minute, with children bearing the brunt of the terrible, protracted and complex conflict. Five million children were affected: 700,000 killed, others tortured, maimed or sexually abused, with all parties detaining children and forcing them to fight. The 'lucky' ones were living in refugee camps in Jordan and Lebanon but 80 per cent of Syrian children were no longer in school, leading to fears of a lost generation.

As the harsh winter progressed, images flooded in of children in flimsy T-shirts and bare feet in the snow. Yet World Vision, along with the other aid agencies, continued to struggle to engage the public with the tragedy. The situation was just too complex for many to be able to see beyond the warring factions to the desperate plight of the innocent.

In a bid for a breakthrough, the United Nations organized a joint social media campaign called *No Lost Generation* to try to get over the message that, no matter the rights and wrongs of the adults involved in the conflict, children must not be allowed to suffer in this way. The campaign resulted in examples of great generosity but most still couldn't see beyond the conflict to the need. It was heartbreaking.

The situation in Syria was front of mind as some staff met in Malaysia to determine how best to use social networks to drive a movement of compassion. One evening, as I walked with a colleague back from a café along the country lane to our hotel, we spotted two men on a motorbike. This was not an unusual sight; the lanes were littered with bikes that spluttered like noisy sewing machines but what caught our eye was the outline of a machete in the hand of the pillion passenger.

'Uh-oh,' groaned my companion.

Within seconds, the men were off the motorbikes, screaming at us and waving a machete and a crowbar over our heads. With their motorbike helmets, they looked like aggressive spacemen. In the first few seconds, I didn't understand what they were saying and feared the worst. Time seemed to slow and I tested out the idea of death in my mind, imagining the pain as iron bit into flesh. We were surrounded by bushes and I realized that it would be very easy to dump our bodies but I felt almost preternaturally calm.

When I made out the words, 'Everything – give us everything,' I carefully took off my backpack and, without looking at my aggressors, nudged it over to them with my foot. Grabbing both my bag, and that of my colleague, our assailants quickly leapt back onto the bike and disappeared around the corner. The whole exercise took just over two minutes.

As their motorbike disappeared from view, I snapped back into real time and, gushing with adrenalin and relief, the two of us ran back to the hotel crying, 'Thank you, Lord. Thank you, Lord, for keeping us safe.'

With so much adrenalin rushing through our systems, we were both wide awake and spent the remainder of the night in a tiny police station. The whole incident had taken on a truly surreal quality, so I was hardly surprised when I received a mobile phone call from the UK and had to deal with a problem at Aly's school surrounded by Malay policemen. And in my heightened state, I couldn't help giggling at the handwritten sign over the bars of a tiny cell which read 'lokup' (sic).

With little sleep, we proceeded with the meetings, and I then flew to Korea to run another workshop. I felt tired but relatively undisturbed and, on return to the UK, went on to present at another key meeting in London.

However, once back home with my family, the incident came back to haunt me. When I closed my eyes to sleep, I would see a raised arm with glittering metal descending upon me. At other times, I saw metal cutting flesh, severed necks, arms and legs hacked from bodies. At first the images only haunted me when asleep but, as the weeks progressed, they began intruding on my waking thoughts, preventing me from thinking straight.

I couldn't understand why on earth I was being plagued in this way. I told myself the attack had only been a robbery, that my assailants had been after my bag not my head and that I had come to no harm but, in those first few seconds, my subconscious had registered my suspicion that I was at the point of death. It didn't matter that my conscious mind had suppressed that thought and just carried on its merry way; my subconscious was still working it all out. I was suffering post-traumatic stress (PTS). My father would have been fascinated.

However, as the winter gave way to spring, the pressure from work became even more intense and I really didn't have the time to succumb to PTS or any other form of illness. At the end of March, I noticed a dull pain in my left breast and made an appointment to see the doctor. I was examined thoroughly and declared free of lumps and bumps, so I simply got on with the job in hand and gave it no further thought. The doctor's note suggesting that I check when the next routine mammograms were taking place became buried under piles of papers on my desk.

The pace of life continued to increase. The work I was leading involved colleagues from all over the world, so calls went on late into the night. After one particularly gruelling forty-eight hour period, I noticed a strange fluttering sensation and tightening in my chest, which grew as the hours progressed. It was a critical day for the project and I really didn't have time to investigate but, as the hours passed, I became more concerned and eventually carved out time to go down to the doctor's surgery again, where my heart was declared sound but my lifestyle less so.

I was given a sternly worded letter stating that I was experiencing the physical symptoms of stress and that I should rest from work for a while. I paused for twenty-four hours but was soon back in the fray, adopting my well-worn strategy of mind over matter. I knew that I thrived on positive 'stress' and that my natural energy had always enabled me to overcome minor stumbling blocks, so I saw no reason why the same should not apply on this occasion.

One day, as I was carrying shopping in from the car, a freak gust of wind blew the car door into my left shoulder. The accident took only a second but the pain that it induced was breathtaking. Even this, however, didn't stop me in my tracks; when the pain became so intense that I could not sleep I just took more painkillers.

At the beginning of April, I took a few days off work and we took the family to Disneyland Paris to celebrate Aly's sixteenth birthday. It was a joyous, almost magical break in a place which seemed to have bottled happiness. I was able to forget about the pressing issues at work as I watched my beautiful girl, savouring the last moments of her childhood as she rushed from ride to ride and embraced the roaming furry cartoon characters with abandon, her eyes sparkling with delight. On a couple of occasions, I felt a wave of fatigue overwhelm me but I pushed any concerns to the back of my mind. I wanted to enjoy the unreality of a world where you could fall off the edge of a cliff and bounce back to fight another day. I wanted to stay in this world of happy endings.

Once back at work, I travelled to meetings in Taipei, Hong Kong and China and, on return to the UK, ran a retreat at the College of the Community of Resurrection in the less exotic location of Mirfield, which was, coincidentally, my mother's birthplace. (I later discovered from her journals that she was actually born in a cottage in the monastery grounds.) I had decided to spend time in retreat with some members of my team to discern our next steps. The monks allowed us to join them in prayer and to eat with them in silence. It was a time of profound insight but, as I relaxed into the rhythm of monastic life, I realized just how desperately tired I was.

One day, deep in prayer, I envisioned myself on my knees exhausted and defeated, but then felt a presence – a familiar figure standing before me. I knew it was Jesus and I wanted to be folded into his arms, to be cared for, but instead he commanded me to stand up, then put his outstretched hand on my left shoulder and said to me, 'Be strong.' I could almost feel the imprint of his hand on my throbbing shoulder and, when I opened my eyes, it was as if the pain was burning a path through my flesh.

On the final evening of our retreat, I sat out in the garden, quietly reflecting, until the sun went down. As I made my way back along the path in the darkness, a black-and-white cat insinuated itself around my legs, almost tripping me over. I bent down low to stroke my new feline friend, who wailed loudly and wrapped itself around me. 'What do you want, little one?' I asked.

As I tried to step forward, the cat once again blocked my pathway wrapping itself around my legs and, once again, I bent down to stroke its fur. We continued in this vein for the next half an hour, as I made my way step by step back to my room, laughing at the contortions of the cat that seemed to want to stop me in my tracks. (It wasn't to be the last time that an animal behaved strangely around me. A ginger tabby performed the same antics a few weeks later as I tried to walk down the road to the fields behind my house.)

The pace continued to be frenetic. Only twenty-four hours after driving back from Mirfield I climbed in the car and set off down to our Heathrow office for a three-day workshop. Then on the Friday I drove home to pack for a family camping holiday in France which seemed doomed from the start.

On the day before our departure, John chopped off the end of his finger with a carving knife and came home from the doctor's with a large dressing on his wounded hand – an obvious handicap when it came to putting up tents. I was also in considerable pain. After examining me, the doctor concluded that I had partly dislocated my shoulder and prescribed stronger pain killers which I was popping like sweets but to no avail. I could hardly lift a bag let alone put up a tent. That evening, we also learnt that a two-week-long storm front was heading for the Jura, the area of France where we had planned to camp.

We nearly gave up on the whole idea but, the following morning, doggedly set out to catch the Eurotunnel train. Having altered our plans, we survived for five soggy days in Burgundy before heading south in search of the sun. In a bid to outrun the storms, we bore our way down through France past Dijon, Lyon and on to Montélimar, where we turned off the autoroute and into the Mediterranean. The hot, dry air and the sound of the cicadas warmed my soul and my heart leapt as we drove through a sea of lavender and dry, pale earth. This was the Provence that I knew from the paintings of Cézanne and Van Gogh – the artists' France that I had read about avidly and always wanted to visit.

We camped deep in the Ardèche Gorge beside the fast-moving river and, each evening, swam in the fresh water. We kayaked rather inelegantly down the gorge beneath the Vallon Pont-d'Arc, which straddled the river like a giant prehistoric rock bridge and all of us ended upside down in the river, apart from Aly who kayaked through the rapids backwards. When my shoulder began to hurt, I leapt into the cool waters. 'This is one of the best days of my life,' Emily cried as she was pulled dripping from the river.

From the Ardèche, we made our way further south to the Luberon where copper-coloured villages draped themselves over the hillsides. On the bridge, in the ancient town of Avignon, I danced with Emily singing the childhood song 'Sur le Pont d'Avigon'. In the cool silence of Van Gogh's room in the asylum of Saint-Rémy-de-Provence, I reflected on the tragic line between genius and madness; a line that the artist and, in a lesser way, my darling father had walked. Outside in the fields, I recognized the landscape that Van Gogh had captured with such intensity.

The experience was quite overwhelming. I had dreamt of travelling to Provence – the inspiration for so many great artists – since studying art at university but it always seemed too far to drive. I was profoundly grateful for the accidents and appalling weather that finally led me to the region.

That night I found it hard to sleep. The day at Saint-Rémy-de-Provence had been intense. That evening I had also had deep discussions with Aly. For some reason, we ended up talking about how much of a loner her father seemed to be. He seemed so content with his own company but deep down we knew that he needed other people, particularly his family. I found myself saying to Aly, 'If anything ever happens to me, you have to promise me that you won't let him be lonely. I don't want you to give up your life to look after him, but include him in it, let him share in your life and happiness.' With a maturity beyond her years she reassured me, 'I will.'

In the small hours of the night, the pain in my shoulder became unbearable as searing arrows shot down my arm. At two o'clock in the morning, I tried to massage under my arm to relieve the pain and there felt a small round, hard lump, deep in the flesh.

In the hours before dawn, I tried to rationalize away my discovery, telling myself that most lumps are benign, that perhaps it was a cyst or a sign of infection in my shoulder, but deep in my heart I knew that it was more.

Exhausted, I eventually fell into a fitful sleep and dreamt that I was being cut into pieces and put back together again. As the first rays of light stole over the horizon, I sat and watched my family sleeping and felt overwhelmed by sadness, but not fear.

John woke before the girls and I told him of my finding. He examined me and pointed out that there was also a telltale dimple under my arm. We decided not to tell the girls but agreed that we needed to get home and see a doctor.

It took us two days to drive up through the centre of France. We spent the night in a beautiful hotel in the stately town of Dijon and then the medieval pearl of Troyes. In the limbo between knowledge and action, once again I felt almost preternaturally calm and was determined to maximize the last days of our holiday together as a family. We wandered the medieval streets and ate opulent and classic French meals of l'escargot, canard and crème brûlée. I drank wine for the first time in years.

On the final afternoon, we took an unaccustomed siesta. I lay in our hotel room in Troyes. Through the open window, I could look down into a small courtyard framed by ancient brick and timber; wooden stairways winding up to small, shuttered windows. The air was still and warm and I could hear the sound of John breathing lightly beside me.

I watched him sleeping, his beautiful olive skin deeply tanned, his hair flecked with grey. And I realized that somewhere along the way, as we had grown together, he had overtaken me in wisdom. I thanked God for bringing us together. I could not have imagined a life with any other.

I lay there in suspended animation as the sun filtered through the shutters, willing time to stop on that perfect afternoon.

28

Shipwrecked

John sat nervously in the waiting room as the surgeon examined me. An uneasy silence hung in the air as I dressed but when I sat back down at his desk, the surgeon looked me directly in the eye and said, 'I'm going to be honest with you. I am concerned it is cancer.'

The crisp clinical room – with its anatomical charts and filing cabinets full of tragedy – momentarily receded. Then a nurse with kind eyes put her hand on mine and asked if there was anyone with me. As she went to collect my husband from the waiting room, the seriousness of the situation sank in.

John slipped in and sat quietly beside me, and the surgeon once again outlined his suspicions. As he explained the various tests that would be undertaken to confirm the diagnosis, I heard a sharp intake of breath to my side.

As the surgeon continued to talk, time seemed to slow down and I felt curiously distant from the events unfolding, as if I were watching a 'film noir' in which two hapless souls are informed about a life-threatening illness. When the meeting was over, we wandered out of the hospital and back out into the summer sunlight like drunken somnambulists.

The following day, we once again huddled like abandoned children in the hospital waiting room. In my hand I held a small wooden cross of the kind that had provided such comfort to my mother in her last hours. As we watched the clock, a young woman emerged from a screening room in tears. I tightened my grip on the cross and opened my Bible.

I began to read the story in the Gospel of Matthew of the centurion who came to Jesus to ask him to heal his servant who was paralysed. The passage recounts how Jesus offered to come to the house of the Roman official but the centurion replied that he was not worthy to have Christ under his roof and insisted that, if Jesus just said the word, his servant would be healed. As I was beckoned into the screening room, Jesus's reply rang in my ears, 'Go! It will be done just as you believed it would' (Matthew 8:13).

In the hours that followed, I was sliced, diced and irradiated. Initially I was given a mammogram, which the nurse told me I should have been offered as part of a routine screening. I recalled, with cold horror, the note reminding me to chase the hospital for an invitation which had become buried under the piles of paper on my desk. With a sick feeling in my stomach, I pushed the thought away; what was done was done and that way madness lay. All I could do was to deal with the reality that presented itself at that moment.

In a second room, an ultrasound was carried out by a female consultant radiologist with a straight-talking bedside manner. 'Well, I don't need to tell you there's a lump . . . but there's actually three or four areas here – quite large masses.'

I couldn't bring myself to look at the screen. I didn't want to be able to visualize the cancer growing inside me. Instead I watched her increasingly furrowed brow. 'If it was just that one lump, I would not be so worried but the other masses make me more concerned,' she told me. I clutched the cross even tighter.

The third step, which was rather grandly described as a fine-needle aspiration, involved sticking a pin into the masses to check if they were fluid-based cysts. I asked the consultant, 'How will you know if it is a cyst?'

'Oh we'll know immediately,' she assured me dryly as she pierced my side with a large needle.

'Well, it's definitely not a cyst.'

So I proceeded to have a series of core biopsies undertaken. The biopsies involved taking samples of the various tumours with an implement that looked like a miniature apple corer. Before the procedure, I was given a rather ineffectual local anaesthetic and, as the metal cut into my flesh, I felt like a fruit that was being eviscerated.

In between the procedures, the consultant and I talked about faith. It wasn't clear whether the consultant was a Christian but she told me that one of her relatives was a Carmelite nun and another was retiring into lay ministry. I told her of my own training and my hope to be authorized as a lay preacher. 'If this is cancer we will get you through this,' she said more gently. 'We are very good at this.' I decided I liked the no-nonsense medic very much.

The final step was a computerized tomography (CT) scan which involved passing my body through a giant hi-tech irradiated doughnut. As I lay surrounded by technology, I once again felt curiously distant, as if I was watching an episode in someone else's drama and my only emotion was one of curiosity. I was mesmerized by the sophistication of the diagnostics equipment and felt a pang of guilt. I knew that in many parts of Africa, cancer was rife and one of the highest causes of morbidity, but machines like the ones that I was being tested with were a rarity. I couldn't help but feel strangely blessed to have access to such medical care.

All I could do then was to go home and wait for the results. I had anticipated that I would be wracked with anxiety but found to my surprise that I was strangely calm. I knew so little about the disease that I had no idea how much time I would have left if cancer was confirmed. A few years before, a friend had been diagnosed with a brain tumour and died only ten days later, but I had no idea if breast cancer destroyed life with the same rapidity. What I did know, however, was that if this was cancer, it obviously hadn't been caught at an early stage. Yet even armed with this knowledge, I found that, in the eye of the hurricane, I was granted a stillness that I knew could only be a gift from God.

As I waited, each moment seemed to take on a precious intensity. I found that I had never felt so alive. I was still officially on holiday from work and was determined to keep the clouds at bay for a few more days. I spent the time of waiting sitting in the sunlit garden watching my children who still had no concept of the storm that threatened to break over their young lives.

I listened intently as they told me about the hopes, concerns and trivia that made up their daily lives. Aly spoke about her nerves and excitement at the prospect of starting at a new school to study for her A levels while Emily spent hours talking to me in an unfamiliar language about the intricacies of computer gaming and her skilful forays into programming. I thanked God for their burgeoning individuality but, beneath, an unbearable sadness lurked as I wondered if I would see them fulfil their dreams and grow to adulthood.

I dug out my old journals and spent bitter-sweet hours flicking my way through a lifetime of preserved memories. I wandered again through the temples of India and the desert wilderness of Australia and relived encounters with the rich, famous, humble and extraordinary. And, as I read, I felt a profound sense of gratitude and wonder at how blessed I had been in my life experiences.

In the evenings, we all ate together around a table in the garden. We told stories and laughed until the light faded from the skies and then, once again, in the middle of the night, I stole into the children's rooms and listened to their gentle breathing as they lay sleeping.

On the morning before I went to hear about the results of the tests, John and I went down to the local Baptist church, where my mother had worshipped, to see Emily take part in a Holiday Bible Club performance. For years I had watched Aly and then Emily take part in the final performance and it felt like a rite of passage. The theme of that year's activities was 'Shipwreck Survivors' and I felt a curious sense of strength as I watched Emily sing her innocent little heart out, belting out the words, 'We will survive this shipwreck. Yes we will, yes, yes, yes.'

When the surgeon came to collect John and me from the hospital waiting room, his expression spoke volumes. Once seated in his office he gently led me. 'You already know that there are masses in the breast and under the arm?'

I nodded mutely and tightened my grip on the ever-present cross in my hands.

'The biopsies confirm that these are cancerous. It is breast cancer.'

John and I sat motionless, paralysed like a couple of rabbits blinded by the glare of car headlights.

In my heart I had known the worst, but once the words were spoken I knew there was no going back. In the space between us, John's pain was palpable.

The surgeon continued, 'It isn't a lymphoma and it hasn't spread to other organs such as your liver but it is present under the collarbone, and there are some enlarged nodes around the lungs and heart. There's also a small amount of fluid around the heart.'

I became conscious of the sound of my own heartbeat and John's breathing.

'We can't get all this out by operating on you but I will be referring you to my colleague, who will start you on chemotherapy.'

I finally found my voice and asked, 'Am I going to die?'

He replied kindly, 'No you are not. We wouldn't even start talking like that until you reached a more advanced stage.'

Outside the hospital, John and I sat in the car holding hands, numbed with emotion, not sure how to move forwards or what to say to each other. Our immediate concern was how we would break the news to the children. Aly was at home but Emily had gone to a friend's house. We reasoned that we needed to tell them together but when we picked up Emily she spotted a cancer care leaflet I had mistakenly left on the front seat of the car. Brandishing the paperwork, she confronted me: 'Is this what is wrong with you?'

Back at home, we sat both girls down and explained that I had breast cancer but had very good doctors and was going to start treatment as soon as possible. I had anticipated hysteria but both girls were surprisingly calm. Their main concern revolved around the fact that I would potentially lose my hair as a result of chemotherapy. 'Mum, you can't walk around with a naked head,' Emily squirmed.

Aly didn't want to talk and shut herself in her room, emerging an hour later to say that she had gone on the internet, had done some research and I was going to be okay. Later that evening, I found her crouched behind her door crying helplessly. I could only hold her and reiterate that I was in good hands.

When I went to sing Emily to sleep she began crying. I asked her to talk to me but she could only sob, 'Everything is changing.'

I desperately wanted to tell them both that everything was going to be all right; that I would be cured and that in years to come this threat would seem like an insignificant shadow that temporarily passed across our lives. But I knew that these were assurances I could not give with any certainty; that these were the words I could not speak. I could only hope that my calm in the face of the storm would reassure them.

I knew that I had to tell the news to others. At first I felt reticent; I didn't know how to put into words how I felt about the situation and I was afraid of others' sympathy when what I really wanted was their prayers and hope. I first rang my sister who was on holiday in France with her husband and two sons, conscious that once again bad news was following her as she tried to escape reality for a while. I could sense her shock even at a distance and her frustration at being so far away. I then rang Theresa in Greece and my parents-in-law in Australia, who had both also been recently treated for cancer. As I watched John on the phone to his mother, I realized that he was surrounded by the threat of death.

When I told my colleagues at work, they came together on an online teleconference and formed a virtual prayer circle, or *caim*, around me and prayed for my protection. Other colleagues skyped me to let me know that they were praying for me in team meetings as far afield as Kenya and Thailand. I was moved beyond belief. As one pointed out, 'There are literally thousands of people praying for you.' It was a remarkable thought; until that point I had not really appreciated how many lives I had come into contact with over the years.

At our local church, my name was added to the weekly list of intercessions for the sick and I had the curious experience of sitting at the back of the church as the congregation prayed for my healing, as I had so many times for others. At one service, a friend handed me a butterfly brooch that had belonged to her late mother, the former curate who had first encouraged me to preach. 'I want you to have this because this period will be hard but you will emerge like a butterfly out of a cocoon at the end,' she told me. 'You won't be the same, but something different and beautiful.'

I felt as if I was being carried on a sea of prayer and from this I drew strength and hope. I clung to Jesus's promise that 'If two of you on earth agree about anything you ask for, it will be done for you by my Father in heaven' (Matthew 18:19).

A week later I met with my assigned oncologist; a gently spoken Scotsman who tempered his sombre occupation with a soft humour. We discussed a plan of treatment which would mainly involve chemotherapy. Once again I asked him, 'Am I going to die?' His response was slightly more measured than that of the surgeon.

'It is treatable and if plan A doesn't work, we have plan B and then plan C,' he reassured me. 'The good news is that it is oestrogen sensitive,' he added.

Oestrogen, it seemed, was my nemesis. Whenever my body let me down, oestrogen always seemed to play a part. It was as if my body was determined to fight against itself.

My oncologist also seemed to be particularly concerned about the layer of fluid around my heart which had shown up in the CT scans. It now seemed likely that this was the cause of the strange chest sensations I had experienced in the spring and some breathlessness that I had attributed to spending too much time in front of a computer. So I was sent to see a cardiologist who undertook more detailed scans and informed me that he had also detected a thickening of the right ventricular wall.

For some reason, the cardiologist also seemed to be very concerned about the presence of the fluid and proposed a procedure to take a sample of the fluid which involved inserting a plastic tube via a large needle into the space around my heart. He explained that this would have to be carried out with minimal anaesthesia, a prospect which played on my mind even more than the cancer diagnosis.

A few days before commencing chemotherapy, I was sent back to see the no-nonsense radiologist who first confirmed the extent of my cancer. As she passed the ultrasound scanner over my skin, she looked confused, 'Have you started chemotherapy yet?' she asked. I shook my head.

It was only at the end of the session that I thought to ask her, 'Why did you ask if I had started treatment yet?'

She glanced at me curiously, 'Well, it's just that it doesn't look as bad as the first time I saw it.'

All I could say was, 'There are a lot of people praying for me.' But I stored up the knowledge like treasure in my heart.

I didn't sleep the night before my first chemotherapy session. I kept on recalling the ghastly list of potential side effects and risks, which included the temporary eradication of your immune system.

The drug that was to be administered was very effective but was also known for reducing your white cell count so I had been coached on looking out for signs of infection which, if left untreated, could be life-threatening.

The first treatment took just over an hour. I sat on a hospital bed with a drip in my arm and my hands buried in bowls of ice to prevent my nails falling out. Some people also applied a freezing cap to their scalps to prevent hair loss but my oncologist had advised against this measure just in case seeds of cancer had spread under my scalp. I didn't argue; my hair was a small price to pay for life.

The treatment itself was painless and I felt a sense of relief that the medical battle against the disease had finally begun. By the time John brought the children to pick me up from the hospital, I was beaming, full of chemicals and hope.

The following day, I had to return to the hospital to have an injection to boost my white blood cell production. I was still feeling quite buoyant and told the oncology nurse that I was being very positive with the family. She agreed that this was the right approach to take at this stage. 'The doctors will tell you if this becomes unmanageable,' she told me.

On the way home, we stopped at a supermarket and bought vast quantities of vegetables known for their anti-cancer properties – carrots, kale, broccoli, and celery – which John passed through a newly acquired single-auger, self-masticating juicer; a silver beast which chewed vegetables like a cow. I had decided that nutrition was to be another weapon in my armoury in the fight against cancer.

The effects of the chemotherapy took forty-eight hours to make themselves felt. Despite the dire warnings, I still had no idea what to expect from the actual experience of chemotherapy so, at first, I dismissed my feverishness as a normal reaction. However, by three o'clock in the morning I was burning up, so we decided to ring the hospital.

I was admitted in a confused state just before dawn. My temperature was off the clock. I had an infection and my immune system was missing in action. Tests showed that I had a neutrophil count of zero and therefore no ability to fight the bacteria attacking my system. All I wanted to do was to go home and the nursing staff had to make me realize the seriousness of the situation: 'It is a good thing that you came in when you did, or it might have been a different story.' It dawned on me that if the cancer didn't kill me, the chemotherapy might.

The following days passed in a blur as I drifted in and out of sleep. At regular intervals, my husband appeared, his face pale and strained, and I could not bear the look of fear on my daughters' faces as they surveyed the mess on the bed they called Mum. I felt as if I were living in a twilight world in which nurses drifted in and out of my room.

One night, a young nurse appeared at my bedside. Spotting my Bible and wooden cross which I kept beside my bed, she asked if I was a Christian and in the early hours we talked about joy, peace and the sensation of being carried at those times when you feel you cannot stand on your own two feet. Then, at my invitation, she held my hand and prayed with me, speaking words of such beauty and power that I felt I had been visited by an angel.

On the third day, John came into the hospital and I roused myself from my hospital bed to go and see the cardiologist for another scan. To my initial relief he told us that the fluid around my heart had reduced but explained that this made it riskier for him to take a sample. 'There are complications with this procedure,' he told us. 'One in a thousand patients may die and one in five hundred may have their heart damaged.'

John sat beside me in a darkened room – the only light emanating from the scanner screen – and asked, 'Why has the fluid reduced?' As the cardiologist replied, the truth that we had been trying to ignore finally clawed its way into our consciousness – the doctors believed that the fluid around the heart had reduced because it was cancerous.

Back in the hospital room, John and I sat on the bed, clinging to each other like passengers on a sinking ship. I comprehended for the first time that my husband was facing head on the very real possibility that he may lose me and I wished with all my heart that I could take the pain from him. It seemed so cruel that he should face the prospect of his mother, father and wife all being claimed by cancer.

My husband had been such a pillar of strength, so calm and reassuring. He was my rock; the anchor that held us together in the storm, providing a sense of normality for the children, easing their fears but, after this latest news, he looked like a frightened child. My heart broke as I watched him crumple and all I could do was tell him how great my love was for him.

On that day, he had been unable to organize childcare so the nurses had looked after Emily. She was sitting just outside the door reading a magazine and I knew that I could not let her or Aly see their father in such pain. It would terrify them. We needed to talk the situation through with the oncologist, to fully understand the implications.

The hours ticked by and eventually the oncologist appeared. As dusk fell, he confirmed that the reason why he had been keen on getting a sample of the fluid around my heart was to diagnose if there were cancer cells present. 'If there is cancer present it changes the staging of the cancer from early to more advanced with a high risk of spreading. It changes the objective of the treatment from cure to control.'

'So without the sample you don't know?' John asked clutching at straws.

The oncologist explained, 'The fact that the fluid has reduced in response to the chemotherapy makes me think that we are dealing with cancer here, but we will confirm that with a CT scan.'

Crushing John's hand in mine, I once again asked, 'Am I going to die?'

This time he said, 'We can get the cancer under control for a worthwhile time – but it will shorten your life.'

It was terrible to watch John's agony. All I could do was hold him as he cried. I kept on wishing that I could somehow make it all go away but the pain in my chest and shoulder told me that it was all too real. One of my greatest fears had always been being alone in old age, losing John after a lifetime of living together. I had come to think of us as one but, now that I had such a vivid reminder of our separateness, I would give anything to outlive him and not leave him alone.

29

Jehova Rapha

The first thing I did after coming out of hospital was to get my head shaved. I had hoped to avoid this obvious badge of the cancer patient but I kept moulting clumps of long blonde hair all over the house. When a shank of hair fell into a bowl of pumpkin soup I was eating, I finally decided to take the matter into my own hands.

The moment that my golden locks fell to the floor was actually strangely liberating, so much so that I posted pictures of my newly-shorn pate on Facebook. The resulting posts likened me to the bald TV private eye Kojak and suggested that 'with a good polish that will come up nicely'. I found that I was still able to laugh.

Emily, who was horrified by the thought of my bald head, helped me to pick out a wig and insisted that I wear one that was long and blonde. The chosen wig, which was christened the 'hairy hat', made me look younger and rather like a 1970s rocker but was intolerably itchy. It also had the tendency to slip, making it obvious that my hair was not my own, so I decided to wear the hairy hat only on special occasions. However, as my children were mortified by the thought of my growing nudity, I wore turbans to preserve my modesty.

The vicar came to see me bringing communion wine and wafers, and together we prayed for fullness of life, whatever that may mean. She also suggested that I draw up a bucket list; not a wish list of daredevil adventures or foreign holidays but a list of those things that I wanted to leave behind, whenever I was scheduled to leave this earth.

At first I resisted the idea as I didn't want to do anything to give the impression that I was giving up but, for practical reasons, I realized that it was necessary for me to imagine a life in which I might not exist; to live balancing two potential realities, planning for the worst and hoping for the best.

I wrote letters to John, Aly and Emily with instructions that they be opened in the event of my death. I told myself that this was something I should have done at an earlier stage given my globe-trotting lifestyle, but when the moment came to put pen to paper it tore my heart out.

I felt strangely at peace about what might happen to me but I found the idea of causing them pain unbearable. I tried to pour all the love in my heart into the words on the paper but I knew that no phrase would be adequate to express what they meant to me and the appalling sadness I felt at the thought that I may have to leave them too soon. As I wrote I tried to assure them that, even if I did eventually succumb to this cancer, one day we would be together again – all they had to do was believe.

I also decided to try to preserve memories of the time I had spent with John and the children for when they were older. John's memory was not good, probably as a result of the head injury and broken neck caused by his drunken, teenage dive into the rock pool in Manly. I found it so sad that he struggled to remember our wedding day or the birth of our children. I had once even said to him – half in jest – that I wasn't sure how much he would remember about me if I died. As a result, I had become an obsessive chronicler of our lives, collecting photographs and mementoes. I was determined to package these so that John and the children would have a visual record to jog many happy memories. So I spent my days making up scrapbooks of old photographs, letters, birthday cards and drawings as evidence of our lives together.

As the treatment progressed, however, I became progressively weaker. On some days I would look at my face in the mirror and hardly recognize myself. My skin looked grey and my eyes sunken; it was as if an old woman was staring back at me, uncomprehending. Every move I made seemed to exhaust me. Every morsel of food and every drink of water tasted metallic and my mouth bled copiously.

The treatments took place in a three-week cycle and even though the dosage had been reduced to avoid another calamity, my neutrophil count remained so low for the two weeks following the treatment that I had to limit my contact with other human beings. When my children came home from school with coughs and sneezes, I was confined to my bedroom to ensure that I wasn't infected.

My world had shrunk so rapidly. Only a few months before I had thought nothing of travelling to Asia one week and Africa the next but, for the first week after each chemotherapy cycle, I could barely lift my battered body off the bed. I would lie on my back watching the sunlight filter through the skylights in our bedroom as I had done when I was pregnant with Aly. I remembered how I used to watch the clouds through the window of our flat in London, feeling the first stirrings of life within me, and recognized with bitter irony that what was now growing within me may well rob me of life.

As I lay in bed in the morning and listened to the house come to life – the children chatting downstairs and the clatter of pots in the kitchen – I also felt an unexpected joy in my heart and thanked God that I was surrounded by family. I was painfully aware that many others were facing cancer alone.

Even when the effects of the chemotherapy were at their worst, when I was so weak I could barely stand, I was grateful for simply being alive and would greet the day praying, 'This is the day the LORD has made; let us rejoice and be glad in it' (Psalm 118:24).

In the early hours of the morning when sleep eluded me, when the pain of the cancer bore into my soul and the chemicals in my veins made me shake uncontrollably, I sometimes felt a comforting presence beside me. One night as I lay wracked and groaning on the bed, I felt a soft touch on my head, as if an unseen hand was stroking my temple, and I felt myself relax into merciful sleep.

On better days, I would force myself out of the house and wander unsteadily up the lane. As I walked in the crispness of the morning, the air seemed electric, sharper and brighter than I ever remembered. It was as if I was seeing the world more clearly: every blade of grass, veined leaf, wheat stalk and gnarled trunk, ripening apple and blackberry stood out in sharp relief.

As the clouds rolled away to reveal an azure sky, I became acutely conscious of the variety of life around me: the butterflies flitting among the late summer blossoms, the song of starlings above, the scuttle of a shrew into the undergrowth, rabbits heading for burrows and deer for the woods. I walked as if in a dream. All I could feel was joy at being alive and the sense of God's presence.

Once again I wandered the fields as I had done as a child, bathing in the sense of the numinous – the God that I now knew. At the top of the field looking out over the valley, a place where I had often gone to pray over the years, I lifted my hands in thanks and felt the pain leaving my body as if I was lifted up by the wind.

As the boundaries of my world narrowed, it was as if my senses became sharper and my ability to feel God's presence more acute. I knew that in some indefinable way he was within me and around me, bringing a sense of wonder at the world and a peace that defied all understanding.

I also felt intuitively that he was there in the wisdom and caring hands of the doctors and in the chemicals that flowed through my veins. I clung to the knowledge that somehow inexplicably he had begun to shrink the cancer even before the conventional medical treatment had begun.

I began to study what the Bible had to say about healing, poring over the thirty-one accounts of Jesus healing individuals and the many references to mass healing. In the first book of the New Testament, I read that immediately after his baptism and time in the wilderness, 'Jesus went throughout Galilee, teaching in their synagogues, preaching the good news of the kingdom, and healing every disease and sickness among the people' (Matthew 4:23). I saw clearly for the first time that, for Christ, healing was a tangible sign of God's will on earth and was bound up in his sacrifice for us on the cross.

One day, I stumbled on an online Bible study series called *God's Healing Journey;* a book and series of videos by an inspirational woman called Cindy Cox from Michigan who had been completely and miraculously healed of stage four melanoma and had since devoted herself to healing ministry. Her studies looked at the meaning of the original Hebrew and Greek words relating to healing in the Bible and I felt a surge of renewed hope as I read that the first time that God talks about who he is, he says, 'I am the LORD, who heals you' (Exodus 15:26) or Jehova Rapha – one of the Old Testament names for God, variously translated as the God who 'heals', 'cures' and 'repairs' – and that '*sozo*', the wonderful Greek word for 'to save' used 110 times in the Bible, encompasses not only the concept of deliverance and the promise of eternal life but also that of healing and being made whole.[1]

My heart filled with hope as I meditated on Isaiah's prophecy about Christ: 'Surely he took up our infirmities and carried our sorrows, yet we considered him stricken by God, smitten by him, and afflicted. But he was pierced for our transgressions, he was crushed for our iniquities; the punishment that brought us peace was upon him, *and by his wounds we are healed*' (Isaiah 53:4–5, my emphasis).

So I became bolder and began to pray for a miracle of healing. Didn't Jesus say in Mark 11:23–24, 'I tell you the truth, if anyone says to this mountain, "Go, throw yourself into the sea," and does not doubt in his heart but believes that what he says will happen, it will be done for him'? I decided I was going to cast this mountain of cancer into the sea and use every tool at my disposal to do so.

I certainly wasn't going to eschew orthodox medical treatment in favour of prayer or a diet of carrots. I was convinced that God works through humanity and that the wonderful medics who were caring for me so skilfully were gifted by him; that the wisdom that has led to such marvellous scientific breakthroughs in the treatment of cancer comes from on high. But it was also obvious that healing was central to Christ's ministry on earth and that he had passed on his gifts of healing to others. Even during his lifetime, when Jesus sent out his followers to share his message, he also gave them the power to heal, telling them, 'Heal the sick, raise the dead, cleanse those who have leprosy, drive out demons. Freely you have received; freely give' (Matthew 10:8).

After Christ's death and resurrection, the apostles carried out so many signs and wonders – including healing – that in Acts it is recorded that people 'brought the sick into the streets and laid them on beds and mats so that at the least Peter's shadow might fall on some of them as he passed by. Crowds gathered also from the towns around Jerusalem, bringing their sick and those tormented by evil spirits, and all of them were healed' (Acts 5:15–16). And as Paul recorded in his letter to the young church in Corinth, Christ's followers were gifted by the Holy Spirit, the manifestations of which included healing: 'to another faith by the same Spirit, to another gifts of healing by that one Spirit' (1 Corinthians 12:9).

I also began to find contemporary stories of people being healed in his name, often from 'incurable' diseases, and examples of Christian healers all over the world employing a range of techniques from the laying-on of hands to the use of prayer cloths (a practice inspired by the woman in the crowd who was healed when she reached to touch the hem of Jesus's garment as well as the various people healed by handkerchiefs and aprons that the evangelist Paul had touched).

I became fascinated by Lourdes, a village in the South of France made famous by the visions of a fourteen-year-old girl in the nineteenth century. Millions who have visited claimed to have been healed and sixty-eight miracles have passed the stringent investigation of the Catholic Church including that of Mademoiselle Dulot, who was cured of stomach and liver cancer in 1925, Rose Martin who was cured of cancer of the uterus in 1947 and Vittorio Micheli, cured of a malignant tumour of the hip in 1963. Many others have claimed to have been granted additional years as a result of visiting the sacred site.

I knew that I wasn't well enough to travel to Lourdes but decided to seek healing closer to home. So I contacted the Christian Healing Mission, who pointed me in the direction of a modern church on the far side of Milton Keynes.

On my first visit to the church, I was greeted at the door by a softly spoken, middle-aged woman with an Aberdeen accent. She invited me in and offered me a cup of tea and a biscuit. Then a couple more women arrived and sat down in the communal area. I hadn't known what to expect from this encounter but, having watched a number of charismatic healers on American television, I had expected something slightly more theatrical. I felt an old scepticism rising in my throat like bile.

When everyone was equipped with tea and biscuits my host, whose name was Kathy, sat down and we exchanged pleasantries. To my astonishment she told me that she had family living in Filgrave, the tiny hamlet where I had spent my childhood. As she talked about her family, my head bowed in shame and humility. I had spent many of my early years running in and out of her sister's house playing with her children. Kathy also explained that the church was ecumenical, and wove together the Baptist and Anglican denominations which had played different but such significant roles in my life. As a teenager, I had turned my back on one, only to be brought back into the arms of the other as an adult, but in this, my moment of need, I had been led to a place where they reconciled in the name of healing. God had taught me a valuable lesson and I was on the edge of my seat and open to whatever he wanted to do.

Two of the women took me into a small room which seemed to serve as office, store room and prayer sanctuary. A small table had been covered with a lace cloth and set up with a wooden cross, Bible and a candle. I sat facing the cross and one woman stood above me with her hand raised over my left shoulder, while Kathy put her hand on my back and began to pray. As she opened her mouth, words poured forth of such beauty and authority that I hardly recognized her and, as she spoke, I felt a surge like electricity pass through my body which left me breathless.

The atmosphere in the room became charged and was so thick with God's presence that I felt as if I could reach out and touch him or cut the air with a knife. I felt so alert. It was as if I was on fire. I could feel a warmth spreading throughout my body, beginning at the site of the cancer and running down my arm. And as the energy spread, I had the strong impression that the cancer cells were leaving my body through my skin, fanning out into the air like golden dust motes in the sunlight and I began to feel lighter.

When Kathy suggested I try to visualize Christ, I was reticent. My experiments with visualization when I had studied meditation had not been successful. I had never been able to conjure up an image in my mind's eye and generally ended up studying the inside of my eyelids. But I suppressed my cynicism and, as I gave myself up to the experience, a face appeared in front of me: a dark-skinned Arabic male with intense eyes, medium-length dark hair and a beard.

I felt quite unnerved and confronted and, as the face began to move towards me, I leant further back in my seat but could not escape. Before I knew it, I was nose to nose with this imposing visage which kept on moving until the face merged with mine, moving onwards until he was inside me, part of me. That night I dreamt that I was swimming in a deep, blue, calm pool of water.

Then, as autumn ushered in the colder weather, John and I stood side by side with our vicar in an empty, echoing church and renewed our wedding vows before the Almighty. We hadn't invited any guests. We hadn't told anyone what we were planning – not even the children. We had not shared the oncologist's latest concerns with them but our children were very bright and we were sure that the significance of this action would not be lost on them. We did not want them living in fear.

So, on the World Vision Day of Prayer, as colleagues from around the globe prayed for the world and its suffering humanity, John and I stood alone before the altar and pledged our lives to each other for a second time. The vicar blessed the wedding ring John had put on my finger twenty years before in the registry office and I felt a sense of completeness as she blessed our love, 'in joy and in sorrow, in life and in death' and prayed, 'Finally, in your mercy, bring them to that banquet where your saints feast for ever in your heavenly home.'

30

Sea Changed

The Gospel of Matthew includes a remarkable story about the disciple Peter. Following the miracle of the feeding of the five thousand, Jesus had sent the disciples back by boat to the other side of the Sea of Galilee, while he went up a mountainside alone to pray.

Night fell and the wind rose. The boat, now far from land, was buffeted by the waves until, in the early hours of the morning, the disciples saw what they thought was a ghost approaching them on the surface of the water. They cried out in terror but heard a voice in the darkness, 'Take courage! It is I. Don't be afraid.'

It sounded like Jesus but they couldn't be sure and Peter replied, 'Lord if it's you . . . tell me to come to you on the water.' And when Jesus said simply 'come', without hesitation Peter climbed out of the boat as the storm raged around him and stepped out in faith towards his saviour (Matthew 14:22–29). It is probably the greatest example of breathtaking, inspiring human trust in Scripture.

The fact that a few moments later he took his eye off Christ, looked down at the churning waves and, overwhelmed by the situation, began to sink, doesn't diminish the extraordinary trust that Peter initially displayed. For a moment he believed that anything was possible and acted on that belief.

All too often we equate the term 'trust' with that of 'faith' but there are fundamental differences. Faith is a noun. It is something that we have; that deep-seated knowledge and sense of God's loving presence. But trust is a verb. It is something that we do; a manifestation of our faith in our actions. Trust is not passive. It is not safe and it requires us to risk all, even if we are afraid.

It demands that we defy a lifetime of logic and step out of the security of ourselves. To abandon the vessel that we have built to carry us on the high seas of life. To step out onto the threatening waters and to keep our eyes on Christ. To trust completely and to ignore the foaming waves that rise around us. To trust in God's promise that, 'When you pass through the waters, I will be with you' (Isaiah 43:2).

All too often, we only learn to do to this when we reach the end of our own resources: our strength, courage and understanding. It is only when we have no option left but to trust in God that we finally begin to learn that having faith means 'being sure of what we hope for and certain of what we do not see' (Hebrews 11:1). Cancer is a great trust teacher.

In early autumn, we were due to meet with the oncologist again to hear the results of the CT scan which would confirm whether or not my cancer was now deemed advanced or stage four. The day before our meeting, I woke from a powerful and vivid dream in which I kept trying to lock a door but failed repeatedly until I awoke. The dream left such a powerful impression that I decided to research its meaning and found that a locked door is believed to be a dream symbol for a situation which you believe is irreversible.

Later that day, I made my way to the healing church. I had begun to go to pray with the healing team before each round of treatment, tests and key meetings with the medical team. On this occasion, we were joined by a lady I had seen at the church but did not really know. She told me that before she had come to church that day, God had given her an image of me and a passage from Psalm 24. She said, 'It seems a very strange passage and I don't know if it means anything to you but what I got was very specific,' and then she opened her Bible and read to me:

> *Lift up your heads, O you gates;*
>   *be lifted up, you ancient doors,*
>   *that the King of glory may come in.*
> *Who is this King of glory?*
>   *The Lord strong and mighty,*
>   *The LORD mighty in battle.*

Psalm 24:7–8

As she read, I felt what was left of the hair on the back of my neck stand up and, in awe, I shared with her my dream of the night before. I knew then that God was telling me clearly to leave the door open to the possibility of his healing; that he was greater than any prognosis and that I just had to trust him.

The following morning, John and I went to the hospital to receive the verdict. 'The good news is the main areas of cancer have shrunk and critically the fluid around the heart has resolved,' the oncologist explained to us. 'But the bad news is that we now have to regard the fluid around the heart as being involved with the cancer. We can't be 100 per cent sure as we didn't get a sample but it has to be a working assumption that it's advanced cancer.'

'But you can't be sure?' John asked with plaintive hope in his voice.

'No, I am sure,' the doctor replied firmly but kindly. 'If it wasn't cancerous it would not have got better. The chemo would have made it worse.'

As he spoke, I realized that I had already assimilated this truth but I could see that John was shaken to the core.

The oncologist then went on to outline a treatment plan aimed at 'control' rather than 'cure' of the disease. 'We will continue on the same chemotherapy drug and we will then look at radiotherapy and hormone treatments which are used to keep cancer in remission.'

'What about surgery?' I asked.

The oncologist looked me in the eye and said gently, 'You seem to be the kind of person who wants me to tell you things straight.'

I nodded.

'The surgeon and I will make a decision on whether it is worth putting your body through surgery depending on how much time we think you have left.'

This time there was no soft-spoken humour to soften the blow. I heard a sob beside me and, turning, watched my darling husband sag like a puppet whose strings had been cut.

I gathered myself, faced the oncologist and said in a steady voice, 'My plea to you is to give me as much time as possible. Help me to be around long enough so that my children can fly on their own.'

John could hardly see through his tears to drive. His pain was terrible and my heart was breaking for him but, strangely, in the midst of this storm, I felt no fear for myself. It wasn't that I was being unrealistic; I knew the implications of what the doctor had told us but was determined to leave the door open for God to heal me.

A couple of weeks before Christmas, after the penultimate chemotherapy cycle, John and I returned to see the oncologist. We had come to dread these meetings as each time a little more of our hope seemed to be taken away from us. We sat outside the hospital on a bench in the rain, praying. As we sat in the waiting room, I felt as if I was heading to the executioner's block.

As we entered the oncologist's office, he shook my hand and I tried fruitlessly to read his expression.

He carried out the customary examination, checking for the telltale signs of disease and, as I replaced my clothes, he studied a pile of papers on his desk.

Then finally, as I sat down on the edge of my seat and faced him expectantly, he smiled broadly, 'The scan was good. You are responding brilliantly to the chemo and there is no new cancer.'

He then leant back in his chair with a quizzical expression.

'In fact, there's no black-and-white guidance on what to do in a situation like yours and given how amazingly you are doing I am anxious not to under-treat you . . . so I am recommending surgery.'

My heart leapt. John squeezed my hand and I could see the strain fall away from him. The oncologist told us that we still had to get agreement from the surgeon who had originally seen me but I knew that a door had been opened.

A few days before Christmas, I sat in the surgeon's office, shaking visibly, weakened following my final chemotherapy treatment, clutching my wooden cross and praying for agreement to undertake the required operation.

This time the surgeon beamed at me and said, 'When oncologists say that someone is doing fantastically, I tend to take it with a pinch of salt but in your case it is true.' He then handed me a Christmas gift, precious beyond measure. As he outlined the procedure which would involve carving me like a turkey, I felt as though I had been given a second chance.

So, on the anniversary of our Saviour's birth, I celebrated like never before, surrounded by family and friends, glowing with the renewed hope I had been given. And as the New Year ushered in, I went under the surgeon's knife.

When I emerged from the fog of anaesthesia, the surgeon told me that he had been able to remove a majority – but not all – of the life-sapping cancer from my body. Apparently, the area of cancer under my collarbone that had caused such agony remained inaccessible but my hopes were not dashed. God had brought me this far. I just had to put myself in his hands and trust that in him all things were possible.

I spent six weeks in painful recovery from the surgery. Like a bird with a broken wing, I had to force movement into my left arm, straining at the scars on my body, before I could undertake a course of intensive radiotherapy.

In preparation for my irradiation, I was then taught to hold my breath for extensive periods as if I were diving for pearls, in order to move my heart and lungs out of the path of the searing beam. For three weeks, on a daily basis, I laid my body down, inhaled and prayed, surfacing for air with gratitude, until my skin was cracked and burnt.

Then, after the very final radiotherapy treatment and follow-up scan, John and I returned to meet up with the surgeon. As I sat down in his office, he simply turned a copy of the report towards me and pointed to the last line, which read: 'There is no evidence of metastatic cancer in her body.'

This was confirmed when, on 8 April 2015, eight months after starting treatment for advanced cancer, the oncologist reported, with an uncharacteristically biblical flourish, that his patient's 'health had been restored'.

***

I used to take issue with my father's poetic assertion that 'you are the only truth one needs to know'. It seemed to advocate a very egocentric approach to life; a fitting justification for astronomical therapist fees and an encouragement towards self-indulgent introspection. But after my own experience of digging into 'desperate troughs' and mounting 'each heady swell', I came to understand that what my father had been saying in his poem 'Sea Change' was that the truth we need to find is God within us.

What my father had been trying to convey was that our life journeys are about discovering the still small voice of God that speaks into the depths of our soul, giving us a glimpse of the infinite and an assurance of a truth 'beyond our knowing'. It is this truth that forms our keel, reaching down into the depths, holding us steady as we navigate the high seas.

I do not know whether the cancer has gone for good. The medics are amazed by my progress but are still managing my expectations in anticipation that the malignancy will reappear one day. I have now started on the hormone treatments which my surgeon and oncologist rely upon to give me as long a life as possible, but the reality is that all of us have to die and none of us know when our own time will come; it is just that survivors of cancer live in greater awareness of the precariousness of existence.

I don't pretend to understand why some are completely – sometimes even miraculously – healed and others are not. Perhaps we are not meant to understand. Doesn't God tell us, 'As the heavens are higher than the earth, so are my ways higher than your ways and my thoughts than your thoughts' (Isaiah 55:9)?

Perhaps we must be wary of making our God too small, trying to limit him to the parameters of our own incomplete understanding. After all, if our inadequate human minds could truly comprehend the mystery, he would not be God. In the end all we can really do is trust.

I don't know whether God has 'cured' me but healing takes many forms and he has healed me in more ways than I could ever have imagined. He has brought me a peace that passes all understanding and, as I have peered into the cracks between the *chronos* and the *kairos*, I recognize that he has always been there waiting patiently for me.

As a child, I sensed him in the wheat fields and woodlands around Larkland and, later, in the deserts and wilderness places of the wider world. I encountered him in so many I have met along the way; people who in their humility were barely even conscious of the God-light that shone through them. I have seen him at work in everyday miracles, synchronicities or God-incidences, and as I look back over the various stages of my life's journey, I recognize his guiding hand as it gently altered my trajectory. And ultimately, when I was faced with my own mortality, I experienced the full wonder of his love.

Of course I wish I had not been diagnosed with cancer but the experience of having come so close to God has been almost incandescent. I feel as if I have lived for a while on the border between the natural and the supernatural.

I have had a truly wonderful life, full of love and learning – a life touched by the infinite – but none of us live a life unscathed. As the ascetic Julian of Norwich so wisely observed, 'God did not say, "You shall not be tempest tossed, you shall not be weary, you shall not be discomforted." But he said, "You shall not be overcome."'[1]

I now sail uncharted waters but will take joy in the journey and the knowledge that I am being Sea Changed.

Glossary

Balalaika: a stringed musical instrument with a characteristic triangular body and three strings.

Bhajan: a Hindu devotional song.

Bhut: a restless ghost in Hindu mythology, believed to be malignant if a person has died a violent death or been denied funeral rites.

Bodhisattva: a Sanskrit term from the Mahayana school of Buddhism for anyone who, motivated by great compassion, is dedicated to attaining enlightenment and Buddhahood.

Chai: an Indian hot drink made of black tea, spices, milk and sweetener.

Charpoy: a bed used especially in India consisting of a frame strung with tapes or light rope.

Dal bhat: a traditional meal consisting of steamed rice and a cooked lentil soup called dal which is popular in many areas of Nepal, Bangladesh and India.

Dhoti: a traditional men's garment worn in the Indian subcontinent consisting of a rectangular piece of unstitched cloth which is wound round the waist and legs and knotted at the waist.

Farang: generic Thai word for someone of European ancestry.

Jackaroo: a young man learning to work on a sheep or cattle station.

Kalimavkion: a cylindrical head covering, similar to a stove pipe hat but without a brim worn by Orthodox Christian and Eastern Catholic clerics.

Losmen: an Indonesian budget hotel without a government rating.

Mandi: traditional Indonesian bath or way of washing using a small scoop dipped into a large tub or container of cold water.

Paseo: a leisurely, usually evening, stroll or promenade, in which young people socialise with each other.

Pecalang: traditional Balinese security guards who work for the benefit of the community, ensuring the security of the village and religious ceremonies.

Puri: an unleavened deep fried Indian bread.

Retablos: small oil paintings on tin, zinc, wood or copper which venerate Catholic saints.

Roundevel: a round native hut of southern Africa usually made of mud with a thatched roof of grass.

Salwar Kameez: traditional South Asian women's dress consisting of a pair of light, loose pleated trousers, tapering to a tight fit around the ankles (*Salwar*) and a shirt of varying length (*Kameez*).

Sati: an ancient Indian funeral custom in which a widow self-immolated on her husband's funeral pyre or committed suicide in another fashion shortly after the death of her husband.

Selamat malam: Malay greeting meaning 'Good night'.

Shikara: a type of wooden boat found on Dal Lake and other bodies of water in India.

Songthaew: a passenger vehicle in Thailand adapted from a pick-up or a larger truck and used as a share taxi or bus.

Thurible: a metal censer suspended from chains, in which incense is burned during worship services.

Contact the Author

If you would like to invite Kate Nicholas to talk about the issues raised in her book, she can be contacted via:

Website: katenicholas.co.uk
Facebook: KateNicholas7363
Twitter: @KateNicholas

'I will not die but live,
and will proclaim what the LORD has done.'
Psalm 118:17

Endnotes

5. The Prow Cracked

[1] Nicholas, Daniel, 'Again I ask', *Disposition of C90* (1998).
[2] Nicholas, Daniel, 'Larkland', *Disposition of C90* (1998).
[3] Nicholas, Daniel, 'Babble', *Disposition of C90* (1998).

9. The Beguiling Soul

[1] p. 9, Ch.2:24 from *The Bhagavad Gita* (Oxford World's Classics), translated by W.J. Johnson (2008). By permission of Oxford University Press.

17. The Thinning of the Veil

[1] Rinpoche, Sogyal (eds. Patrick Gaffney and Andrew Harvey), *The Tibetan Book of Living and Dying* (Rider, an imprint of Random House UK Ltd 1992), p. 289.

18. Rebuilding

[1] Nicholas, Kate, 'To Di For: A Right Royal Job', *PRWeek UK*, (Haymarket Publishing, 23 August 1996).
[2] Nicholas, Kate, 'Sophie's World', *PRWeek UK*, (Haymarket Publishing, 28 May 1999).
[3] Nicholas, Kate, 'Wessex Breaks Own PR Rules' *PRWeek UK*, (Haymarket Publishing, 5 April 2001).

22. The Call in the Night

[1] Extract from 'Here I Am, Lord' (80670) © 1981, OCP, 5536 NE Hassalo, Portland, OR97213. All rights reserved. Used by permission. Text based on Isaiah 6.

24. Crossroads

[1] Nouwen, Henri J.M. (ed. Michael Ford), *Eternal Seasons: A Spiritual Journey Through the Church's Year*, (Ave Maria Press, 2007), p. 38.

26. Through the Valley

[1] Moll, Rob (foreword by Lauren Winner), *The Art of Dying: Living Fully into the Life to Come* (InterVarsity Press, 2010), p. 40. Republished with permission of IVP Books. Permission conveyed through Copyright Clearance Center, Inc.

[2] Moll, Rob, *The Art of Dying*, p. 43 [quoting *The Divine Conspiracy* by Dallas Willard. Reprinted by permission of HarperCollins Publishers, Ltd. Copyright © Dallas Willard 1998].

[3] Moll, Rob, *The Art of Dying*, p. 45 [quoting from LAST RIGHTS © 2006 by Stephen P. Kiernan. Reprinted by permission of St. Martin's Press, LLC. All Rights Reserved].

[4] Nicholas, Kate, *Report from the Edge* (www.youtube.com/watch?v=Agky0Vo9KmU, 2014).

29. Jehova Rapha

[1] Cox, Cindy, *A Healing Journey* (Christian Illness Support, 2009).

30. Sea Changed

[1] Julian of Norwich (ed. Robert Llewelyn), *Enfolded in Love, Daily Readings with Julian of Norwich* (Darton, Longman and Todd Ltd, 2004). p. 47 [Translations in book have been made from Julian of Norwich, *Revelations of Divine Love* (ed. Marian Glasscoe), (Exeter Medieval Texts: Liverpool University Press)].